Aris & Phillips Classical Texts

GREEK ORATORS VI

Apollodoros Agains Neaira

[Demosthenes] 59

Edited with an introduction, translation and notes by

Christopher Carey

Aris & Phillips is an imprint of Oxbow Books

First published in the United Kingdom in 1992. Reprinted 2007, 2015 by
OXBOW BOOKS
10 Hythe Bridge Street, Oxford OX1 2EW

and in the United States by
OXBOW BOOKS
908 Darby Road, Havertown, PA 19083

Paperback Edition: ISBN 978-0-85668-526-2

A CIP record for this book is available from the British Library

For a complete list of Aris & Phillips titles, please contact:

UNITED KINGDOM
Oxbow Books
Telephone (01865) 241249
Fax (01865) 794449
Email: oxbow@oxbowbooks.com
www.oxbowbooks.com

UNITED STATES OF AMERICA
Oxbow Books
Telephone (800) 791-9354
Fax (610) 853-9146
Email: queries@casemateacademic.com
www.casemateacademic.com/oxbow

Oxbow Books is part of the Casemate Group

Contents

IN MEMORY OF MY PARENTS

CHRISTOPHER CAREY 1914 - 1989

ALICE MAY CAREY 1923 - 1992

Preface

Firstly, a note about the title. It has been suggested since late antiquity that the *Neaira* is not the work of Demosthenes. It is widely believed that the speech was written by the principal speaker, Apollodoros, himself. Since I share that belief, I felt that after two and a half millenia Apollodoros should finally be given star billing.

The *Neaira* is one of the most fascinating texts from fourth century Athens which have come down to us. It is all the more unfortunate therefore that no commentary is readily available in English. This book seeks to supply that need. It is aimed principally at undergraduates and senior pupils in high schools. With that audience in mind, and in view of the fact that I have undertaken no independent collation of the manuscripts, I have not included an apparatus, which would merely reproduce information available elsewhere. Departures from the Oxford text are noted at the end of the Introduction. As far as possible the commentary confines itself to literary and historical matters; textual problems have been addressed rarely, and only where absolutely necessary. I have sought to produce a readable and accurate translation, while at the same time conveying something of the inelegance of Apollodoros' Greek.

The book was completed more or less in its present form by September 1991. Subsequent progress was slowed significantly by the administrative and other duties of a new appointment. However, delay offered a compensatory advantage, since I was able to subject the typescript in its entirety to the scrutiny of my colleagues at Royal Holloway and Bedford New College, Dr. Stephen Usher and Dr. Rosalind Thomas, and Dr. Stephen Todd of the University of Keele. I am grateful to them for drawing my attention to inadequacies. I have not always followed their advice; so for any remaining defects the responsibility rests with the author. I am also very grateful to Tig Lang and Lynne Grierson for putting on disk the first drafts of the Greek text and the English translation respectively, to Jeremy Trevett for sending me a copy of the proofs of his forthcoming book as I was preparing the final draft, and to Prof. U. Albini for the gift of a copy of Avezzù's commentary.

Christopher Carey,

Royal Holloway and Bedford New College,

University of London,

May 1992

ABBREVIATIONS

Avezzù	E. Avezzù, *Demostene, Processo a una cortigiana (contro Neera)* (Venice 1986)
Blass	F. Blass, *Die attische Beredsamkeit*[2], vol.ii (Leipzig 1887)
Bonner-Smith	R.J. Bonner and G. Smith, *The administration of justice from Homer to Aristotle*, 2 vols. (Chicago 1930, 1938)
Carey	C. Carey, *Lysias, selected speeches* (Cambridge 1990)
Carey-Reid	C. Carey and R.A. Reid, *Demosthenes: selected private speeches* (Cambridge 1985)
Davies *APF*	J.K. Davies, *Athenian propertied families, 600-300 B.C.* (Oxford 1971)
Dover *GPM*	K.J. Dover, *Greek popular morality in the time of Plato and Aristotle* (Oxford 1974)
Drerup	E. Drerup, *Uber die bei den attischen Rednern eigelegten Urkunden* (*Jahrb. für cl. Phil.* Suppl. 24, 1898)
Gernet	L. Gernet, *Demosthene, plaidoyers civils* IV (Paris 1959)
Gomme	A.W. Gomme, *A historical commentary on Thucydides* vol. II (Oxford 1956)
Harrison	A.R.W. Harrison, *The law of Athens*, 2 vols. (Oxford 1968, 1971)
IG	*Inscriptiones Graecae* (Berlin 1873-)
Kirchner *PA*	J. Kirchner, *Prosopographia Attica* (Berlin 1901-3)
Lacey	W.K. Lacey, *The family in Classical Greece* (Auckland 1983)
Lipsius	J.H. Lipsius, *Das attische Recht und Rechtsverfahren* (Leipzig 1905-15)
MacDowell *Andok.*	D.M. MacDowell, *Andokides on the Mysteries* (Oxford 1962)
MacDowell *Meidias*	D.M. MacDowell, *Demosthenes against Meidias (oration 21)* (Oxford 1990)
MacDowell *AHL*	D.M. MacDowell, *Athenian homicide law in the age of the orators* (Manchester 1963)
MacDowell *Law*	D.M. MacDowell, *The law in classical Athens* (London 1978)

Meiggs-Lewis	R. Meiggs and D.M. Lewis, *A selection of Greek historical inscriptions* (Oxford 1969)
Millett	P. Millett, *Lending and borrowing in ancient Athens* (Cambridge 1991)
Osborne	M.J. Osborne, *Naturalization in Athens*, 4 vols. (Brussels 1981-3)
Parke,	H.W. Parke, *Festivals of the Athenians* (London 1977)
Patteson	A.J. Patteson, *A commentary on [Demosthenes] LIX: Against Neaira* (Diss. Pennsylvania 1978)
Rhodes	P.J. Rhodes, *A commentary on the Aristotelian Athenaion Politeia* (Oxford 1981)
Rhodes *AB*	P.J. Rhodes, *The Athenian Boule* (Oxford 1972)
Simon	E. Simon, *Festivals of Attica* (Wisconsin 1983)
Thomas	R. Thomas, *Oral tradition and written record in classical Athens* (Cambridge 1989)
Travlos *PDA*	J. Travlos, *Pictorial dictionary of Athens* (London 1971)
Trevett *Apollodoros*	J.C. Trevett, *Apollodoros the son of Pasion* (Oxford 1992)

INTRODUCTION

1. Dramatis personae

Apollodoros

Apollodoros is well known to us from a number of speeches preserved in the Demosthenic corpus. He was born in 394. His father Pasion[1] was originally a slave in a bank. He was freed and became a banker himself. He was subsequently granted Athenian citizenship.[2] When he died in 370 Pasion left a vast fortune.

About Apollodoros' personal life we know only the sort of scandalous and unreliable detail which was standard ammunition in Greek litigation.[3] We are better informed about his public activities. Partly no doubt out of genuine gratitude to Athens for the gift of citizenship, partly because he wished to ingratiate himself with the people as a foundation for a political career, Apollodoros was especially diligent in performing *leitourgiai*.[4] In 368 he served as trierarch of a ship in Peloponnesian waters. In 366/5 he was joint trierarch on two ships in succession. He was joint trierarch of a ship in the north Aegaean from autumn 362 to February 360. In 362 he was also one of the rich men charged with making advance payment of the war levy; such men would pay the tax in advance and recoup the appropriate amount from others liable to the tax. He served as joint trierarch of the ship *Phosphoros* in 356. He was chorus producer (*choregos*) for his tribe in the boys' dithyramb at the Dionysia in 352/1. The only office he is known to have held is that of member of the Council of Five Hundred in 349-8.

Apollodoros was involved in an unusual amount of litigation. Pasion had bequeathed his wife Archippe to a former slave of his, Phormion, who was named guardian of Pasion's younger son Pasikles in Pasion's will. Apollodoros quarrelled with Phormion over Pasion's estate soon after the latter's death; the quarrel lasted for nearly two decades. Apollodoros also sued, and was sued by, people who had dealt with his father's bank and who owed money to Pasion's estate or were owed money. His public career was another source of litigation. The trierarchy of 362-60 led to his suing his successor for failure to relieve him on time. After the same trierarchy he prosecuted the three successive commanders of the fleet; he secured the execution of one. He also brought other public indictments and was himself prosecuted on at least one occasion.[5]

Theomnestos

[Dem.]59 is really two speeches. §§16-126 were delivered by Apollodoros. §§1-15 were delivered by his kinsman by marriage, Theomnestos. All we learn about him is that he was younger than Apollodoros and less confident of his powers of speech. He came from a propertied family of which little is known.[6]

Stephanos

Most of our knowledge of Stephanos' career comes from the present speech. Like Apollodoros he belongs to the host of lesser politicians who attached themselves to the major political figures. He is represented as politically active by the late 370s, but not yet playing any significant role (§§39, 43). We should probably place his birth in the period 410-400. By 369 (§43) he appears to have attached himself to the politician Kallistratos. In §§72ff. he is represented as acting as assessor to the King-Archon Theogenes, at a date which cannot be fixed with certainty but probably belongs to the period 360-355. By 349/8 he appears to have aligned himself with Euboulos, who dominated Athenian politics for a decade or so from the mid 350s.[7] Outside the speech, we know Stephanos as the proposer of a motion in 347/6 renewing a treaty with Mytilene, and possibly as the proposer of a motion praising the people of Mytilene in 368.[8] His political affiliations suggest that he may be (but cannot be shown to be) identical with the Stephanos who served with Aischines as ambassador to the Amphictyonic Council in 346.[9]

Neaira

All we know about Neaira derives from this speech.[10] The broad outlines of the account are likely to be correct. She began her career as a slave prostitute in Corinth, and was subsequently acquired for sexual purposes by two men, Timanoridas of Corinth and Eukrates of Leukas. She was able to purchase her freedom with the aid of an Athenian lover named Phrynion, with whom she lived for a while in Athens. Tired of his abusive treatment, she fled to Megara, where she met Stephanos, whose mistress she became and under whose protection she returned to Athens. According to the speech she continued to work as a prostitute while living with Stephanos in Athens; we have no means to verify this claim. One or two details in the speech provide a rough indication of her age at the date of the trial. i) She was associated indirectly with the speechwriter Lysias (who is represented in §§20-2 as having a strong attachment to one of her fellow slaves, Metaneira). Unfortunately, this is of limited use, since Lysias' own dates are disputed.[11] If we accept the date of 459 for Lysias' birth, following the ancient tradition, 395 is probably the latest plausible date for the incident in question, since he is sexually potent, and has a mother who is still alive. However, many modern writers are inclined to date Lysias' birth to the mid-440s. On this dating we should probably place the incident in 380 at the latest. At the time Neaira had not reached puberty; we should probably place her age at 10-12, and her birth between 405 and 390, depending on our dating of Lysias' birth. ii) The second detail is more useful. According to §37, while working as a prostitute in Megara she was still able to attract a permanent lover in 371; probably therefore she was no older than 30 at that time. But to accommodate the vicissitudes narrated in §§18-36 we should not place her age much below 25. Probably therefore we should place her birth between 400 and 395 and the incident in §§20-22 between 390 and 385. At the date of the trial therefore she was probably in her fifties, possibly in her late fifties.

2. Date

Neaira's trial can be dated with some confidence to the period 343-40. §§3-8 describe an unsuccessful attempt by Apollodoros to divert money from the theoric to the military fund. In 339 Demosthenes succeeded in carrying this measure.[12] Apollodoros' failure to mention this in retrospective justification has reasonably been taken as evidence that the speech precedes Demosthenes' successful proposal; which suggests 340 as the lower terminus. §26, which implies that his disfranchisement is the only factor preventing the poet Xenokleides from testifying, appears to suggest that Xenokleides is in Athens; he was ejected from Macedon in 343.[13]

3. The law

Theomnestos is prosecuting Neaira for living in marriage with Stephanos, despite being a foreigner, in contravention of the law. Greek states were extremely jealous of the privileges of citizen status. Athens in fact appears to have become increasingly restrictive in this respect during the century preceding Neaira's trial. During the first half of the fifth century any marriage was valid (for the purposes of producing citizen issue) in which the father was of Athenian birth. But in 451/0 Perikles sponsored a decree limiting citizenship to children born of two Athenian parents. In the closing phase of the Peloponnesian War this requirement was allowed to lapse because of shortage of manpower. It was revived in 403 after the overthrow of the régime of the Thirty. At some stage in the fourth century the law became more severe.[14] While the effect of the decree of 451/0 was to make all unions between citizens and non-citizens invalid for purposes of legitimacy and citizenship of issue, in the fourth century such relationships were actually punishable. Under the law cited in §16 of our speech, the foreigner who married an Athenian citizen was liable to enslavement and confiscation of property, the penalty for conviction on an indictment for illegal use of citizen rights (*graphe xenias*).

There is in fact a superficial ambiguity in the law under which Neaira was indicted by Theomnestos. The law literally defines the offence as follows (§16): 'if any foreigner lives with an Athenian by any manner or means ...', which might suggest informal cohabitation as well as marriage. However, the verb *synoikein*, translated here 'lives with', is frequently used of formal marriage. That this was the meaning of the verb in the context of the law is indicated by two facts. Firstly, Apollodoros when defining the relationship covered by the verb (§122) singles out the acts which distinguish formal marriage. Since it is in his interests to minimize, not to maximize, the criteria which would allow for conviction, we may take his definition seriously. Secondly, Apollodoros gives us to understand at §119 that Stephanos will argue that Neaira lives in his house not as his wife but as his mistress. The alleged line of defence indicates that it is perfectly legitimate for Stephanos to have a foreign mistress living with him. It was formal marriage, or the pretence of formal marriage, between citizen and alien which the law forbad, since unlike informal cohabitation this involved the pretence of citizen status on the part of the foreigner and the bestowal of citizen status on any issue. Although there were no marriage certificates in ancient Athens, it was relatively easy in practice to distinguish marriage from informal cohabitation, for marriage was distinguished not only by the formalities of bride bestowal but also by a series of acts recognizing the legitimacy of the offspring.[15]

4. The hidden agenda

i Apollodoros' feud with Stephanos

Formally Theomnestos is Neaira's prosecutor. Although the case against Neaira is presented by Apollodoros, he appears only as supporting speaker (*synegoros*),[16] ostensibly because of Theomnestos' youth and inexperience (§§14-15). However in §§121, 124, 125 and 126 Apollodoros makes clear that the initiative to prosecute comes from him. This is as one would expect from Theomnestos' account of the motives for bringing the action. In §§3-10 he describes two attacks by Stephanos. The first of these was in 348 when Stephanos prosecuted Apollodoros for putting an illegal motion before the Assembly. The second was a malicious charge of homicide. In the first trial, according to Theomnestos, having secured the conviction of Apollodoros, Stephanos proposed a penalty of fifteen talents, with the intention of ruining Apollodoros and his family. If the second trial had resulted in conviction, Apollodoros might have faced exile. Theomnestos claims in §12 that many people urged him to take revenge on Stephanos. The insistence on the duty to avenge is entirely in accordance with Greek belief. But in fact Theomnestos would have been affected only indirectly by Stephanos' attacks. It was Apollodoros who was directly threatened by Stephanos, and the duty to avenge was primarily his.

We can guess at Apollodoros' reasons for inducing Theomnestos to play the part of official prosecutor. Athenian public opinion was generally hostile to people who resorted regularly to the courts; Apollodoros may have felt that the prosecution would stand a better chance of success if he played a slightly less prominent role. Apollodoros may also have felt that a prosecution under laws relating to citizen rights would carry more weight if initiated by a man of pure Athenian birth than by an enfranchised alien like himself. More significant perhaps is the fact that in most public actions there were penalties for prosecutors who failed to obtain one fifth of the votes cast. There was a fine of one thousand drachmas, and it seems that in certain circumstances at least the prosecutor lost the right to bring the same type of action again.[17] For an active politician like Apollodoros this would be a severe limitation, since the lawcourts provided an important arena for settling political feuds.

Just as Theomnestos is only formally the prosecutor, so Neaira is only the intermediate, not the real, target. Her conviction is primarily a means to an end, not an end in itself. The real target is Stephanos, as is made clear right at the outset (§1). Virtually the whole of Theomnestos' speech is devoted to Stephanos' actions and the imperative to punish him. Stephanos is again explicitly the target at the opening of Apollodoros' speech (§16). The early part of his narrative (§§18-36) deals exclusively with Neaira. But from the point where her relationship with Stephanos begins, Apollodoros is careful to treat Stephanos as an active collaborator, not as Neaira's dupe. Thus in §§41-3 and 64-70 it is alleged that Stephanos was her partner in blackmail. In §§49-61 he is represented as breaching marriage/citizenship law, and in §§72-84 not only as breaching this law but also committing impiety. It is clear that Neaira was represented in court by Stephanos.[18] In a sense therefore he too is on trial, though if the prosecution is successful he will face only a fine, while Neaira will be sold into slavery.

However, probably there is more at issue than personal satisfaction, important though that undoubtedly was. The interval between Stephanos' attack and Apollodoros' retaliation, combined with their political careers and known affiliations, suggests that the trial may have a political as well as a personal motivation.

ii The political dimension

Upon his accession to the throne of Macedon in 359 Philip II set about securing his own position in Macedon and Macedon's position in Greece. The second objective inevitably involved a conflict of interest with Athens, which had a number of dependencies in the north. In rapid succession Philip took Amphipolis (357), which the Athenians had always regarded as theirs, even though it had not been subject to Athenian control since the fifth century, Pydna and Poteidaia (356). Athens at this period was distracted by war with her allies (357-5) and her attempts to regain control of Euboia (357), and so was unable to deal effectively with the threat posed by Macedon. Philip now began to extend his influence southwards.

From the mid 350s, the dominant political figure in Athens was Euboulos,[19] whose policy towards Macedon appears to have been one of cautious pragmatism. He was not a pacifist in the modern sense. Under his leadership attention was paid to the navy, the dockyards and the city walls. But he was opposed to long-distance, expensive operations against Philip in pursuit of unrealistic objectives. An important part of his political strategy was the organization and use of the theoric fund.[20] Theoric distributions may have been instituted early in the fourth century.[21] The aim was to provide the theatre entrance fee to enable poorer citizens to attend the Dionysia;[22] subsequently distributions were extended to other festivals, providing in effect several days paid holiday per year. Euboulos appears to have been responsible for a major reorganization in the 350s.[23] The creation of a distinct theoric fund may belong to this period. In addition to the festival distributions, the fund was also used to finance major public works.[24] To meet the increased costs, in addition to receiving its own allocation under the annual financial distribution the theoric fund received the surplus of public money after the administrative costs of the state had been met.[25] This arrangement was protected by laws prescribing penalties for anyone attempting to divert the surplus from the theoric fund.[26] Unfortunately, we have no means of knowing how much the fund received either from the distribution or from the surplus in any one year.[27] And any attempt to determine the amounts spent either on festival distributions or on public works must be largely conjectural.[28] But the arrangements for the theoric fund were an important element in the political influence of Euboulos. Festival distributions were popular with the citizenry at large, while building projects provided a source of employment. Hence those who were associated with the fund had a ready means of maintaining their own popularity. At the same time, the potential impact of expensive military operations on the fund could be used to undermine popular support for more grandiose foreign adventures.[29]

There were however other politicians, including Demosthenes and Apollodoros, who had a grander view of Athens' destiny and favoured more vigorous opposition to Macedonian expansion. An opportunity for action was presented in 349 when Olynthos in the north, under threat from Philip, sought Athenian aid. At the instigation of Demosthenes, among others, Athens made an alliance with Olynthos, and provided military aid on a small scale, to no effect; Olynthos fell in 348.[30] In 349, in the context of an appeal for vigorous aid to Olynthos, Demosthenes twice suggested circumspectly (without making a formal proposal) that the surplus monies should be diverted to military use.[31] In 348 even the limited aid to Olynthos became difficult to sustain, when Athens sent a force to Euboia to support the tyrant Ploutarchos; the cost of operations on two fronts led to a shortage of funds for other administrative purposes.[32] At this point Apollodoros, who was serving on the Council, made a formal proposal that the Assembly should decide whether the administrative surplus should be put to military or theoric use.[33] In the subsequent vote the Assembly decided to use the surplus for war. If the decision had been put into effect, it would have meant a major change of direction in foreign affairs, since Demosthenes and his associates would have had the means, and the popular support, to pursue a more adventurous policy; it would also have marked the eclipse of Euboulos and his associates. However, Apollodoros' proposal was indicted as illegal by Stephanos; Apollodoros was convicted and fined one talent.[34] Political trials in Athens settled more than questions of fact; they also served as a test of the popularity of opposing political interests and rival policies. The aim, and the effect, of the prosecution was both to block the diversion of funds and the general shift of policy it implied and to preserve the power of the dominant political faction.

It is however easier to posit political motives in the prosecution of Neaira than to identify specific political aims. 343-40 were eventful years, which saw Demosthenes' enemy Aischines decline in importance and Demosthenes reach the peak of his influence, which saw the Athenians become progressively more disillusioned with the Peace of Philokrates with Macedon of 346, convinced of the inevitability of war and finally committed formally to war with Philip. Since we cannot locate the speech precisely within this period, its relation to the immediate political climate must be a matter for conjecture.

Macurdy[35] emphasizes the appearance of Demosthenes' enemy Euboulos as witness for Apollodoros in §48. It is probable that Euboulos was the instigator of Stephanos' attack on Apollodoros in 348. Yet here he appears for Stephanos enemy, in the same camp as Demosthenes, who appears in support of Apollodoros later (§123). In 343, when Euboulos appeared for Demosthenes' enemy, Aischines, the two were still implacably opposed. Macurdy attributes Euboulos' appearance for Apollodoros to a drawing together of rival political groups in 340 in preparation for the struggle against Macedon. This is not without problems. The evidence for this rapprochement between opposing groups is both slender and ambiguous.[36] Moreover, Stephanos was not a major political figure. When he attacked Apollodoros he was probably merely the agent for vested interests. It is difficult to see why Stephanos should remain obdurate in his attachment to the peace of 346 if its main supporters had now decided that war should be pursued vigorously; if the rival groups had joined forces it would be exceedingly dangerous for Stephanos to remain outside the coalition. Finally, Theomnestos' historical sketch in §§4ff., while clearly drawing on Athenian disenchantment with the Peace of Philokrates, gives no hint of a conviction that war with Philip is inevitable or imminent.

The alternative is to link the speech with developments in and after 343. At this point those who believed that the peace had failed were seeking to take control of policy. It was in this year that Philokrates was impeached and fled. In the same year Demosthenes prosecuted Aischines for his part in the peace negotiations. This had been attempted prematurely in 345, with disastrous consequences for Demosthenes' associate, Timarchos. Demosthenes returned to the attack in 343 and almost secured Aischines' conviction. The attack on Stephanos through Neaira may be part of the same political assault. It could for instance be a preliminary engagement to test public opinion prior to the more serious prosecutions; alternatively it may have followed the major prosecutions of 343. Influential voices could be raised against war as late as 341,[37] and presumably later. The mopping up operation may have continued for some time.[38]

5. Apollodoros' case

In order to prove that Neaira is guilty under the law, Apollodoros needs to demonstrate two things, firstly that Neaira is a foreigner, secondly that she is not merely living with Stephanos as his mistress but is actually married to him. To prove the second point, Apollodoros needs to demonstrate that Stephanos contracted a formal marriage with Neaira and/or that he has both had children by Neaira and bestowed on those children the acts of recognition which distinguish marriage.

On the first count Apollodoros' case is conclusive. In §§17-48 he gives an account of Neaira's career, from the point when she was bought by a brothelkeeper as a child, through various vicissitudes as a prostitute or concubine in several states and with various lovers. In fact, Apollodoros' attempt to prove the first count extends to §87, though much of the detail concerns Neaira's daughter Phano. However, there is no indication anywhere that Stephanos intends to deny Neaira's non-citizen status. From §119 it is clear that the defence will be based on the nature of the relationship. Stephanos proposes to argue that Neaira is simply his mistress, and that his children are the issue not of his liaison with Neaira but of a marriage to a female of citizen status. Since there is no suggestion in the speech of any formal contraction of marriage, the case turns on the parentage and declared status of Stephanos' children. Apollodoros identifies (§§121, 124) three male offspring, Proxenos, Ariston and Antidorides, and a female, Phano (also known as Strybele); three of these offspring are also mentioned in §38. Apollodoros' allegations concerning these children are in fact ambiguous. §§38 and 51 treat them as children of Neaira, not Stephanos, while §§121 and 124 treat them as Stephanos' children by Neaira.

In assessing the strength of Apollodoros' case, it is useful to distinguish between the three males and Phano. As far as the male offspring are concerned, there is no support in the speech for Apollodoros' claims. The only evidence presented is a formal challenge (§§123-4) in which Apollodoros alleged that these were Stephanos' sons by Neaira. It seems clear from the terms of Apollodoros' challenge that the males were enjoying citizen rights and that Stephanos claimed that they were his legitimate children by an Athenian wife. Yet at no point does Apollodoros seek to prove that these sons were not entitled to citizen status. There is no deposition at any point in the speech to link them with Neaira. The cursory treatment of an issue of central importance to Apollodoros' case is a fair indication that Stephanos is telling the truth. This supposition is supported by the fact that one of the sons bore the name of Stephanos' father, Antidorides. Given the tendency of Athenians to name the first legitimate son after the paternal grandfather, it seems clear that here at least we have a legitimate son.

Apollodoros does however devote a great deal of space to the female, Phano. So it is on the Stephanos' treatment of Phano that the factual case must rest. There is reason to believe that Phano was Neaira's daughter.[39] Yet if Apollodoros is to be believed Stephanos has consistently represented her as his legitimate daughter. The account of Phano's career is introduced (§49) to prove that Neaira is a foreigner, but it is also relevant to the question of the nature of Neaira's relationship with Stephanos. Apollodoros narrates three scandalous incidents. The first of these (§§49-61) concerns an Athenian citizen of modest means named Phrastor, to whom Stephanos gave Phano in marriage. Because of her dissolute ways and because he had discovered that she was Neaira's daughter, Phrastor ejected Phano after a year of marriage, by which time she was pregnant, refusing to return the dowry of thirty minas provided by Stephanos. Stephanos brought a private suit to compel him to return the dowry or pay interest on it for Phano's maintenance. Phrastor replied by indicting Stephanos under the law forbidding an Athenian citizen to bestow a foreign female in marriage on another Athenian citizen, the penalty for this offence being disfranchisement with confiscation of property. Stephanos took fright and made a deal: he would cede the dowry to Phrastor if Phrastor withdrew his prosecution. Subsequently Phrastor fell ill; being childless, he was inveigled by Phano and Neaira into acknowledging as legitimate his son by Phano. However, when he tried to introduce the child into his genos it was rejected. Phrastor brought a suit against the genos to compel them to admit the child, but on being challenged to swear an oath that the child was his legitimate issue by a woman of citizen status he declined.

The second incident concerns a man from Andros named Epainetos (§§64-71). Stephanos invited Epainetos to the countryside in order to engineer a situation in which he could catch Epainetos in bed with Phano. Athenian law gave a male considerable powers over another male whom he caught in illicit sex (*moicheia*) with a female under his protection and control.[40] This included the right to hold the offender to ransom. On the basis of this right Stephanos imprisoned Epainetos and extorted the promise of a ransom of thirty minas. Upon release, however, Epainetos brought an action for wrongful imprisonment against Stephanos. He argued that since Stephanos was not Phano's father he had no rights in the matter, that Neaira was aware of his relationship with Phano, and that the law on *moicheia* explicitly excluded women working in a brothel, which is what Stephanos' house was. Stephanos once more took fright, and a deal was struck under which Epainetos would provide ten minas for Phano's dowry, in return for the right to have sex with her whenever he was in Athens.

The third, and most scandalous, incident (§§72-87) concerned an Athenian named Theogenes, to whom Stephanos gave Phano in marriage while Theogenes was serving as King-Archon and Stephanos was his assistant. This was another breach of citizenship/marriage law. In addition, a law prescribed that the wife of the King-Archon should not have been married previously. Finally, as Apollodoros shows (§§85-7), it was illegal for a woman who had been caught in illicit sex to enter the public temples, let alone carry out sacrifices as the King-Archon's wife had to do. On all these counts Phano could not legally be given in marriage to Theogenes. But since the King-Archon and his wife carried out religious duties on behalf of the city, Stephanos' alleged breach of the laws impinged on the city's relationship with its gods and therefore placed the whole community at risk. Stephanos' deception came to light when the Areopagos inquired into the identity of the King-Archon's wife. On learning the truth, the Areopagos threatened to punish Theogenes but refrained when he divorced Phano and dismissed Stephanos from the post of assistant.

For the reader the presentation of the case for the prosecution is unconvincing. The problems are discussed in detail in the commentary. At this point it is sufficient to stress the lack of independent support for Apollodoros' allegations. We are given only Phrastor's evidence that he was ever married to Phano, though there should be abundant testimony to support the claim. For the Epainetos affair we are given only two witnesses, though again testimony should have been readily available, and we have no evidence from Epainetos himself. Most strikingly, for the third and most shocking affair we have only the evidence of Theogenes, though here we might have had evidence for the marriage of Phano to Theogenes, her performance of religious rites, and the threatened punishment of Theogenes by the Areopagos. The paucity of testimony does not inspire confidence. It is to be borne in mind moreover that conviction on any of the offences alleged in relation to Phrastor and Theogenes would have led to severe punishment for Stephanos. Since Stephanos is the real target, we might expect Apollodoros to prosecute him directly for these offences if he were confident of his case, instead of introducing the allegations tangentially into a prosecution of Neaira.

Thus even with reference to Phano the case is factually weak. It is hardly surprising that Apollodoros devotes so much space to the first part of his case, Neaira's foreign origin. To the modern reader the case is also juristically weak. It is made clear that Stephanos represented Phano as his daughter by an Athenian wife, not Neaira. Neither Phrastor nor Theogenes, even on Apollodoros' account, was left in any doubt that Neaira was a foreigner.[41] For Stephanos to be representing Neaira as his wife, he should be passing the girl off as his legitimate daughter by Neaira, and thereby claiming that the latter was his wife and of citizen status; Apollodoros' account if true indicates illegality by Stephanos, but not Neaira's guilt under the law cited against her. So at least it seems to the modern reader, accustomed to the precise interpretation of law and to consistency of application created by precedent. But since each Athenian jury was its own interpreter of the law, and since juries were not impressed by fine distinctions, it is not inconceivable that the jury might convict if they were satisfied that Stephanos was treating Neaira's children as his legitimate issue. It is striking however that Apollodoros does not explicitly use these incidents as proof of Neaira's relationship with Stephanos but as proof that Neaira is a foreigner He is content to imply that the incidents prove the second half of his case and at the same time to rely on scandal to submerge questions of law. This unwillingness to confront the issue directly suggests that even an Athenian jury might be disinclined to stretch the law to fit Stephanos' alleged conduct.

However, in assessing Apollodoros' prospects for success it is also necessary to bear in mind the political climate. Athenian juries did not confine their attention to the factual issue, particularly in trials with a political dimension, covert or explicit. In the context of the late 340s the reminder of Stephanos' prevention of more vigorous action against Macedon, irrespective of its likelihood of success, would harness anti-Macedonian sentiment. There was moreover another source of resentment to tap. In 346/5 a politician named Demophilos carried a decree arranging for a scrutiny to be held in all the demes to test the citizenship qualifications of deme members. Evidently there was a generally shared suspicion that the citizenship laws were being flouted. The scrutiny resulted in a substantial number of ejections by the demes and raised strong hostility against individuals who were ejected.[42] We cannot determine whether the internal and external political context was sufficient to secure Neaira's conviction. However, for Apollodoros' purposes conviction may not have been necessary. If the trial was part of an attack on the opponents of vigorous action against Macedon or (if we follow Macurdy) a preparation for the proposed attack on the theoric fund, near-conviction of Neaira on a flimsy prosecution like this might suffice as an index of the unpopularity of Stephanos, his associates and their policies.

6. The speech

i. Structure

The speeches of Theomnestos and Apollodoros against Neaira are clearly conceived as a unity. Although variations, and further subdivisions, are possible, typically a Greek forensic speech contains four elements: introduction (*proioimion*), narrative (*diegesis*), proofs (*pisteis*), conclusion (*epilogos*). Apollodoros' speech (§§16-126) has no formal introduction, merely a brief reference to the legal grounds for the prosecution (§§16-7). This element is provided by Theomnestos' speech (§§1-15), which justifies the decision to prosecute. Apollodoros' speech contains the other three elements, narrative of the case against Neaira (§§18-84), proofs (§§85-125) and a brief conclusion (§126). However, any attempt to detect a neat division between the contituent parts is frustrated by the formal resemblance between the narrative and proof sections. A substantial proportion of the proof section consists of narrative: §§88-93 detail the procedures for the enfranchisement of aliens in order to demonstrate how seriously the Athenian people takes the rights which Stephanos has (allegedly) bestowed so casually on Neaira; §§94-106 amplify this point by describing the sevices and reward of the Plataians, who were given Athenian citizenship for outstanding loyalty to Athens, but subject to strict limitations. As a result the transition between narrative and proof becomes blurred.

ii. Methods of persuasion

Aristotle in the *Rhetoric*[43] distinguishes two categories of proof, 'artless' (*atechnoi pisteis*) and 'artificial' or 'rhetorical' (*entechnoi pisteis*). The former consists of documentary proof (depositions etc.) presented in court, the latter of proofs advanced through the medium of the speech. Aristotle divides these into three categories, argument, the moral character of the speaker (*ethos*) and the emotional effect of the speech on the hearer (*pathos*). Of these, little of Apollodoros' argument in the proof section relates to questions of fact: §§85-7, on Phano's disqualification for any religious duty, and §§119-125, the refutation of Stephanos' arguments, together make up only 25% of the proof section and less than 8% of the case presented by the prosecution. The rest of the proof section is devoted to the need for severity. The cursory nature of Apollodoros' refutation of Stephanos is particularly noteworthy. It consists of a single argument, based on Stephanos' refusal of a formal challenge from Apollodoros for the submission of Neaira's slaves for torture in order to prove the parentage of Stephanos' children. As far as the factual issue is concerned, Apollodoros relies on the vividness and internal consistency of the narrative[44] to carry conviction.

The function of moral character is to present the speaker as a trustworthy person and also to establish a claim on the goodwill of the jury. This element figures only indirectly in Apollodoros' speech, not surprisingly, since he does not touch on his own dealings with Stephanos. His stance is consistently that of the decent citizen, and there is much righteous indignation at Stephanos' conduct. At the same time, his persistent reticence on sexual matters suggests the propriety of the speaker and helps to create a bond between speaker and hearer. Moral character is more obviously present in Theomnestos' speech. Since the law offered rewards for successful prosecutors, it was important to disclaim any desire for gain, for Athenian public opinion disapproved of manipulation of the lawcourts for personal profit. Theomnestos meets this problem head-on by stressing the desire for revenge as a motive for prosecuting. However, since Athenian jurors did not approve of people who resorted casually to litigation, he is careful to demonstrate that the prosecutors are retaliating to systematic persecution of Apollodoros by Stephanos.

The impression created is that they have been provoked beyond endurance. Theomnestos thus claims sufficient tolerance to win the respect of the jury without going so far as to present himself as weak.

The third type of proof, emotion, is based on common sense and experience. Litigants, politicians and poets had appreciated long before Aristotle that the process of inducing an audience to vote in one's favour is only partly rational. The aim of *pathos* is to induce the audience to vote subjectively, that is, to view the factual issue through a filter coloured by emotion. Appeals to emotion in the orators are often explicit. It is in *pathos* that the strength of this speech resides, and much of the prosecution case is calculated to have an emotional effect. In the case of Neaira, Apollodoros seeks to arouse in the jurors a mixture of contempt and hostility, based primarily on her past life. Though much of the narrative is ostensibly offered to prove that Neaira is a foreigner, what emerges most clearly is the scandalous nature of her past life. Apollodoros presents a picture of degradation, by repeatedly emphasizing her status as a sexual plaything, both during her time as a slave, first prostitute (§§18-28) and then concubine (§§29-32), and later as a free prostitute and as a mistress used for sexual purposes by her lovers and others (§§33-48). He depicts a woman who is sexually insatiable and tolerant of any degree of humiliation. This element reaches a climax in §§107-8, where she is presented as someone who has prostituted herself over the whole of the Greek world. Apollodoros also associates her with a blackmail technique routinely practised by Stephanos (§§41-2). The aim of all of this is to create an ambiguous response, a combination of titillation and disapproval. The titillation keeps the audience attentive, while at the same time diverting that attention from awkward questions of fact. The disapproval causes the audience to despise her and take especial offence at the alleged attempt to usurp citizen rights. The shocked disapproval aroused by the career of her daughter Phano (§§49-84) increases audience hostility to Neaira.

The other target for audience anger is Stephanos, who is represented as contemptuous of both law and morality, a politician and prosecutor for hire (§§39, 43), a blackmailer (§§42, 64-71), a man who casually (§38) gives citizen status to a foreign prostitute and equally casually breaks the solemn laws governing the worship of the city's gods (§§72-84).

The other emotional vein mined by Apollodoros is fear. The account of the Theogenes affair (§§72-84) is meant to cause a frisson of horror as well as a surge of hostility, for it represents Stephanos as endangering the city's relationship with its gods, thus placing the whole population at risk. This fear recurs in another form in §§109 and 126, where Apollodoros threatens the juries with divine anger if they vote for acquittal.

A different source of fear is exploited in §§111-114, where Apollodoros argues that the acquittal of Neaira would create a precedent by legitimizing Neaira's conduct. Poor women of citizen status will be unable to marry if they have to compete for husbands with prostitutes who can provide a substantial dowry; they will therefore be forced to turn to prostitution. The jurors are meant to feel afraid for their female relatives, and for the future of Athenian society.

7. Women in Athens

Apollodoros' narrative has much to say about the lives of and attitudes to women in ancient Athens.

i. Women of citizen status

Of women of citizen status[45] Apollodoros has little to say directly. However, the ideal of Athenian womanhood is invoked implicitly throughout Apollodoros' account of Neaira's career. His use of her presence at male gatherings as evidence of her status as a prostitute rests on the fact, confirmed by other sources, that an Athenian male avoided as far as possible bringing his female relatives into contact with males outside the family. This image of Athenian womanhood is exploited more directly in §§110-111, where the jurors are reminded of their womenfolk, waiting at home for news of the outside world. His insistence on Neaira's sexual promiscuity relies for its power to shock on an ideal of female conduct derived from the wives and daughters of citizens.

ii. Non-citizen women

The speech has rather more to say about non-citizen women, more specifically independent non-citizen women. Athenian law assumed that every female of citizen status had a male protector/controller, her *kyrios*, who acted for her in any significant financial transactions and represented her in court, whether for prosecution, defence, or simply as witness. The same almost certainly applied to the vast majority of women of resident alien ('metic', *metoikos*) status, who would be part of a family unit and under the protection and control of a male relative from birth until death. However, some female metics had no male *kyrios*. Most women in this category would be freed slaves, who unless they chose to marry would not be part of a family unit. Female metics who had no adult male relative to take responsibility for them were registered as metics in their own right and were liable to the metics' tax in Athens alongside male metics but at a lower rate.[46] As an unmarried freedwoman, Neaira belonged to this category. Hence we hear of a dispute about her status (§46) resulting in a decision that she was kyria of herself, that is her own mistress.[47] A woman in this category enjoyed considerably more freedom of movement than the average woman of either citizen or metic status. And if like Neaira she was also a prostitute she would enjoy considerably more freedom of association. But the cost in insecurity was high. It might be difficult for a woman in this position to defend her free status from attack without a male protector, as Neaira found (§§40, 45-6), or indeed to obtain redress when wronged. Women did not appear in Athenian courts, as witnesses, plaintiffs or defendants. Moreover, although such a woman was legally free and subject to no male control, we find in the case of both Neaira and her daughter Phano arrangements being made by males which effectively disposed of the sexual favours of the woman. The legal force of such arrangements was no doubt questionable. But there was evidently a gap between the legal and the practical position. The independent non-citizen female probably envied the security and status enjoyed by the citizen female, irrespective of social class and property.

iii. Prostitutes

This speech provides our most detailed account of the life of a prostitute in ancient Greece. The terms normally used for a woman who provided sex in return for money were *porne* and *hetaira*. The former term is the more coarse. The latter is slightly more delicate; euphemistic in origin, literally it means 'companion', and it is used not only of the prostitute but also of a woman engaged in an informal semi-permanent sexual relationship with a man. In an attempt to represent the register of the latter term in English, I have consistently translated *hetaira* as 'courtesan'.

Prostitutes varied widely in terms of cost, status and skills. At the lowest end of the scale was the woman who simply provided sex, the streetwalker or the prostitute in a brothel. At the close of Aristophanes' *Knights* (1400, 1403), when the demagogue Kleon (dramatized as a Paphlagonian slave) loses power and prestige, he is left to squabble at the city gates with the *pornai*, the implication being that he has fallen from the highest to the lowest position in city life. At this level the women would commonly, though not inevitably, be slaves. It was in a brothel that Neaira began her career, though not a common brothel, for her original owner Nikarete maintained the fiction of running a respectable house (§§18ff.). At a higher level were the women who provided elegant and witty companionship as well as sex. The most accomplished and ambitious of these women became both celebrated and sought after. There is no equivalent in modern western society, though we can recognize a similar world in the France of Zola's *Nana*. These women too might be of servile status, though they were more commonly freedwomen or women of free (foreign) birth. We find Neaira while still a slave (§26) achieving a degree of celebrity in Corinth.

8. Authorship and Style

At least seven, and possibly nine, of the speeches preserved in the Demosthenic corpus were delivered by Apollodoros. Certain are 45 and 46 *Against Stephanos*,[48] 49 *Against Timotheos*, 50 *Against Polykles*, 52 *Against Kallippos*, 53 *Against Nikostratos*, and 59 *Against Neaira*; possible are 47 *Against Euergos and Mnesiboulos* and 51 *On the Trierarchic Crown*. Two, possibly three, of these can be dissociated from Demosthenes on chronological grounds. 52 was written in 369/8, when Demosthenes (who was born in 384) was below the age of majority. 53 can be dated to about 366. Demosthenes was by now of age; but since immediately on attaining his majority he became embroiled in a legal dispute with his guardians, who had misappropriated his inheritance, it is unlikely that he had the time to devote to producing speeches for others. Since the legal battle dragged on for some time, we should probably dismiss also 49 (written c.362) as undemosthenic on chronological grounds. There is no external evidence to determine the authorship of the other speeches probably or certainly delivered by Apollodoros. However, scholars in the nineteenth century noted marked differences in style between most members of this group and those speeches which are certainly by Demosthenes. Because the data collected was either unquantified or unquantifiable, the conclusions though suggestive remained highly subjective. The degree of subjectivity has been reduced by the application of modern statistical methods by McCabe, whose work has been supplemented by some useful numerical data from Trevett.[49]

i. Rhythm

Blass found that in his mature period Demosthenes tended to avoid successions of three or more short syllables.[50] McCabe's analysis indicates a significant difference between the genuine demosthenic speeches and 46, 49, 50, 52, 53 and 59; 47 agrees with this group, 45 and 51 with the genuine Demosthenes.

ii. Hiatus

It was observed in antiquity that Demosthenes sought to avoid hiatus. McCabe's analysis confirms the conclusions of scholars in the last century that most speeches in the Apollodoros group are less sensitive in this respect, with 46, 49, 50, 52, 53, 59 showing a significant difference from Demosthenes; 45 agrees with genuine Demosthenes, 47 with the Apollodoros speeches, 51 with neither.

iii. Sentence length

Trevett compares the sentence word-count of the Apollodoros group with a demosthenic sample and concludes that 'the sentences in the speeches delivered by Apollodoros ... are noticeably longer than those in the genuine speeches of Demosthenes'. Exceptions are 45 and 46.

iv. Pronouns *houtos* and *autos*

Trevett finds *houtos* markedly less frequent in the Apollodoros group than in Demosthenes, with 47 agreeing with the Apollodoros group, 45 with Demosthenes, 51 occupying an intermediate position. He finds *autos* strikingly more frequent in the Apollodoros group, with 47 agreeing with this group, 45 and 49 occupying an intermediate position.

The statistical evidence tends to support the conclusion reached by nineteenth century scholars that 46, 49, 50, 52, 53 and 59 are the work of a single author, and that this was not Demosthenes. 47 may belong with the Apollodoros group, though in default of external evidence we cannot be confident; 51 probably does not belong with the Apollodoros group, to which it was linked by some scholars in the last century. Demosthenes was probably the author of 45.[51] We cannot pronounce with certainty on the identity of the author of the bulk of the Apollodoros speeches. However, since Apollodoros was himself an active politician, there is much to recommend the widely held view that these speeches were his own work. This is especially suggested by the period (almost three decades) over which the speeches were delivered. It is unlikely that Apollodoros could draw on a single speechwriter over such a period.[52]

The following features of Apollodoros' style and manner have been emphasized by scholars over the last hundred years or so:

1. Repetition

There is in the Apollodoros group a desire for precision which causes the author to restate the obvious. The result is a tendency toward flabbiness. The opening of the speech offers a typical example; the words 'we were placed [by him] in the most serious danger' occur twice in close proximity in §1. §63 has three subordinate clauses in succession introduced by the same conjunction. This insensitivity to repetition is particularly visible in the tendency to repeat proper names or pronouns. For instance, in §2 the name Apollodoros occurs four times, in §§59-60 the name Phrastor six times; in §31 the pronoun *autos* occurs six times (3X masculine, 3X feminine).

2. Longwindedness

Reference has already been made to sentence length in the Apollodoran speeches. In particular, several of the Apollodoros speeches show a tendency to extend sentences by stringing together participles. Against Neaira has some particularly striking examples; extreme cases are §§3-4, 62-3. Sometimes this tendency to crowd ideas in the sentence causes Apollodoros to lose his way. Examples are §§12-13, 36-7, 38, 96-7.

3. Narrative

The speeches written by Apollodoros tend to contain a lengthy and circumstantial narrative. 46 (which as a second speech has no use for narrative) is an exception. Trevett finds that the average narrative content for Apollodoros is 54.4%, as against 14.6% for a sample from Demosthenes.[53] This is however not just a matter of quantity but of emphasis. Apollodoros relies heavily on narrative to perform the task of persuasion, giving far less weight to argumentation. The argument section is not infrequently weak as well as brief.

4. Direct statement

Apollodoros shows a predilection for introducing direct quotation into his speeches. The narrative of our speech contains no fewer than three examples, §§70, 82, 111-2.

5. Self-importance

There is a tendency on occasion to parade knowledge. This is true of speech 46, which is a shallow display of legal expertise, and also of the present speech, where as well as paraphrasing laws at length beyond his immediate requirements Apollodoros also explicitly gives the jurors a lesson in the law (§89), and makes a display of his historical knowledge (§§74-7, 94ff.). At 46.17 Apollodoros compliments himself on his cleverness.

Not all these features are to be dismissed as flaws. Certainly not the use of direct statement, which contributes to vividness, a quality which can enhance plausibility. The same can be said of a detailed narrative, though over-reliance on narrative would be very dangerous when matched against an opponent skilled in argument (especially when prosecuting, since the prosecutor spoke first). The repetition can be decidedly tedious for the reader; but it may well have been welcome to an audience seeking to keep the facts and issues clear in their minds. Taken together, they may indicate a lack of formal rhetorical training, as has recently been suggested.[54]

9. The documents

A separate question of authenticity concerns the documents which survive in the manuscript tradition. Some speeches survive with documents at all points where we expect them, some with an incomplete set of documents, some with none at all. Of the documents which survive, some are likely to be genuine while others are patent forgeries.[55] The documents are an important means of testing the strength of a litigant's case, since they enable us to establish the degree of support he can muster. The importance of the documentary evidence is increased for the modern reader by the accident of survival; only rarely have both sides of a dispute come down to us. It is therefore vital for us to determine as far as possible whether the documents offered by the manuscripts are those which were presented in court. Since the fluctuation in the reliability of the tradition on this issue does not allow us either to accept or to reject documents *en masse*, either within the corpus as a whole or within the individual speech, the only effective method is to assess each document on its own merits. Striking divergences from the conventions governing the form of a particular kind of document, where these are known, should make us suspicious. Major factual discrepancies between a document and the surrounding text, or between the content of a document and independent evidence for legal provisions and procedures, likewise suggest spuriousness. However, since the most obvious source of information for a forger is the surrounding text, information contained in a document beyond what could be derived from the context may be taken as evidence of authenticity, if it is either verified by an independent source or is inherently plausible. In the case of depositions inscriptions offer an important means of authentication: where the manuscript text of a deposition contains the names of witnesses known to us only from inscriptions we may reasonably conclude that the document is genuine, given the intrinsic improbability that such a source would, or often could, be consulted by a later forger.

10. The text

Of the older medieval manuscripts of Demosthenes, five offer the speech

Against Neaira: **D** (tenth or eleventh century), **F** (tenth century), **Q** (tenth or eleventh century), **S** (ninth or tenth century), and **Y** (tenth century). Of these, **S**, **FQD**, and **Y** are representatives of three of the four families into which the Demosthenic corpus is conventionally divided.[56] The oldest representative of the fourth family, **A** (tenth or eleventh century) does not contain *Against Neaira* (nor the two following speeches), but the speech is included in the fourteenth century manuscript **R**, which evidently comes from an exemplar derived from **A** while the latter was intact.

For a full apparatus Rennie's Oxford text should be consulted. In the following places I have departed from the Oxford text.[57]

10 δραχμῶν FQSYR: δικαστῶν Qγρ.D: del. Reiske.

13 καὶ ὥσπερ codd.: ὥσπερ καὶ Hude.

32 τῶι τε Εὐκράτει R: τῶι Εὐκράτει cett., Bekker Anecd.151.31.

51 δ' ὁ DRY: δὲ SFQ.

53 καὶ del. Reiske.

54 Στέφανον del. Blass.

78 ἐν κανοῖς codd.: τὰς ἐν κανοῖς Rennie

82 ἔστωσαν codd.: ὄντων Rennie.

85 ἐπὶ τούτοις codd.: τὸν ἐπὶ τούτοις Rennie

89 lacunam statuit Herwerden.

99 αὐτῶν (ante τὴν πόλιν) codd.: del. Rennie.

102 δὲ (post ἀφίστασθαι) codd.: del. Rennie:: δέκα codd.: δύο Palmer.

104 lacunam statuit Riehemann.

124 τῶν ὄντων Στεφάνωι Baiter: τῶν ὄντων Νεαίραι FQ: τῶν ὄντων Νεαίρας DRSY:: ὅτι ἐκ Νεαίρας εἰσιν Baiter: ὅτι ἐκ Στεφάνου εἰσιν codd.: οὐκ ante ἐκ add. Voemel:: ἐκ Στεφάνου εἶναι καὶ Νεαίρας codd.: ἐκ Στ. et καὶ del. Blass.

NOTES TO INTRODUCTION

1 For Pasion and his family see Davies *APF* 427-42 and Trevett *Apollodoros* ch.1.

2 Cf. §2. For an attempt to date Pasion's receipt of citizenship see *CQ* 41 (1991) 84-9.

3 According to the speaker of speech 36 (§45) Apollodoros was extravagant, licentious, ostentatious and violent in his private life. Apollodoros' self-description at 45.77 ('In my appearance, men of Athens, and my rapid walk and loud voice, I do not consider myself one of those blessed by nature.') suggests that his manner was brash and boorish.

4 For the term see on §117. For a list of Apollodoros' *leitourgiai* with references see Davies *APF* 440-2.

5 For an account of Apollodoros' litigation see R.J. Bonner, *Lawyers and litigants in ancient Athens* (Chicago 1927) ch. 7.

6 For Theomnestos' family see Davies *APF* 437-8.

7 For Euboulos see further p.6.

8 *IG* ii^2 213.5, 107.8.

9 Aischin.2.140. This Stephanos should not be confused with Apollodoros' target in Dem.45 and 46; see n. 48 below.

10 For Athenaios' allusions to Neaira and her associates see on §18.

11 See most recently Carey 1.

12 Philochoros F56a *FGH*.

13 19.231.

14 Gernet 67 n.3 suggests a date c.350. See also *CQ* 41 (1991) 85 n.10.

15 See on §122.

16 For this term see on §14.

17 See on §53. For the possibility that Apollodoros originally indicted Neaira himself see on §124.

18 The capacity in which Stephanos acted for Neaira is not clear. Whether or not Stephanos regarded himself as Neaira's *kyrios* (for this term see below p.15), his name will have figured in the indictment, since Apollodoros claims they are married, for in the case of a woman the charge was made against 'X and her *kyrios*' (schol.Ar.*Knights* 969). Stephanos may have represented her in court not as her *kyrios* but as her citizen patron (see on §37), as G. Thür, *Die Beweisführung vor den Schwurgerichtshöfen Athens* (Vienna 1977) 68 suggests. The role of the patron is disputed (see Harrison II 190ff., D. Whitehead, *The ideology of the Athenian metic* (*PCPS* Suppl. 4, 1977) 90-1), but in the case of the female metic at least it may have included legal representation. It is possible however that Stephanos was legally her *kyrios* even if as he claims she was only his *pallake* (for this term see on §122), as Patteson 11 supposes.

19 For Euboulos' career and policies see G.L. Cawkwell, *JHS* 83 (1963) 47-67.

20 Owing to the lack of reliable information on the origin, scale and administration of the theoric monies, the brief account which follows is necessarily tentative. See further A.H.M. Jones, *Athenian democracy* (Oxford 1957) 33-5, J.J. Buchanan, *Theorika. A study of monetary distributions to the Athenian citizenry during the fourth and fifth centuries B.C.* (New York 1962), Cawkwell, *JHS* 83 (1963) 55-61, G.E.M. de Ste Croix, *CR* 14 (1964) 190-2, Rhodes *AB* 235-40 and note on *Ath.Pol.* 43.1, M.H. Hansen, *GRBS* 17 (1976) 235-46.

21 Harpokration s.v. *theorika*.

22 Harpokration and Souda s.v. *theorika*, citing the fourth century orator Philinos.

23 Aischines 3.25, Harpokration and Souda s.v. *theorika*.

24 Aischines 3.25, Dem.3.29, Deinarchos 1.96, Harpokration and Souda s.v. *theorika.*

25 My account of the financing of the fund follows Hansen, *GRBS* 17 (1976) 240-3.

26 The laws governing the theoric fund are discussed in detail in the Appendix.

27 The issue is important. If the bulk of the money disbursed from the fund was derived from the surplus, then any attempt to divert the surplus would severely limit the potential of the theoric fund and the activity of its administrators.

28 Two sources from the 320s give a figure of five drachmas for the annual amount received per capita (Hypereides *Dem.* col.26, Deinarchos 1.56). This would suggest a maximum outlay of 25 talents in distributions. However, we cannot retroject this figure twenty or thirty years with confidence. The sums spent on public works must have been substantial, not enough to wage a major war, but probably enough for the initial financing of an expedition with a limited military purpose.

29 At 19.291 Demosthenes represents Euboulos as arguing in support of Philokrates' peace proposal of 346 that the alternative was to use the theoric money for military purposes.

30 See in general G.L. Cawkwell, *CQ* 1 (1962) 122-40.

31 1.19, 3.11.

32 Dem.39.17.

33 On the chronology of the proposals, Trevett *Apollodoros* 143 notes that Demosthenes' silence about Euboia in the Third Olynthiac indicates that his attack on the fund predates the Euboian campaign, while 59.4 explicitly connects Apollodoros' proposal with both campaigns.

34 For the problems presented by Stephanos' action see Appendix.

35 G.H. Macurdy, *AJP* 63 (1942) 257-71. Trevett *Apollodoros* 150 also inclines to a date c.339 for the prosecution of Neaira.

[36] Macurdy cites Phokion's appointment to the highest naval command and the selection of Demosthenes' enemies Aischines and Meidias as envoys to the Amphictyonic Council. As to the latter point, even in 339 Demosthenes cannot have had such positions in his gift. It is also easy to imagine good pragmatic reasons why Demosthenes should acquiesce in Aischines' appointment (for instance Aischines, as a man who had continued to support peace with Philip when it had become unpopular, might be a useful negotiator with a body which had close links with Philip, with a view to buying time to build up an anti-Macedonian coalition). At 18.83 Demosthenes represents himself and Aischines as still enemies in 340.

[37] Cf. 8.4-5.

[38] This alternative also presents a problem. How do we account for Euboulos' appearance for Apollodoros? It is important in this connection to note the different roles of Aischines and Demosthenes. Anyone approaching a matter which might involve litigation would normally arm himself with friendly witnesses. In other cases, including matters relating to the past, he would have to make do with such witnesses as he could get. Demosthenes, who voluntarily accompanied Apollodoros when he served his challenge, clearly falls into the former category; Euboulos may belong to the latter. That is, he may appear for Apollodoros because the details he is called to attest are true. He could of course have refused to appear and accepted the penalty for this (see on §28 for the procedure of *kleteusis*; if S.C. Todd (cited on §28) is correct to argue that this procedure was only available against recalcitrant witnesses actually in court, Euboulos could have evaded the penalty simply by refusing to turn up; but Dem.32.30 is decisive against his view). But since the events he attests are tangential to the main charge, he may have felt that his name would be of little use to the prosecution. It may also be significant that it is not Stephanos who is under direct threat. How much would Euboulos risk for an aging ex-prostitute?

[39] See on §61.

[40] D. Cohen *RIDA* 31 (1984) 147-50 rejects the generally accepted view that the offence of *moicheia* under Athenian law covered other dependent female relatives as well as wives. However, §67 of our speech makes it abundantly clear that Stephanos' seizure of Epainetos is based on a claim that she is his daughter.

41 This is made clear at §§51 and 81; §61 suggests that Neaira's non-citizen status was common knowledge.

42 Cf. 57.2, Aischines 1.78.

43 *R.*1355b35-1356a4.

44 See on §27.

45 Since women did not exercise citizen rights in Athens, I use the terms 'women/females of citizen status' consistently in preference to 'citizen women/females'.

46 Cf. Harpokration, M. Clerc, *Les métèques athéniens* (Paris 1893) 15, Whitehead (cited above n.18) 75.

47 By the time of the present trial this situation may have changed; see n.18 above.

48 This Stephanos (son of Menekles of Acharnai) should not be confused with the target of the present speech (Stephanos son of Antidorides of Eroiadai).

49 See D.F. McCabe, *The prose-rhythm of Demosthenes* (New York 1981), especially 152-74, Trevett *Apollodoros* 62-70. For nineteenth century discussion see especially J. Sigg, *Der Verfasser neun angeblich von Demosthenes für Apollodor geschriebener Reden* (*Jahrbücher für classische Philologie* Suppl. 6 (1873) 395-434) , A. Schäfer, *Demosthenes und seine Zeit* IIIB (Leipzig 1858) 184-93 and Blass III.1 539ff.

50 Blass III.1 105.

51 The conclusion that Demosthenes composed speech 45 for Apollodoros casts an interesting light on the relationship between Demosthenes' activities as politician and logographer. Speech 45 was delivered in 349 in the prosecution of Stephanos of Acharnai for allegedly giving false testimony for Apollodoros' stepfather Phormion in 350. Speech 36, composed by Demosthenes for delivery by a supporter of Phormion at the trial of 350, contains a fierce attack on Apollodoros (§§41-2, 45-7, 52, 53, 56, 61). Demosthenes' change of sides involved a vigorous attack on his

former client (45.71-82). Given its speed and proximity in time to the attack on the theoric fund, it is reasonable to suppose that the change of sides was the result of a political connection forged with Apollodoros. Whether speech 45 was more specifically Apollodoros' reward for agreeing to expose himself to attack in a cause he shared with (and perhaps as agent for) Demosthenes is impossible to say.

52 So most recently Trevett *Apollodoros* 74.

53 Trevett *Apollodoros* 82 n.26.

54 Trevett *Apollodoros* 116ff. This does not apply to the use of direct statement, which is also put to good use by the professional speechwriter Lysias.

55 The authenticity of the documents has been much discussed. I have found Drerup and J. Kirchner, *RhM* 40 (1855) 377-86 particularly valuable.

56 See in general Rennie v-xiv with references, G. Pasquali, *Storia della tradizione e critica del testo* (Florence 1952) 269ff.

57 Changes of punctuation and corrections of spelling and diacritical marks are not noted.

Apollodoros Against Neaira

[Demosthenes] 59

Text and Translation

ΚΑΤΑ ΝΕΑΙΡΑΣ

1 Πολλά με τὰ παρακαλοῦντα ἦν, ὦ ἄνδρες Ἀθηναῖοι, γράψασθαι Νέαιραν
τὴν γραφὴν ταυτηνὶ καὶ εἰσελθεῖν εἰς ὑμᾶς. καὶ γὰρ ἠδικήμεθα ὑπὸ Στεφάνου
μεγάλα, καὶ εἰς κινδύνους τοὺς ἐσχάτους κατέστημεν ὑπ' αὐτοῦ, ὅ τε κηδέστης
καὶ ἐγὼ καὶ ἡ ἀδελφὴ καὶ ἡ γυνὴ ἡ ἐμή, ὥστε οὐχ ὑπάρχων ἀλλὰ τιμωρούμενος
ἀγωνιοῦμαι τὸν ἀγῶνα τουτονί· τῆς γὰρ ἔχθρας πρότερος οὗτος ὑπῆρξεν, οὐδὲν
ὑφ' ἡμῶν πώποτε οὔτε λόγωι οὔτε ἔργωι κακὸν παθών. βούλομαι δ' ὑμῖν
προδιηγήσασθαι πρῶτον ἃ πεπόνθαμεν ὑπ' αὐτοῦ, ἵνα μᾶλλόν μοι συγγνώμην
ἔχητε ἀμυνομένωι, καὶ ὡς εἰς τοὺς ἐσχάτους κινδύνους κατέστημεν περί τε τῆς
πατρίδος καὶ περὶ ἀτιμίας.
2 ψηφισάμενου γὰρ τοῦ δήμου τοῦ Ἀθηναίων Ἀθηναῖον εἶναι Πασίωνα καὶ
ἐκγόνους τοὺς ἐκείνου διὰ τὰς εὐεργεσίας τὰς εἰς τὴν πόλιν, ὁμογνώμων καὶ ὁ
πατὴρ ἐγένετο ὁ ἐμὸς τῆι τοῦ δήμου δωρεᾶι, καὶ ἔδωκεν Ἀπολλοδώρωι τῶι υἱεῖ
τῶι ἐκείνου θυγατέρα μὲν αὐτοῦ, ἀδελφὴν δὲ ἐμήν, ἐξ ἧς Ἀπολλοδώρωι οἱ
παῖδές εἰσιν. ὄντος δὲ χρηστοῦ τοῦ Ἀπολλοδώρου περί τε τὴν ἀδελφὴν τὴν ἐμὴν
καὶ περὶ ἡμᾶς ἅπαντας, καὶ ἡγουμένου τῆι ἀληθείαι οἰκείους ὄντας κοινωνεῖν
πάντων τῶν ὄντων, ἔλαβον καὶ ἐγὼ γυναῖκα Ἀπολλοδώρου μὲν θυγατέρα,
3 ἀδελφιδῆν δ' ἐμαυτοῦ. προεληλυθότος δὲ χρόνου λαγχάνει βουλεύειν Ἀπολλό-
δωρος· δοκιμασθεὶς δὲ καὶ ὀμόσας τὸν νόμιμον ὅρκον, συμβάντος τῆι πόλει
καιροῦ τοιούτου καὶ πολέμου, ἐν ὧι ἦν ἢ κρατήσασιν ὑμῖν μεγίστοις τῶν
Ἑλλήνων εἶναι καὶ ἀναμφισβητήτως τά τε ὑμέτερα αὐτῶν κεκομίσθαι καὶ
καταπεπολεμηκέναι Φίλιππον, ἢ ὑστερίσασι τῆι βοηθείαι καὶ προεμένοις τοὺς
συμμάχους, δι' ἀπορίαν χρημάτων καταλυθέντος τοῦ στρατοπέδου, τούτους τ'
ἀπολέσαι καὶ τοῖς ἄλλοις Ἕλλησιν ἀπίστους εἶναι δοκεῖν, καὶ κινδυνεύειν περὶ
4 τῶν ὑπολοίπων, περί τε Λήμνου καὶ Ἴμβρου καὶ Σκύρου καὶ Χερρονήσου, καὶ
μελλόντων στρατεύεσθαι ὑμῶν πανδημεὶ εἴς τε Εὔβοιαν καὶ Ὄλυνθον, ἔγραψε
ψήφισμα ἐν τῆι βουλῆι Ἀπολλόδωρος βουλεύων καὶ ἐξήνεγκε προβούλευμα εἰς
τὸν δῆμον, λέγον διαχειροτονῆσαι τὸν δῆμον εἴτε δοκεῖ τὰ περιόντα χρήματα τῆς
διοικήσεως στρατιωτικὰ εἶναι εἴτε θεωρικά, κελευόντων μὲν τῶν νόμων, ὅταν
πόλεμος ἦι, τὰ περιόντα χρήματα τῆς διοικήσεως στρατιωτικὰ εἶναι, κύριον δ'
ἡγούμενος δεῖν τὸν δῆμον εἶναι περὶ τῶν αὑτοῦ ὅ τι ἂν βούληται πρᾶξαι,
ὀμωμοκὼς δὲ τὰ βέλτιστα βουλεύσειν τῶι δήμωι τῶι Ἀθηναίων, ὡς ὑμεῖς πάντ-
5 ες ἐμαρτυρήσατε ἐν ἐκείνωι τῶι καιρῶι. γενομένης γὰρ τῆς διαχειροτονίας,
οὐδεὶς ἀντεχειροτόνησεν ὡς οὐ δεῖ τοῖς χρήμασι τούτοις στρατιωτικοῖς χρῆσθαι,
ἀλλὰ καὶ νῦν ἔτι, ἄν που λόγος γένηται, παρὰ πάντων ὁμολογεῖται ὡς τὰ
βέλτιστα εἰπὼν ἄδικα πάθοι. τῶι οὖν ἐξαπατήσαντι τῶι λόγωι τοὺς δικαστὰς

AGAINST NEAIRA

1 There were many reasons which induced me, men of Athens, to bring this
indictment against Neaira, and to come before you. We have been grieviously
wronged by Stephanos, and we were placed by him in the most serious danger,
my father-in-law, myself, my sister and my wife, so that I shall present this
case not as an aggressor but in retaliation; for it was this man who first started
the quarrel, though he had never suffered any harm from us either in word or
deed. I wish first of all to give you an account of what we have suffered from
him, so that you will feel more sympathy for me as I seek to defend myself,
and to show how we were placed in the most serious danger of losing both
homeland and citizen rights.

2 When the Athenian people passed a decree granting Athenian citizenship
to Pasion and his descendants because of his benefactions to the city, my father
agreed with the people's gift, and he gave Pasion's son Apollodoros his
daughter, my sister, in marriage; and she is the mother of Apollodoros' children.
Since Apollodoros treated my sister and all of us well, and as he felt that true
relatives share all they have, I took as wife Apollodoros' daughter, my niece.
3 After a time Apollodoros was drawn as member of the Council. When he had
passed the examination and sworn the customary oath, a war crisis befell the
city such that it was open to you, if you won, to be the most powerful state in
Greece and to recover once for all your possessions beyond dispute and finally
put down Philip, or if you were late in sending aid and abandoned your allies,
once the army was disbanded for lack of money, to destroy them and be judged
untrustworthy by the rest of Greece, and to risk the loss of your remaining
4 possessions, Lemnos, Imbros, Skyros and the Chersonese. When you were
about to march out in full force to Euboia and Olynthos, Apollodoros as
councillor drafted a decree in the Council and brought a resolution before the
Assembly proposing that the people decide by show of hands whether the
surplus from the administration should be used for military or festival purposes.
For the laws prescribed that in time of war the surplus from the administration
should be used for military purposes; he thought that the people should have
the power to do what it wished with its own property, and he had sworn to act
as councillor for the best interests of the Athenian people, as you all bore wit-
5 ness on that occasion. For when the vote took place, nobody voted against the
use of this money for military purposes; and even now, if ever the subject is
discussed, it is agreed by all that he was unjustly treated for offering the best
advice. So it is the man who deceived the jurors with his arguments who

δίκαιον ὀργίζεσθαι, οὐ τοῖς ἐξαπατηθεῖσιν. γραψάμενος γὰρ παρανόμων τὸ ψήφισμα Στέφανος οὑτοσὶ καὶ εἰσελθὼν εἰς τὸ δικαστήριον, ἐπὶ διαβολῆι ψευδεῖς μάρτυρας παρασχόμενος ὡς ὤφλε τῶι δημοσίωι ἐκ πέντε καὶ εἴκοσιν ἐτῶν, καὶ
6 ἔξω τῆς γραφῆς πολλὰ κατηγορῶν, εἷλε τὸ ψήφισμα. καὶ τοῦτο μὲν εἰ αὐτῶι ἐδόκει διαπράξασθαι, οὐ χαλεπῶς φέρομεν· ἀλλ' ἐπειδὴ περὶ τοῦ τιμήματος ἐλάμβανον τὴν ψῆφον οἱ δικασταί, δεομένων ἡμῶν συγχωρῆσαι οὐκ ἤθελεν, ἀλλὰ πεντεκαίδεκα ταλάντων ἐτιμᾶτο, ἵνα ἀτιμώσειεν αὐτὸν καὶ παῖδας τοὺς ἐκείνου, καὶ τὴν ἀδελφὴν τὴν ἐμὴν καὶ ἡμᾶς ἅπαντας εἰς τὴν ἐσχάτην ἀπορίαν
7 καταστήσειεν καὶ ἔνδειαν ἁπάντων. ἡ μὲν γὰρ οὐσία οὐδὲ τριῶν ταλάντων πάνυ τι ἦν, ὥστε δυνηθῆναι ἐκτεῖσαι τοσοῦτον ὄφλημα· μὴ ἐκτεισθέντος δὲ τοῦ ὀφλήματος ἐπὶ τῆς ἐνάτης πρυτανείας, διπλοῦν ἔμελλεν ἔσεσθαι τὸ ὄφλημα καὶ ἐγγραφήσεσθαι Ἀπολλόδωρος τριάκοντα τάλαντα ὀφείλων τῶι δημοσίωι· ἐγγεγραμμένου δὲ τῶι δημοσίωι, ἀπογραφήσεσθαι ἔμελλεν ἡ ὑπάρχουσα οὐσία Ἀπολλοδώρωι δημοσία εἶναι, πραθείσης δ' αὐτῆς εἰς τὴν ἐσχάτην ἀπορίαν κατα-
8 στήσεσθαι καὶ αὐτὸς καὶ παῖδες οἱ ἐκείνου καὶ γυνὴ καὶ ἡμεῖς ἅπαντες. ἔτι δὲ καὶ ἡ ἑτέρα θυγάτηρ ἀνέκδοτος ἔμελλεν ἔσεσθαι· τίς γὰρ ἄν ποτε παρ' ὀφείλοντος τῶι δημοσίωι καὶ ἀποροῦντος ἔλαβεν ἄπροικον; οὐκοῦν τηλικούτων κακῶν αἴτιος ἡμῖν πᾶσιν ἐγίγνετο, οὐδὲν πώποτε ὑφ' ἡμῶν ἠδικημένος. τοῖς μὲν οὖν δικασταῖς τοῖς τότε δικάσασι πολλὴν χάριν κατά γε τοῦτο ἔχω, ὅτι οὐ περιεῖδον αὐτὸν ἀναρπασθέντα, ἀλλ' ἐτίμησαν ταλάντου, ὥστε δυνηθῆναι ἐκτεῖσαι μόλις· τούτωι δὲ δικαίως τὸν αὐτὸν ἔρανον ἐνεχειρήσαμεν ἀποδοῦναι.

9 Καὶ γὰρ οὐ μόνον ταύτηι ἐζήτησεν ἀνελεῖν ἡμᾶς, ἀλλὰ καὶ ἐκ τῆς πατρίδος αὐτὸν ἐβουλήθη ἐκβαλεῖν. ἐπενέγκας γὰρ αὐτῶι αἰτίαν ψευδῆ ὡς Ἀφίδναζέ ποτε ἀφικόμενος ἐπὶ δραπέτην αὑτοῦ ζητῶν πατάξειε γυναῖκα καὶ ἐκ τῆς πληγῆς τελευτήσειεν ἡ ἄνθρωπος, παρασκευασάμενος ἀνθρώπους δούλους καὶ κατασκευάσας ὡς Κυρηναῖοι εἴησαν, προεῖπεν αὐτῶι ἐπὶ Παλλαδίωι φόνου.
10 καὶ ἔλεγεν τὴν δίκην Στέφανος οὑτοσί, διομοσάμενος ὡς ἔκτεινεν Ἀπολλόδωρος τὴν γυναῖκα αὐτοχειρίαι, ἐξώλειαν αὑτῶι καὶ γένει καὶ οἰκίαι ἐπαρασάμενος, ἃ οὔτ' ἐγένετο οὔτ' εἶδεν οὔτ' ἤκουσεν οὐδενὸς πώποτε ἀνθρώπων. ἐξελεγχθεὶς δ' ἐπιορκῶν καὶ ψευδῆ αἰτίαν ἐπιφέρων, καὶ καταφανὴς γενόμενος μεμισθωμένος ὑπὸ Κηφισοφῶντος καὶ Ἀπολλοφάνους ὥστ' ἐξελάσαι Ἀπολλόδωρον ἢ ἀτιμῶσαι ἀργύριον εἰληφώς, ὀλίγας ψήφους μεταλαβὼν ἐκ πεντακοσίων δραχμῶν, ἀπῆλθεν ἐπιωρκηκὼς καὶ δόξας πονηρὸς εἶναι.

11 Σκοπεῖτε δὴ αὐτοί, ὦ ἄνδρες δικασταί, ἐκ τῶν εἰκότων λογιζόμενοι πρὸς ὑμᾶς αὐτούς, τί ἂν ἐχρησάμην ἐμαυτῶι καὶ τῆι γυναικὶ καὶ τῆι ἀδελφῆι, εἴ τι

deserves our anger, not the ones who were deceived. This man Stephanos
indicted the decree as illegal and came to court; he produced false witnesses to
support the slanderous charge that Apollodoros had been a debtor to the
Treasury for twenty-five years, made many accusations irrelevant to the indict-
6 ment and secured a verdict against the decree. On this count, if this is what he
chose to do, we have no complaint. But when the jurors were voting on the
penalty assessment, though we urged him to compromise he refused, and
proposed a penalty of fifteen talents with the intention of disfranchising
Apollodoros himself and his children and reducing my sister and all of us to
7 absolute poverty and complete destitution. For Apollodoros' property did not
amount even to three talents, to enable him to pay so large a fine; and if the
debt was not paid by the ninth prytany, the debt would be doubled and
Apollodoros would be listed as owing thirty talents to the Treasury; and once
he was listed as a debtor to the Treasury, all the property Apollodoros owns
would be inventoried as belonging to the state, and once it was sold
Apollodoros himself, his children, his wife and all of us would be reduced to
8 absolute poverty. Furthermore, his second daughter would be unmarriageable.
For who would ever have accepted a girl without dowry from a father who was
a debtor to the Treasury and a pauper? Such then, were the calamities he tried
to inflict on us, without ever having been wronged by us. To the jurors who
tried the case then I am deeply grateful for this at least, that they did not leave
Apollodoros to be plundered, but imposed a fine of one talent, so that he was
just able to pay it; but as for Stephanos, we have, as is just, sought to pay him
back in the same coin.

9 For he not only tried to destroy us like this, but also wanted to exile him
from his homeland. He brought a false charge against him that once when he
had gone to Aphidna in search of a runaway slave of his he struck a woman
and the person died from the blow; he produced some slaves and represented
them as Cyrenaeans, and publicly summonsed him for murder at the
10 Palladion. And Stephanos here conducted the prosecution, having taken an oath
that Apollodoros killed the woman with his own hand, invoking destruction on
himself, his race and his household, though it had not happened, nor had he
seen it or heard it ever from any living man. It was proved that he was lying
on oath and bringing a false charge, and it was shown that he had been hired
by Kephisophon and Apollophanes to secure Apollodoros' exile or
disfranchisement for pay; he received few votes from his five hundred
drachmas, and left the court a perjurer with a base reputation.

11 Consider for yourselves, men of Athens, reflecting on the probable
consequences in your own minds, what I could have done with myself and my

Ἀπολλοδώρωι συνέβη παθεῖν ὧν Στέφανος οὑτοσὶ ἐπεβούλευσεν αὐτῶι, ἢ ἐν
τῶι προτέρωι ἢ ἐν τῶι ὑστέρωι ἀγῶνι; ἢ ποίαι αἰσχύνηι οὐκ ἂν καὶ συμφορᾶι
12 περιπεπτωκὼς ἦν; παρακαλούντων δή με ἁπάντων, ἰδίαι προσιόντων μοι, ἐπὶ
τιμωρίαν τρέπεσθαι ὧν ἐπάθομεν ὑπ' αὐτοῦ, καὶ ὀνειδιζόντων μοι ἀνανδρότατον
ἀνθρώπων εἶναι, εἰ οὕτως οἰκείως ἔχων τὰ πρὸς τούτους μὴ λήψομαι δίκην ὑπὲρ
ἀδελφῆς καὶ κηδεστοῦ καὶ ἀδελφιδῶν καὶ γυναικὸς ἐμαυτοῦ, μηδὲ τὴν
περιφανῶς εἰς τοὺς θεοὺς ἀσεβοῦσαν καὶ εἰς τὴν πόλιν ὑβρίζουσαν καὶ τῶν
νόμων καταφρονοῦσαν τῶν ὑμετέρων εἰσαγαγὼν εἰς ὑμᾶς καὶ ἐξελέγξας τῶι
13 λόγωι ὡς ἀδικεῖ, κυρίους καταστήσω ὅ τι ἂν βούλησθε χρῆσθαι αὐτῆι, καὶ
ὥσπερ Στέφανος οὑτοσὶ ἐμὲ ἀφηιρεῖτο τοὺς οἰκείους παρὰ τοὺς νόμους καὶ τὰ
ψηφίσματα τὰ ὑμέτερα, οὕτω καὶ ἐγὼ τοῦτον ἥκω ἐπιδείξων εἰς ὑμᾶς ξένηι μὲν
γυναικὶ συνοικοῦντα παρὰ τὸν νόμον, ἀλλοτρίους δὲ παῖδας εἰσαγαγόντα εἴς τε
τοὺς φράτερας καὶ εἰς τοὺς δημότας, ἐγγυῶντα δὲ τὰς τῶν ἑταιρῶν θυγατέρας
ὡς αὑτοῦ οὔσας, ἠσεβηκότα δ' εἰς τοὺς θεούς, ἄκυρον δὲ ποιοῦντα τὸν δῆμον
τῶν αὑτοῦ, ἄν τινα βούληται πολίτην ποιήσασθαι· τίς γὰρ ἂν ἔτι παρὰ τοῦ
δήμου ζητήσειε λαβεῖν δωρεάν, μετὰ πολλῶν ἀναλωμάτων καὶ πραγματείας
πολίτης μέλλων ἔσεσθαι, ἐξὸν παρὰ Στεφάνου ἀπ' ἐλάττονος ἀναλώματος, εἴ γε
τὸ αὐτὸ τοῦτο γενήσεται αὐτῶι;
14 Ἃ μὲν οὖν ἀδικηθεὶς ἐγὼ ὑπὸ Στεφάνου πρότερος ἐγραψάμην τὴν γραφὴν
ταύτην, εἴρηκα πρὸς ὑμᾶς· ὡς δ' ἐστὶν ξένη Νέαιρα αὑτηὶ καὶ συνοικεῖ
Στεφάνωι τουτωὶ καὶ πολλὰ παρανενόμηκεν εἰς τὴν πόλιν, ταῦτ' ἤδη δεῖ μαθεῖν
ὑμᾶς. δέομαι οὖν ὑμῶν, ὦ ἄνδρες δικασταί, ἅπερ ἡγοῦμαι προσήκειν δεηθῆναι
νέον τε ὄντα καὶ ἀπείρως ἔχοντα τοῦ λέγειν, συνήγορόν με κελεῦσαι καλέσαι
15 τῶι ἀγῶνι τούτωι Ἀπολλόδωρον. καὶ γὰρ πρεσβύτερός ἐστιν ἢ ἐγώ, καὶ
ἐμπειροτέρως ἔχει τῶν νόμων, καὶ μεμέληκεν αὐτῶι περὶ τούτων ἁπάντων
ἀκριβῶς, καὶ ἠδίκηται ὑπὸ Στεφάνου τουτουί, ὥστε καὶ ἀνεπίφθονον αὐτῶι
τιμωρεῖσθαι τὸν ὑπάρξαντα. δεῖ δ' ὑμᾶς ἐξ αὐτῆς τῆς ἀληθείας, τὴν ἀκρίβειαν
ἀκούσαντας τῆς τε κατηγορίας καὶ τῆς ἀπολογίας, οὕτως ἤδη τὴν ψῆφον φέρειν
ὑπέρ τε τῶν θεῶν καὶ τῶν νόμων καὶ τοῦ δικαίου καὶ ὑμῶν αὐτῶν.

ΣΥΝΗΓΟΡΙΑ

16 Ἃ μὲν ἠδικημένος, ὦ ἄνδρες Ἀθηναῖοι, ὑπὸ Στεφάνου ἀναβέβηκα
κατηγορήσων Νεαίρας ταυτησί, Θεόμνηστος εἴρηκεν πρὸς ὑμᾶς· ὡς δ' ἐστὶ ξένη
Νέαιρα καὶ παρὰ τοὺς νόμους συνοικεῖ Στεφάνωι, τοῦτο ὑμῖν βούλομαι σαφῶς
ἐπιδεῖξαι. πρῶτον μὲν οὖν τὸν νόμον ὑμῖν ἀναγνώσεται, καθ' ὃν τήν τε γραφὴν

wife and my sister, if Apollodoros had actually suffered any of the injuries
which Stephanos plotted against him, either in the first or in the second trial?
12 What disgrace, what disaster would not have befallen me? Since people on all
sides urged me, approaching me privately, to seek revenge for what was done
to us by him and condemned me as the most cowardly man alive, if though so
closely related to them I failed to exact punishment for my sister, father-in-law,
nieces and wife, and by bringing before you the woman who is so blatantly
committing impiety against the gods and outrage against the city and showing
contempt for your laws, and by proving her guilt in my speech, enable you to
13 treat her as you wish – and just as Stephanos tried to deprive me of my
relatives, contrary to your laws and decrees, so I too have come before you to
prove that this man is living in marriage with a foreign woman contrary to the
law, that he introduced another's children into his phratry and deme, that he
gives the daughters of courtesans in marriage as though they were his own,
that he has committed impiety against the gods and deprives the people of its
privilege of granting citizenship to anyone it wishes. For who would seek to
obtain this gift from the people, when it would cost much expense and trouble
to become a citizen, if he can get it from Stephanos with less expense, provided
that the result for him will be exactly the same.

14 The wrongs inflicted by Stephanos without provocation which induced me
to bring this indictment, I have explained to you. You must now be convinced
that this woman Neaira is a foreigner and that she is living in marriage with
Stephanos here and has committed many crimes against the city. So I put to
you, gentlemen of the jury, a request which I think appropriate for a young
man inexperienced in speaking, that you bid me call Apollodoros as my sup-
15 porter for this trial. For he is older than I and has more experience in the laws;
he has studied all these matters carefully, and he has been wronged by
Stephanos, so that there can be no objection if he seeks revenge on the man
who started it. It is your duty to listen to the detailed presentation of
prosecution and defence and then on the basis of the actual truth to cast your
vote on behalf of the gods, the laws, justice and yourselves.

SUPPORTING SPEECH

16 The wrongs inflicted by Stephanos here, men of Athens, which induced me to take the stand to accuse this woman Neaira, have been explained to you by Theomnestos; what I wish to prove clearly to you is that Neaira is a foreigner and is living in marriage with Stephanos contrary to the laws. First of all the clerk will read you the law under which Theomnestos brought this

ταυτηνὶ Θεόμνηστος ἐγράψατο καὶ ὁ ἀγὼν οὗτος εἰσέρχεται εἰς ὑμᾶς.

ΝΟΜΟΣ

Ἐὰν δὲ ξένος ἀστῆι συνοικῆι τέχνηι ἢ μηχανῆι ἡιτινιοῦν, γραφέσθω πρὸς τοὺς θεσμοθέτας Ἀθηναίων ὁ βουλόμενος οἷς ἔξεστιν. ἐὰν δὲ ἁλῶι, πεπράσθω καὶ αὐτὸς καὶ ἡ οὐσία αὐτοῦ, καὶ τὸ τρίτον μέρος ἔστω τοῦ ἑλόντος. ἔστω δὲ καὶ ἐὰν ἡ ξένη τῶι ἀστῶι συνοικῆι κατὰ ταὐτά, καὶ ὁ συνοικῶν τῆι ξένηι τῆι ἁλούσηι ὀφειλέτω χιλίας δραχμάς.

17 Τοῦ μὲν νόμου τοίνυν ἀκηκόατε, ὦ ἄνδρες δικασταί, ὃς οὐκ ἐᾶι τὴν ξένην τῶι ἀστῶι συνοικεῖν οὐδὲ τὴν ἀστὴν τῶι ξένωι, οὐδὲ παιδοποιεῖσθαι, τέχνηι οὐδὲ μηχανῆι οὐδεμιᾶι· ἐὰν δέ τις παρὰ ταῦτα ποιῆι, γραφὴν πεποίηκεν κατ' αὐτῶν εἶναι πρὸς τοὺς θεσμοθέτας, κατά τε τοῦ ξένου καὶ τῆς ξένης, κἂν ἁλῶι, πεπρᾶσθαι κελεύει. ὡς οὖν ἐστι ξένη Νέαιρα αὑτηί, τοῦθ' ὑμῖν βούλομαι ἐξ ἀρχῆς ἀκριβῶς ἐπιδεῖξαι.

18 Ἑπτὰ γὰρ ταύτας παιδίσκας ἐκ μικρῶν παιδίων ἐκτήσατο Νικαρέτη, Χαρισίου μὲν οὖσα τοῦ Ἠλείου ἀπελευθέρα, Ἱππίου δὲ τοῦ μαγείρου τοῦ ἐκείνου γυνή, δεινὴ δὲ [καὶ δυναμένη] φύσιν μικρῶν παιδίων συνιδεῖν εὐπρεπῆ, καὶ ταῦτα ἐπισταμένη θρέψαι καὶ παιδεῦσαι ἐμπείρως, τέχνην ταύτην κατεσκευασ-
19 μένη καὶ ἀπὸ τούτων τὸν βίον συνειλεγμένη. προσειποῦσα δ' αὐτὰς ὀνόματι θυγατέρας, ἵν' ὡς μεγίστους μισθοὺς πράττοιτο τοὺς βουλομένους πλησιάζειν αὐταῖς ὡς ἐλευθέραις οὔσαις, ἐπειδὴ τὴν ἡλικίαν ἐκαρπώσατο αὐτῶν ἑκάστης, συλλήβδην καὶ τὰ σώματα ἀπέδοτο ἁπασῶν ἑπτὰ οὐσῶν, Ἄντειαν καὶ Στρατόλαν καὶ Ἀριστόκλειαν καὶ Μετάνειραν καὶ Φίλαν καὶ Ἰσθμιάδα καὶ Νέ-
20 αιραν ταυτηνί. ἣν μὲν οὖν ἕκαστος αὐτῶν ἐκτήσατο καὶ ὡς ἠλευθερώθησαν ἀπὸ τῶν πριαμένων αὐτὰς παρὰ τῆς Νικαρέτης, προϊόντος τοῦ λόγου, ἂν βούλησθε ἀκούειν καί μοι περιουσία ἦι τοῦ ὕδατος, δηλώσω ὑμῖν· ὡς δὲ Νέαιρα αὑτηὶ Νικαρέτης ἦν καὶ ἠργάζετο τῶι σώματι μισθαρνοῦσα τοῖς βουλομένοις
21 αὐτῆι πλησιάζειν, τοῦθ' ὑμῖν βούλομαι πάλιν ἐπανελθεῖν. Λυσίας γὰρ ὁ σοφιστὴς Μετανείρας ὢν ἐραστὴς ἐβουλήθη πρὸς τοῖς ἄλλοις ἀναλώμασιν οἷς ἀνήλισκεν εἰς αὐτὴν καὶ μυῆσαι, ἡγούμενος τὰ μὲν ἄλλα ἀναλώματα τὴν κεκτημένην αὐτὴν λαμβάνειν, ἃ δ' ἂν εἰς τὴν ἑορτὴν καὶ τὰ μυστήρια ὑπὲρ αὐτῆς ἀναλώσηι, πρὸς αὐτὴν τὴν ἄνθρωπον χάριν καταθήσεσθαι. ἐδεήθη οὖν τῆς Νικαρέτης ἐλθεῖν εἰς τὰ μυστήρια ἄγουσαν τὴν Μετάνειραν, ἵνα μυηθῆι, καὶ
22 αὐτὸς ὑπέσχετο μυήσειν. ἀφικομένας δ' αὐτὰς ὁ Λυσίας εἰς μὲν τὴν αὑτοῦ

indictment and this trial comes before you.

LAW

If an alien lives in marriage with an Athenian woman by any manner or means, any Athenian at all who possesses the right may indict him before the Thesmothetai. If he is convicted, both he and his property are to be sold, and one third is to go to the successful prosecutor. The same is to apply if an alien woman lives in marriage with an Athenian man, and the man who lives with the alien woman so convicted is to be fined one thousand drachmas.

17 You have heard the law, gentlemen of the jury, which forbids an alien woman to live in marriage with an Athenian or an Athenian woman with an alien, or to produce children, by any manner or means. If anyone breaks this law, it allows for an indictment against them, the alien man or woman, before the Thesmothetai, and it instructs that if convicted the person is to be sold. So then, I wish to prove to you in detail, starting at the beginning, that this woman Neaira is an alien.

18 There were seven girls acquired as small children by Nikarete, a freedwoman of Charisios of Elis and the wife of his cook Hippias, an expert judge of beauty in small children who knew how to bring them up and train
them skilfully, for she had made this her trade and she obtained her living by
19 this means. She called them by the name of daughters, so that she could charge the maximum possible fees from men who wished to have relations with them, on the pretext that they were free girls, and when she had made her
profit from the youth of each of them she sold them off together, all seven,
20 Anteia, Stratola, Aristokleia, Metaneira, Phila, Isthmias and Neaira here. Which of them each purchaser acquired and how they obtained their freedom from those who bought them from Nikarete I shall inform you further on in my speech, if you wish to hear and I have water to spare; but the fact that this woman Neaira belonged to Nikarete and worked as a courtesan on hire to all
who wished to have relations with her, this is the point to which I wish to re-
21 turn. Lysias the sophist, who was a lover of Metaneira, wanted to initiate her, in addition to the other sums he had paid out on her; for he thought that while her owner received the rest of the money he paid out anything he spent on the festival and the Mysteries for her sake would win him the gratitude of the girl herself. He therefore asked Nikarete to come to the Mysteries and bring
Metaneira, so that she could be initiated, and he promised to initiate her per-
22 sonally. When they arrived Lysias did not bring them into his own house, out

οἰκίαν οὐκ εἰσάγει, αἰσχυνόμενος τήν τε γυναῖκα ἣν εἶχε, Βραχύλλου μὲν θυγατέρα, ἀδελφιδῆν δὲ αὐτοῦ, καὶ τὴν μητέρα τὴν αὐτοῦ πρεσβυτέραν τε οὖσαν καὶ ἐν τῶι αὐτῶι διαιτωμένην· ὡς Φιλόστρατον δὲ τὸν Κολωνῆθεν, ἤιθεον ἔτι ὄντα καὶ φίλον αὐτῶι, καθίστησιν ὁ Λυσίας αὐτάς, τήν τε Μετάνειραν καὶ τὴν Νικαρέτην. συνηκολούθει δὲ καὶ Νέαιρα αὐτηί, ἐργαζομένη μὲν ἤδη τῶι σώματι, νεωτέρα δὲ οὖσα διὰ τὸ μήπω τὴν ἡλικίαν αὐτῆι παρεῖναι.
23 ὡς οὖν ἀληθῆ λέγω, ὅτι Νικαρέτης ἦν καὶ ἠκολούθει ἐκείνηι καὶ ἐμισθάρνει τῶι βουλομένωι ἀναλίσκειν, τούτων ὑμῖν αὐτὸν τὸν Φιλόστρατον μάρτυρα καλῶ.

ΜΑΡΤΥΡΙΑ.

Φιλόστρατος Διονυσίου Κολωνῆθεν μαρτυρει εἰδέναι Νέαιραν Νικαρέτης οὖσαν, ἧσπερ καὶ Μετάνειρα ἐγένετο, καὶ κατάγεσθαι παρ' αὐτῶι, ὅτε εἰς τὰ μυστήρια ἐπεδήμησαν ἐν Κορίνθωι οἰκοῦσαι· καταστῆσαι δὲ αὐτὰς ὡς αὐτὸν Λυσίαν τὸν Κεφάλου, φίλον ὄντα ἑαυτῶι καὶ ἐπιτήδειον.

24 Πάλιν τοίνυν, ὦ ἄνδρες Ἀθηναῖοι, μετὰ ταῦτα Σῖμος ὁ Θετταλὸς ἔχων Νέαιραν ταυτηνὶ ἀφικνεῖται δεῦρο εἰς τὰ Παναθήναια τὰ μεγάλα. συνηκολούθει δὲ καὶ ἡ Νικαρέτη αὐτῆι, κατήγοντο δὲ παρὰ Κτησίππωι τῶι Γλαυκωνίδου τῶι Κυδαντίδηι, καὶ συνέπινεν καὶ συνεδείπνει ἐναντίον πολλῶν Νέαιρα αὐτηὶ ὡς ἂν
25 ἑταίρα οὖσα. καὶ ὅτι ἀληθῆ λέγω, τούτων τοὺς μάρτυρας καλῶ. καὶ μοι κάλει Εὐφίλητον Σίμωνος Αἰξωνέα καὶ Ἀριστόμαχον Κριτοδήμου Ἀλωπεκῆθεν.

ΜΑΡΤΥΡΕΣ

Εὐφίλητος Σίμωνος Αἰξωνεύς, Ἀριστόμαχος Κριτοδήμου Ἀλωπεκῆθεν, μαρτυροῦσιν εἰδέναι Σῖμον τὸν Θετταλὸν ἀφικόμενον Ἀθήναζε εἰς τὰ Παναθήναια τὰ μεγάλα, καὶ μετ' αὐτοῦ Νικαρέτην καὶ Νέαιραν τὴν νυνὶ ἀγωνιζομένην· καὶ κατάγεσθαι αὐτοὺς παρὰ Κτησίππωι τῶι Γλαυκωνίδου, καὶ συμπίνειν μετ' αὐτῶν Νέαιραν ὡς ἑταίραν οὖσαν καὶ ἄλλων πολλῶν παρόντων καὶ συμπινόντων παρὰ Κτησίππωι.

26 Μετὰ ταῦτα τοίνυν ἐν τῆι Κορίνθωι αὐτῆς ἐπιφανῶς ἐργαζομένης καὶ οὔσης λαμπρᾶς ἄλλοι τε ἐρασταὶ γίγνονται καὶ Ξενοκλείδης ὁ ποιητὴς καὶ Ἵππαρχος ὁ ὑποκριτής, καὶ εἶχον αὐτὴν μεμισθωμένοι. καὶ ὅτι ἀληθῆ λέγω, τοῦ μὲν Ξενοκλείδου οὐκ ἂν δυναίμην ὑμῖν μαρτυρίαν παρασχέσθαι· οὐ γὰρ ἐῶσιν
27 αὐτὸν οἱ νόμοι μαρτυρεῖν· ὅτε γὰρ Λακεδαιμονίους ὑμεῖς ἐσώιζετε πεισθέντες ὑπὸ Καλλιστράτου, τότε ἀντειπὼν ἐν τῶι δήμωι τῆι βοηθείαι, ἐωνημένος τὴν

of respect for his wife, the daughter of Brachyllos and his own niece, and for his mother, who was somewhat elderly and who lived with him. He lodged them, Metaneira and Nikarete, at the house of Philostratos of Kolonai, who was still unmarried and a friend of his. Neaira here accompanied them; she was already working as a prostitute, though she was too young as she had not yet
23 reached puberty. To prove the truth of my statements, that she belonged to Nikarete and accompanied her and was hired out to anyone willing to pay, I shall call Philostratos himself as witness to these facts.

DEPOSITION

Philostratos the son of Dionysios of Kolonai deposes that he knows that Neaira belonged to Nikarete, who also owned Metaneira, and that they stayed with him when they were in town for the Mysteries while they were residing in Corinth; that they were lodged at his house by Lysias the son of Kephalos, a close personal friend of his.

24 Again, men of Athens, subsequently Simos of Thessaly came here for the Great Panathenaia and brought this woman Neaira. Nikarete came with her too, and they stayed with Ktesippos the son of Glaukonides of Kydantidai; and Neaira here drank and dined with them in the presence of a number of men as though she were a courtesan. And to prove the truth of my statements I shall
25 call witnesses of these facts for you. Call Euphiletos the son of Simon of Aixone and Aristomachos the son of Kritodemos of Alopeke.

WITNESSES

Euphiletos the son of Simon of Aixone and Aristomachos the son of Kritodemos of Alopeke depose that they know that Simos of Thessaly came to Athens for the Great Panathenaia, and with him Nikarete and Neaira the defendant in this case, that they stayed with Ktesippos the son of Glaukonides, and that Neaira drank with them like a courtesan in the presence of many others who were drinking at Ktesippos' house.

26 Subsequently she carried on her trade openly in Corinth and was a celebrity; her many lovers included Xenokleides the poet and Hipparchos the actor, who hired and had her. To prove the truth of this statement I cannot
27 provide the testimony of Xenokleides; the laws do not allow him to testify. For when you were rescuing the Spartans at the instigation of Kallistratos, initially he opposed the sending of aid in the Assembly. As he had bought the

πεντηκοστὴν τοῦ σίτου ἐν εἰρήνηι καὶ δέον αὐτὸν καταβάλλειν τὰς καταβολὰς εἰς τὸ βουλευτήριον κατὰ πρυτανείαν, καὶ οὔσης αὐτῶι ἀτελείας ἐκ τῶν νόμων οὐκ ἐξελθὼν ἐκείνην τὴν στρατείαν, γραφεὶς ὑπὸ Στεφάνου τουτουὶ ἀστρατείας
28 καὶ διαβληθεὶς τῶι λόγωι ἐν τῶι δικαστηρίωι ἑάλω καὶ ἠτιμώθη. καίτοι πῶς οὐκ οἴεσθε δεινὸν εἶναι, εἰ τοὺς μὲν φύσει πολίτας καὶ γνησίως μετέχοντας τῆς πόλεως ἀπεστέρηκε τῆς παρρησίας Στέφανος οὑτοσί, τοὺς δὲ μηδὲν προσήκοντας βιάζεται Ἀθηναίους εἶναι παρὰ πάντας τοὺς νόμους; τὸν δ' Ἵππαρχον αὐτὸν ὑμῖν καλῶ, καὶ ἀναγκάσω μαρτυρεῖν ἢ ἐξόμνυσθαι κατὰ τὸν νόμον, ἢ κλητεύσω αὐτόν. καί μοι κάλει Ἵππαρχον.

ΜΑΡΤΥΡΙΑ

Ἵππαρχος Ἀθμονεὺς μαρτυρεῖ Ξενοκλείδην καὶ αὐτὸν μισθώσασθαι Νέαιραν ἐν Κορίνθωι τὴν νῦν ἀγωνιζομένην, ὡς ἑταίραν οὖσαν τῶν μισθαρνουσῶν, καὶ συμπίνειν ἐν Κορίνθωι Νέαιραν μεθ' αὐτοῦ καὶ Ξενοκλείδου τοῦ ποιητοῦ.

29 Μετὰ ταῦτα τοίνυν αὐτῆς γίγνονται ἐρασταὶ δύο, Τιμανορίδας τε ὁ Κορίνθιος καὶ Εὐκράτης ὁ Λευκάδιος, οἳ ἐπειδήπερ πολυτελὴς ἦν ἡ Νικαρέτη τοῖς ἐπιτάγμασιν, ἀξιοῦσα τὰ καθ' ἡμέραν ἀναλώματα ἅπαντα τῆι οἰκίαι παρ' αὐτῶν λαμβάνειν, κατατιθέασιν αὐτῆς τιμὴν τριάκοντα μνᾶς τοῦ σώματος τῆι Νικαρέτηι, καὶ ὠνοῦνται αὐτὴν παρ' αὐτῆς νόμωι πόλεως καθάπαξ αὐτῶν
30 δούλην εἶναι. καὶ εἶχον καὶ ἐχρῶντο ὅσον ἐβούλοντο αὐτῆι χρόνον. μέλλοντες δὲ γαμεῖν, προαγορεύουσιν αὐτῆι, ὅτι οὐ βούλονται αὐτὴν σφῶν αὐτῶν ἑταίραν γεγενημένην ὁρᾶν ἐν Κορίνθωι ἐργαζομένην οὐδ' ὑπὸ πορνοβοσκῶι οὖσαν, ἀλλ' ἡδέως ἂν αὐτοῖς εἴη ἔλαττόν τε τἀργύριον κομίσασθαι παρ' αὐτῆς ἢ κατέθεσαν, καὶ αὐτὴν ταύτην ὁρᾶν τι ἀγαθὸν ἔχουσαν. ἀφιέναι οὖν αὐτῆι ἔφασαν εἰς ἐλευθερίαν χιλίας δραχμάς, πεντακοσίας ἑκάτερος· τὰς δ' εἴκοσι μνᾶς ἐκέλευον αὐτὴν ἐξευροῦσαν αὐτοῖς ἀποδοῦναι. ἀκούσασα δ' αὕτη τοὺς λόγους τούτους τοῦ τε Εὐκράτους καὶ Τιμανορίδου, μεταπέμπεται εἰς τὴν Κόρινθον ἄλλους τε τῶν ἐραστῶν τῶν γεγενημένων αὐτῆι καὶ Φρυνίωνα τὸν Παιανιέα, Δήμωνος μὲν ὄντα υἱόν, Δημοχάρους δὲ ἀδελφόν, ἀσελγῶς δὲ καὶ πολυτελῶς διάγοντα
31 τὸν βίον, ὡς ὑμῶν οἱ πρεσβύτεροι μνημονεύουσιν. ἀφικομένου δ' ὡς αὐτὴν τοῦ Φρυνίωνος, λέγει πρὸς αὐτὸν τοὺς λόγους οὓς εἶπον πρὸς αὐτὴν ὅ τε Εὐκράτης καὶ Τιμανορίδας, καὶ δίδωσιν αὐτῶι τὸ ἀργύριον ὃ παρὰ τῶν ἄλλων ἐραστῶν ἐδασμολόγησεν ἔρανον εἰς τὴν ἐλευθερίαν συλλέγουσα, καὶ εἴ τι ἄρα αὐτὴ περιεποιήσατο, καὶ δεῖται αὐτοῦ προσθέντα τὸ ἐπίλοιπον, οὗ προσέδει εἰς τὰς εἴκοσι μνᾶς, καταθεῖναι αὐτῆς τῶι τε Εὐκράτει καὶ τῶι Τιμανορίδαι ὥστε ἐλευθ-

two-percent tax on grain during the peace and was required to pay his instalments to the Council-chamber each prytany, and he was exempted under the law, he did not join in that expedition; but he was indicted for failure to serve by this man Stephanos, slandered by him in his speech in court, convicted
28 and disfranchised. And yet don't you think it appalling that this man Stephanos has robbed of their right to speak citizens by birth who have a legitimate claim to citizenship while he forces in as Athenian citizens people who do not belong, in defiance of all the laws? I shall call Hipparchos in person for you, and compel him to give evidence or take the oath of disclaimer as the law prescribes, or I shall subpoena him. Please call Hipparchos.

DEPOSITION

Hipparchos of Athmone deposes that Xenokleides the poet and he hired Neaira, the defendant in this case, in Corinth as a courtesan who worked for hire, and that Neaira drank with himself and Xenokleides the poet in Corinth.

29 Subsequently she had two lovers, Timanoridas of Corinth and Eukrates of Leukas; since Nikarete was extravagant in her demands, expecting them to meet all the daily expenses of her household, they paid Nikarete thirty minas for Neaira's person and bought her outright from her in accordance with the law of the city to be their slave. And they kept her and used her for as long as
30 they pleased. But when they were about to marry they declared to her that since she had been their mistress they did not wish to see her working in Corinth or under the control of a brothelkeeper, and that they would be content to receive less money for her than they had paid and see her get some personal advantage. So they offered to remit her one thousand drachmas towards her freedom, five hundred each, and told her to find the other twenty minas herself and pay them. After listening to what Eukrates and Timanoridas said, she invited to Corinth several of her former lovers, including Phrynion of Paiania, the son of Demon and father of Demochares, a man with an outrageous and ex-
31 travagant way of life, as the older among you remember. When Phrynion arrived, she told him what Eukrates and Timanoridas had said to her and gave him the money which she had collected in contributions from her other lovers towards the cost of her freedom and whatever she had saved herself, and begged him to add the rest needed to make up the twenty minas and pay it for

32 έραν εἶναι. ἄσμενος δ' ἀκούσας ἐκεῖνος τοὺς λόγους τούτους αὐτῆς, καὶ λαβὼν τἀργύριον ὃ παρὰ τῶν ἐραστῶν τῶν ἄλλων εἰσηνέχθη αὐτῆι, καὶ προσθεὶς τὸ ἐπίλοιπον αὐτός, κατατίθησιν αὐτῆς τὰς εἴκοσι μνᾶς τῶι τε Εὐκράτει καὶ τῶι Τιμανορίδαι ἐπ' ἐλευθερίαι καὶ ἐφ' ὧι ἐν Κορίνθωι μὴ ἐργάζεσθαι. καὶ ὅτι ταῦτ' ἀληθῆ λέγω, τούτων ὑμῖν τὸν παραγενόμενον μάρτυρα καλῶ. καί μοι κάλει Φίλαγρον Μελιτέα.

ΜΑΡΤΥΡΙΑ

Φίλαγρος Μελιτεὺς μαρτυρεῖ παρεῖναι ἐν Κορίνθωι, ὅτε Φρυνίων ὁ Δημοχάρους ἀδελφὸς κατετίθει εἴκοσι μνᾶς Νεαίρας τῆς νῦν ἀγωνιζομένης Τιμανορίδαι τῶι Κορινθίωι καὶ Εὐκράτει τῶι Λευκαδίωι, καὶ καταθεὶς τὸ ἀργύριον ὤιχετο ἀπάγων 'Αθήναζε Νέαιραν.

33 'Αφικόμενος τοίνυν δεῦρο ἔχων αὐτὴν ἀσελγῶς καὶ προπετῶς ἐχρῆτο αὐτῆι, καὶ ἐπὶ τὰ δεῖπνα ἔχων αυτὴν πανταχοῖ ἐπορεύετο ὅπου πίνοι, ἐκώμαζέ τ' ἀεὶ μετ' αὐτοῦ, συνῆν τ' ἐμφανῶς ὁπότε βουληθείη πανταχοῦ, φιλοτιμίαν τὴν ἐξουσίαν πρὸς τοὺς ὁρῶντας ποιούμενος. καὶ ὡς ἄλλους τε πολλοὺς ἐπὶ κῶμον ἔχων ἦλθεν αὐτὴν καὶ ὡς Χαβρίαν τὸν Αἰξωνέα, ὅτε ἐνίκα ἐπὶ Σωκρατίδου ἄρχοντος τὰ Πύθια τῶι τεθρίππωι ὃ ἐπρίατο παρὰ τῶν παίδων τῶν Μίτυος τοῦ 'Αργείου, καὶ ἥκων ἐκ Δελφῶν εἱστία τὰ ἐπινίκια ἐπὶ Κωλιάδι. καὶ ἐκεῖ ἄλλοι τε πολλοὶ συνεγίγνοντο αὐτῆι μεθυούσηι καθεύδοντος τοῦ Φρυνίωνος καὶ οἱ διά-
34 κονοι οἱ Χαβρίου τράπεζαν παραθέμενοι. καὶ ὅτι ταῦτ' ἀληθῆ λέγω, τοὺς ὁρῶντας ὑμῖν καὶ παρόντας μάρτυρας παρέξομαι. καί μοι κάλει Χιωνίδην Ξυπεταιόνα καὶ Εὐθετίωνα Κυδαθηναιᾶ.

ΜΑΡΤΥΡΙΑ

Χιωνίδης Ξυπεταιών, Εὐθετίων Κυδαθηναιεὺς μαρτυροῦσι κληθῆναι ὑπὸ Χαβρίου ἐπὶ δεῖπνον, ὅτε τὰ ἐπινίκια εἱστία Χαβρίας τῆς νίκης τοῦ ἅρματος, καὶ ἑστιᾶσθαι ἐπὶ Κωλιάδι, καὶ εἰδέναι Φρυνίωνα παρόντα ἐν τῶι δείπνωι τούτωι ἔχοντα Νέαιραν τὴν νυνὶ ἀγωνιζομένην, καὶ καθεύδειν σφᾶς αὐτοὺς και Φρυνίωνα καὶ Νέαιραν, καὶ αἰσθάνεσθαι αὐτοὶ ἀνισταμένους τῆς νυκτὸς πρὸς Νέαιραν ἄλλους τε καὶ τῶν διακόνων τινάς, οἳ ἦσαν Χαβρίου οἰκέται.

35 Ἐπειὴ τοίνυν ἀσελγῶς προὐπηλακίζετο ὑπὸ τοῦ Φρυνίωνος καὶ οὐχ ὡς ὤιετο ἠγαπᾶτο, οὐδ' ὑπηρέτει αὐτῆι ἃ ἐβούλετο, συσκευασαμένη αὐτοῦ τὰ ἐκ τῆς οἰκίας καὶ ὅσα ἦν αὐτῆι ὑπ' ἐκείνου περὶ τὸ σῶμα κατεσκευασμένα ἱμάτια καὶ χρυσία, καὶ θεραπαίνας δύο, Θρᾶιτταν καὶ Κοκκαλίνην, ἀποδιδράσκει εἰς

32 her to Eukrates and Timanorides to free her. He listened readily to her tale, and taking the money which had been contributed by her other lovers and adding the rest personally he paid Eukrates and Timanoridas the twenty minas to secure her freedom on condition that she did not work in Corinth. To prove the truth of these statements I shall call as witness someone who was present. Call Philagros of Melite.

DEPOSITION

Philagros of Melite deposes that he was present in Corinth when Phrynion the brother of Demochares paid twenty minas for Neaira the defendant in this case to Timanoridas of Corinth and Eukrates of Leukas, and when he had paid the money he went off to Athens with Neaira.

33 When he came here with her he treated her in an outrageous and reckless way; he took her to dinner with him everywhere wherever he was drinking, she joined in all his carousals, and he had intercourse with her in public anywhere whenever he pleased, making a display of his privilege in front of onlookers. The many people to whom he took her carousing included Chabrias of Aixone, when he won in the Pythian games in the archonship of Sokratidas with the chariot he bought from the sons of Mitys of Argos, and on his return from Delphoi held a victory feast at Kolias. There were many there who had intercourse with her when she was drunk, while Phrynion was asleep, includ-
34 ing the servants who had served Chabrias' meal. To prove the truth of these statements, I shall provide as witnesses the people who were there and saw it. Please call Chionides of Xypete and Euthetion of Kydathenaion.

DEPOSITION

Chionides of Xypete and Euthetion of Kydathenaion depose that they were invited to dinner by Chabrias, when he was celebrating his chariot victory, and they were entertained at Kolias; that they know that Phrynion was at that dinner with Neaira the defendant in this case; that they and Phrynion and Neaira went to sleep and they noticed several people get up in the night and visit Neaira, including some of the servants, who were Chabrias' household slaves.

35 So then, since she was mistreated outrageously by Phrynion instead of being cherished as she expected, and he did not grant all her wishes, she gathered the property in his house and all the clothing and gold jewellery he had bought to adorn her and two maidservants, Thratta and Kokkaline, and ran

Μέγαρα. ἦν δὲ ὁ χρόνος οὗτος ὧι Ἀστεῖος μὲν ἦν ἄρχων Ἀθήνησιν, ὁ καιρὸς δ'
36 ἐν ὧι ἐπολεμεῖθ' ὑμεῖς πρὸς Λακεδαιμονίους τὸν ὕστερον πόλεμον. διατρίψασα δ' ἐν τοῖς Μεγάροις δύ' ἔτη, τόν τ' ἐπ' Ἀστείου ἄρχοντος καὶ Ἀλκισθένους ἐνιαυτόν, ὡς αὐτῆι ἡ ἀπὸ τοῦ σώματος ἐργασία οὐχ ἱκανὴν εὐπορίαν παρεῖχεν ὥστε διοικεῖν τὴν οἰκίαν (πολυτελὴς δ' ἦν, οἱ Μεγαρεῖς δ' ἀνελεύθεροι καὶ μικρολόγοι, ξένων δὲ οὐ πάνυ ἐπιδημία ἦν αὐτόθι διὰ τὸ πόλεμον εἶναι καὶ τοὺς μὲν Μεγαρέας λακωνίζειν, τῆς δὲ θαλάττης ὑμᾶς ἄρχειν· εἰς δὲ τὴν Κόρινθον οὐκ ἐξῆν αὐτῆι ἐπανελθεῖν διὰ τὸ ἐπὶ τούτωι ἀπηλλάχθαι ἀπὸ τοῦ Εὐκράτους
37 καὶ τοῦ Τιμανορίδου, ὥστ' ἐν Κορίνθωι μὴ ἐργάζεσθαι), ὡς οὖν γίγνεται ἡ εἰρήνη ἡ ἐπὶ Φρασικλείδου ἄρχοντος καὶ ἡ μάχη ἡ ἐν Λεύκτροις Θηβαίων καὶ Λακεδαιμονίων, τότε ἐπιδημήσαντα Στέφανον τουτονὶ εἰς τὰ Μέγαρα καὶ καταγόμενον ὡς αὐτὴν ἑταίραν οὖσαν καὶ πλησιάσαντα αὐτῆι, διηγησαμένη πάντα τὰ πεπραγμένα καὶ τὴν ὕβριν τοῦ Φρυνίωνος, καὶ ἐπιδοῦσα ἃ ἐξῆλθεν ἔχουσα παρ' αὐτοῦ, ἐπιθυμοῦσα μὲν τῆς ἐνθάδε οἰκήσεως, φοβουμένη δὲ τὸν Φρυνίωνα διὰ τὸ ἠδικηκέναι μὲν αὐτή, ἐκεῖνον δὲ ὀργίλως ἔχειν αὐτῆι, σοβαρὸν δὲ καὶ ὀλίγωρον εἰδυῖα αὐτοῦ τὸν τρόπον ὄντα, προΐσταται Στέφανον τουτονὶ
38 αὑτῆς. ἐπάρας δὲ αὐτὴν οὗτος ἐν τοῖς Μεγάροις τῶι λόγωι καὶ φυσήσας, ὡς κλαύσοιτο ὁ Φρυνίων εἰ ἅψοιτο αὐτῆς, αὐτὸς δὲ γυναῖκα αὐτὴν ἕξων, τούς τε παῖδας τοὺς ὄντας αὐτῆι τότε εἰσάξων εἰς τοὺς φράτερας ὡς αὑτοῦ ὄντας καὶ πολίτας ποιήσων, ἀδικήσει δὲ οὐδεὶς ἀνθρώπων, ἀφικνεῖται αὐτὴν ἔχων δεῦρο ἐκ τῶν Μεγάρων, καὶ παιδία μετ' αὐτῆς τρία, Πρόξενον καὶ Ἀρίστωνα καὶ θυγ-
39 ατέρα, ἣν νυνὶ Φανὼ καλοῦσιν· καὶ εἰσάγει αὐτὴν καὶ τὰ παιδία εἰς τὸ οἰκίδιον ὃ ἦν αὐτῶι παρὰ τὸν ψιθυριστὴν Ἑρμῆν, μεταξὺ τῆς Δωροθέου τοῦ Ἐλευσινίου οἰκίας καὶ τῆς Κλεινομάχου, ἣν νυνὶ Σπίνθαρος παρ' αὐτοῦ ἐώνηται ἑπτὰ μνῶν. ὥστε ἡ μὲν ὑπάρχουσα Στεφάνωι οὐσία αὕτη ἦν καὶ ἄλλο οὐδέν· δυοῖν δ' ἕνεκα ἦλθεν ἔχων αὐτήν, ὡς ἐξ ἀτελείας τε ἕξων καλὴν ἑταίραν, καὶ τὰ ἐπιτήδεια ταύτην ἐργασομένην καὶ θρέψουσαν τὴν οἰκίαν· οὐ γὰρ ἦν αὐτῶι ἄλλη πρόσοδ-
40 ος, ὅ τι μὴ συκοφαντήσας τι λάβοι. πυθόμενος δὲ ὁ Φρυνίων ἐπιδημοῦσαν αὐτὴν καὶ οὖσαν παρὰ τούτωι, παραλαβὼν νεανίσκους μεθ' ἑαυτοῦ καὶ ἐλθὼν ἐπὶ τὴν οἰκίαν τὴν τοῦ Στεφάνου ἦγεν αὐτήν. ἀφαιρουμένου δὲ τοῦ Στεφάνου κατὰ τὸν νόμον εἰς ἐλευθερίαν, κατηγγύησεν αὐτὴν πρὸς τῶι πολεμάρχωι. καὶ ὡς ἀληθῆ λέγω, τούτων αὐτὸν μάρτυρα ὑμῖν τὸν τότε πολέμαρχον παρέξομαι. καί μοι κάλει Αἰήτην Κειριάδην.

off to Megara. This was the time when Asteios was archon at Athens, and it
was the period in which you were involved in your second war with Sparta.
36 She spent two years in Megara, that of Asteios' archonship and the year of
Alkisthenes. But since her trade as a prostitute did not provide enough money
to maintain her household - she was extravagant, while the Megarians are
mean and petty, and there were few foreigners in town at that time because
there was a war on, the Megarians were on the Spartan side and you had
control of the sea; but she could not return to Corinth because the condition on
which she was quit of Eukrates and Timanoridas was that she would not carry
37 on her trade in Corinth. Well, when the peace came in the archonship of
Phrasikleides and the battle was fought at Leuktra between the Thebans and
the Spartans, at that point this Stephanos came to town and stayed with her as
a courtesan and had relations with her. She told him all that happened and
Phrynion's insulting treatment, she gave him besides all she had brought from
Phrynion's house, and since she was eager to live here but afraid of Phrynion
because she had done him wrong and he was angry with her, and she knew
his temper was violent and arrogant, she made Stephanos here her patron.
38 Stephanos spoke encouragement to her in Megara and inflated her confidence,
saying that Phyrnion would regret it if he laid hands on her; he would keep her
as his wife and introduce the children she had at that time into his phratry as
his own and give them citizenship; nobody in the world would harm her. So he
brought her here from Megara and three children with her, Proxenos and Arist-
39 on and a daughter who is now known as Phano. He established her and her
children in the small house he had by the Whispering Hermes, between the
houses of Dorotheos of Eleusis and Kleinomachos, the house which Spintharos
has since bought from him for seven minas. So this was the sum total of
Stephanos' property. His two aims in bringing her here were so that he should
have a beautiful mistress for free and so that her trade should pay for the
necessities and maintain the house; for he had no other source of income, apart
40 from what he could obtain as a sycophant. But Phyrnion learned that she was
in town and staying with Stephanos, and bringing some young men with him
he went to Stephanos' house and tried to drag her off. When Stephanos
asserted her freedom according to the law, Phyrnion compelled her to post bail
before the Polemarchos. To prove the truth of this statement, I shall provide
the man who was Polemarchos then in person as witness. Please call Aietes of
Keiriadai.

ΜΑΡΤΥΡΙΑ

Αἰήτης Κειριάδης μαρτυρεῖ πολεμαρχοῦντος αὐτοῦ κατεγγυηθῆναι Νέαιραν τὴν νυνὶ ἀγωνιζομένην ὑπὸ Φρυνίωνος τοῦ Δημοχάρους ἀδελφοῦ, καὶ ἐγγυητὰς γενέσθαι Νεαίρας Στέφανον Ἐροιάδην, Γλαυκέτην Κηφισιέα, Ἀριστοκράτην Φαληρέα.

41 Διεγγυηθεῖσα δ' ὑπὸ Στεφάνου καὶ οὖσα παρὰ τούτωι τὴν μὲν αὐτὴν ἐργασίαν οὐδὲν ἧττον ἢ πρότερον ἠργάζετο, τοὺς δὲ μισθοὺς μείζους ἐπράττετο τοὺς βουλομένους αὐτῆι πλησιάζειν, ὡς ἐπὶ προσχήματος ἤδη τινὸς οὖσα καὶ ἀνδρὶ συνοικοῦσα. συνεσυκοφάντει δὲ καὶ οὗτος, εἴ τινα ξένον ἀγνῶτα πλούσιον λάβοι ἐραστὴν αὐτῆς, ὡς μοιχὸν ἐπ' αὐτῆι ἔνδον ἀποκλείων καὶ ἀργ-
42 ύριον πραττόμενος πολύ, εἰκότως· οὐσία μὲν γὰρ οὐχ ὑπῆρχεν Στεφάνωι οὐδὲ Νεαίραι, ὥστε τὰ καθ' ἡμέραν ἀναλώματα δύνασθαι ὑποφέρειν, ἡ δὲ διοίκησις συχνή, ὁπότ' ἔδει τοῦτόν τε καὶ αὐτὴν τρέφειν καὶ παιδάρια τρία, ἃ ἦλθεν ἔχουσα ὡς αὐτόν, καὶ θεραπαίνας δύο καὶ οἰκέτην διάκονον, ἄλλως τε καὶ μεμαθηκυῖα μὴ κακῶς ἔχειν τὰ ἐπιτήδεια ἑτέρων ἀναλισκόντων αὐτῆι τὸ πρότ-
43 ερον. οὔτε γὰρ ἀπὸ τῆς πολιτείας προσήιει Στεφάνωι τουτωὶ ἄξιον λόγου· οὐ γάρ πω ἦν ῥήτωρ, ἀλλ' ἔτι συκοφάντης τῶν παραβοώντων παρὰ τὸ βῆμα καὶ γραφομένων μισθοῦ καὶ φαινόντων καὶ ἐπιγραφομένων ταῖς ἀλλοτρίαις γνώμαις, ἕως ὑπέπεσε Καλλιστράτωι τῶι Ἀφιδναίωι· ἐξ ὅτου δὲ τρόπου καὶ δι' ἣν αἰτίαν, ἐγὼ ὑμῖν καὶ περὶ τούτου διέξειμι, ἐπειδὰν περὶ ταυτησὶ Νεαίρας ἐπιδείξω ὡς ἔστι ξένη καὶ ὡς μεγάλα ὑμᾶς ἠδίκηκεν καὶ ὡς ἠσέβηκεν εἰς τοὺς
44 θεούς, ἵν' εἰδῆτε ὅτι καὶ αὐτὸς οὗτος ἄξιός ἐστιν οὐκ ἐλάττω δοῦναι δίκην ἢ καὶ Νέαιρα αὑτηί, ἀλλὰ καὶ πολλῶι μείζω καὶ μᾶλλον, ὅσωι Ἀθηναῖος φάσκων εἶναι οὕτω πολὺ τῶν νόμων καταπεφρόνηκεν καὶ ὑμῶν καὶ τῶν θεῶν, ὥστ' οὐδ' ὑπὲρ τῶν ἡμαρτημένων αὐτῶι αἰσχυνόμενος τολμᾶι ἡσυχίαν ἄγειν, ἀλλὰ συκοφαντῶν ἄλλους τε καὶ ἐμέ, τουτονὶ πεποίηκεν αὐτὸν καὶ ταύτην εἰς τηλικοῦτον ἀγῶνα καταστῆσαι, ὥστ' ἐξετασθῆναι μὲν ταύτην ἥτις ἐστίν, ἐξελεγχθῆναι δὲ τὴν αὐτοῦ πονηρίαν.

45 Λαχόντος τοίνυν αὐτῶι τοῦ Φρυνίωνος δίκην, ὅτι αὐτοῦ ἀφείλετο Νέαιραν ταυτηνὶ εἰς ἐλευθερίαν, καὶ ὅτι, ἃ ἐξῆλθεν ἔχουσα παρ' αὐτοῦ αὕτη, ὑπεδέξατο, συνῆγον αὐτοὺς οἱ ἐπιτήδειοι καὶ ἔπεισαν δίαιταν ἐπιτρέψαι αὐτοῖς. καὶ ὑπὲρ μὲν τοῦ Φρυνίωνος διαιτητὴς ἐκαθέζετο Σάτυρος Ἀλωπεκῆθεν ὁ Λακεδαιμονίου ἀδελφός, ὑπὲρ δὲ Στεφάνου τουτουὶ Σαυρίας Λαμπτρεύς· κοινὸν δὲ αὐτοῖς προσ-

DEPOSITION

Aietes of Keiriadai deposes that when he was Polemachos Neaira the defendant in this case was compelled to post bail by Phrynion the brother of Demochares, and Stephanos of Eroiadai, Glauketes of Kephisia and Aristokrates of Phaleron went bail for Neaira.

41 After being bailed by Stephanos, while she was staying with him she
continued to carry on the same trade no less than before, though she charged
larger fees from people who wanted to have relations with her, since she
enjoyed a degree of respectability and was living with a man in marriage.
Stephanos too used to help her in blackmail; if he caught any rich and
unknown alien making love to her, he would lock him up indoors and demand a
42 large sum of money. Not surprisingly; for neither Stephanos nor Neaira had
any property to enable them to meet their daily expenses, and the cost of
maintenance was high, since she had to keep him and herself and three children
which she brought with her to his house, and two maidservants and a
manservant, especially as she had become used to living comfortably before,
43 with other people paying for her needs. Stephanos here had no income worth
mentioning from political activity; he was not yet a public speaker but still only
a sycophant, the sort who shout by the speaker's platform and hire themselves
to bring indictments and denunciations and put their names to other people's
proposals, until he fell under the influence of Kallistratos of Aphidna. How and
why that happened I shall tell you, when I have told Neaira's tale and
demonstrated that she is an alien, and has committed serious offences against
44 you and impiety against the gods; then you will know that this man is himself
no less deserving of punishment than Neaira, but much more so, and all the
more for the fact that while claiming to be an Athenian citizen he has shown
so much contempt for the laws, for you and for the gods that he cannot bring
himself to keep quiet for shame at his misdeeds, but by persecuting myself and
others he has caused Theomnestos here to subject him and the defendent to
such a serious trial, with the result that her origin has been examined and his
criminality exposed.

45 So then, Phrynion brought a suit against him for asserting the freedom of
this woman Neaira and for receiving the property which she took from
Phrynion's house, but their acquaintances brought them together and persuaded
them to submit the dispute to their arbitration. And Satyros of Alopeke, the
brother of Lakedaimonios, sat as arbitrator representing Phrynion, while
Saurias of Lamptrai sat for Stephanos here; as impartial arbitrator they chose

46 αιροῦνται Διογείτονα Ἀχαρνέα. συνελθόντες δ' οὗτοι ἐν τῶι ἱερῶι, ἀκούσαντες ἀμφοτέρων καὶ αὐτῆς τῆς ἀνθρώπου τὰ πεπραγμένα, γνώμην ἀπεφήναντο, καὶ οὗτοι ἐνέμειναν αὐτῆι, τὴν μὲν ἄνθρωπον ἐλευθέραν εἶναι καὶ αὐτὴν αὑτῆς κυρίαν, ἃ δ' ἐξῆλθεν ἔχουσα Νέαιρα παρὰ Φρυνίωνος χωρὶς ἱματίων καὶ χρυσίων καὶ θεραπαινῶν, ἃ αὐτῆι τῆι ἀνθρώπωι ἠγοράσθη, ἀποδοῦναι Φρυνίωνι πάντα· συνεῖναι δ' ἑκατέρωι ἡμέραν παρ' ἡμέραν· ἐὰν δὲ καὶ ἄλλως πως ἀλλήλους πείθωσι, ταῦτα κύρια εἶναι· τὰ δ' ἐπιτήδεια τῆι ἀνθρώπωι τὸν ἔχοντα ἀεὶ παρέχειν, καὶ ἐκ τοῦ λοιποῦ χρόνου φίλους εἶναι ἀλλήλοις καὶ μὴ
47 μνησικακεῖν. ἡ μὲν οὖν γνωσθεῖσα διαλλαγὴ ὑπὸ τῶν διαιτητῶν Φρυνίωνι καὶ Στεφάνωι περὶ Νεαίρας ταυτησὶ αὕτη ἐστίν. ὅτι δ' ἀληθῆ λέγω ταῦτα, τούτων ὑμῖν τὴν μαρτυρίαν ἀναγνώσεται. κάλει μοι Σάτυρον Ἀλωπεκῆθεν, Σαυρίαν Λαμπτρέα, Διογείτονα Ἀχαρνέα.

ΜΑΡΤΥΡΙΑ

Σάτυρος Ἀλωπεκῆθεν, Σαυρίας Λαμπτρεύς, Διογείτων Ἀχαρνεὺς μαρτυροῦσι διαλλάξαι διαιτηταὶ γενόμενοι περὶ Νεαίρας τῆς νυνὶ ἀγωνιζομένης Στέφανον καὶ Φρυνίωνα· τὰς δὲ διαλλαγὰς εἶναι, καθ' ἃς διήλλαξαν, οἵας παρέχεται Ἀπολλόδωρος.

ΔΙΑΛΛΑΓΑΙ

Κατὰ τάδε διήλλαξαν Φρυνίωνα καὶ Στέφανον, χρῆσθαι ἑκάτερον Νεαίραι τὰς ἴσας ἡμέρας τοῦ μηνὸς παρ' ἑαυτοῖς ἔχοντας, ἂν μή τι ἄλλο αὐτοὶ αὑτοῖς συγχωρήσωσιν.

48 Ὡς δ' ἀπηλλαγμένοι ἦσαν, οἱ παρόντες ἑκατέρωι ἐπὶ τῆι διαίτηι καὶ τοῖς πράγμασιν, οἷον οἶμαι φιλεῖ γίγνεσθαι ἑκάστοτε, ἄλλως τε καὶ περὶ ἑταίρας οὔσης αὐτοῖς τῆς διαφορᾶς, ἐπὶ δεῖπνον ἦισαν ὡς ἑκάτερον αὐτῶν, ὁπότε καὶ Νέαιραν ἔχοιεν, καὶ αὐτὴ συνεδείπνει καὶ συνέπινεν ὡς ἑταίρα οὖσα.. καὶ ὅτι ταῦτ' ἀληθῆ λέγω, κάλει μοι μάρτυρας τοὺς συνόντας αὐτοῖς, Εὔβουλον Προβαλίσιον, Διοπείθην Μελιτέα, Κτήσωνα ἐκ Κεραμέων.

ΜΑΡΤΥΡΕΣ

Εὔβουλος Προβαλίσιος, Διοπείθης Μελιτεύς, Κτήσων ἐκ Κεραμέων μαρτυροῦσιν, ἐπειδὴ αἱ διαλλαγαὶ ἐγένοντο αἱ περὶ Νεαίρας Φρυνίωνι καὶ Στεφάνωι, πολλάκις συνδειπνῆσαι αὐτοῖς καὶ συμπίνειν μετὰ Νεαίρας τῆς νυνὶ ἀγωνιζομένης, καὶ ὁπότε παρὰ Στεφάνωι εἴη Νέαιρα καὶ ὁπότε παρὰ Φρυνίωνι.

46 Diogeiton of Acharnai. They met in the temple and after hearing the facts from both parties and the woman herself they announced their decision, which the parties accepted, that the woman was to be free and her own mistress, but that Neaira should give back to Phrynion all that she took with her from Phrynion's house, except for clothing and jewellery and maidservants, which had been bought for the woman herself; she was to live with each of them day for day; but any other arrangement arrived at by mutual agreement should be binding; the one who at the time had her in his keeping was to provide for her mainten-
47 ance; and for the future they were to be friends and bear no grudge. This then was the settlement determined by the arbitrators for Phrynion and Stephanos over this woman Neaira. To prove the truth of my statements, he will read out to you the deposition concerning these events. Please call Satyros of Alopeke, Saurias of Lamptrai and Diogeiton of Acharnai.

DEPOSITION

Satyros of Alopeke, Saurias of Lamptrai and Diogeiton of Acharnai depose that they effected a settlement between Stephanos and Phrynion when acting as arbitrators in the matter of Neaira the defendent in this case; and that the terms on which they affected the settlement were such as Apollodoros produces.

SETTLEMENT

They affected a settlement between Phrynion and Stephanos on the following terms, that each is to keep Neaira at his house and have the use of her for an equal number of days each month, unless they reach any other agreement themselves.

48 Once the settlement was affected, the people who had supported each party in the arbitration and the whole affair, as often, I think, happens, especially when the dispute is about a courtesan, went to dinner at the house of each when he had Neaira with him, and she dined and drank with them as if she were a courtesan. To prove the truth of my statements, please call the witnesses who were with them, Euboulos of Probalinthos, Diopeithes of Melite, Kteson of Kerameis.

WITNESSES

Euboulos of Probalinthos, Diopeithes of Melite and Kteson of Kerameis depose that when the settlement was made between Phrynion and Stephanos in the matter of Neaira, they often dined with them and drank with Neaira, the defendant in this case, both when Neiara was at Stephanos' house and when she was at

49 Ὅτι μὲν τοίνυν ἐξ ἀρχῆς δούλη ἦν καὶ ἐπράθη δὶς καὶ ἠργάζετο τῶι
σώματι ὡς ἑταίρα οὖσα, καὶ ἀπέδρα τὸν Φρυνίωνα εἰς Μέγαρα, καὶ ἥκουσα
κατηγγυήθη ὡς ξένη οὖσα πρὸς τῶι πολεμάρχωι, τῶι τε λόγωι ἀποφαίνω ὑμῖν
καὶ μεμαρτύρηται. βούλομαι δ' ὑμῖν καὶ αὐτὸν Στέφανον τουτονὶ ἐπιδεῖξαι κατα-
50 μεμαρτυρηκότ' αυτῆς ὡς ἔστι ξένη. τὴν γὰρ θυγατέρα τὴν ταυτησὶ Νεαίρας, ἣν
ἦλθεν ἔχουσα ὡς τουτονὶ παιδάριον μικρόν, ἣν τότε μὲν Στρυβήλην ἐκάλουν,
νυνὶ δὲ Φανώ, ἐκδίδωσι Στέφανος οὑτοσὶ ὡς οὖσαν αὑτοῦ θυγατέρα ἀνδρὶ
Ἀθηναίωι Φράστορι Αἰγιλιεῖ, καὶ προῖκα ἐπ' αὐτῆι δίδωσι τριάκοντα μνᾶς. ὡς
δ' ἦλθεν ὡς τὸν Φράστορα, ἄνδρα ἐργάτην καὶ ἀκριβῶς τὸν βίον συνειλεγμένον,
οὐκ ἠπίστατο τοῖς τοῦ Φράστορος τρόποις ἀρέσκειν, ἀλλ' ἐζήτει τὰ τῆς μητρὸς
51 ἔθη καὶ τὴν παρ' αὐτῆι ἀκολασίαν, ἐν τοιαύτηι οἶμαι ἐξουσίαι τεθραμμένη. ὁρῶν
δ' ὁ Φράστωρ αὐτὴν οὔτε κοσμίαν οὖσαν οὔτ' ἐθέλουσαν αὑτοῦ ἀκροᾶσθαι, ἅμα
δὲ καὶ πεπυσμένος σαφῶς ἤδη ὅτι Στεφάνου μὲν οὐκ εἴη θυγάτηρ, Νεαίρας δέ,
τὸ δὲ πρῶτον ἐξηπατήθη, ὅτ' ἠγγυᾶτο ὡς Στεφάνου θυγατέρα λαμβάνων καὶ οὐ
Νεαίρας, ἀλλὰ τούτωι ἐξ ἀστῆς αὐτὴν γυναικὸς οὖσαν πρότερον πρὶν ταύτηι
συνοικῆσαι, ὀργισθεὶς δ' ἐπὶ τούτοις ἅπασιν, καὶ ὑβρίσθαι ἡγούμενος καὶ
ἐξηπατῆσθαι, ἐκβάλλει τὴν ἄνθρωπον ὡς ἐνιαυτὸν συνοικήσας αὐτῆι, κυοῦσαν,
52 καὶ τὴν προῖκα οὐκ ἀποδίδωσιν. λαχόντος δὲ τοῦ Στεφάνου αὐτῶι δίκην σίτου
εἰς Ὠιδεῖον κατὰ τὸν νόμον ὃς κελεύει, ἐὰν ἀποπέμπηι τὴν γυναῖκα, ἀποδιδόναι
τὴν προῖκα, ἐὰν δὲ μή, ἐπ' ἐννέ' ὀβολοῖς τοκοφορεῖν, καὶ σίτου εἰς Ὠιδεῖον εἶναι
δικάσασθαι ὑπὲρ τῆς γυναικὸς τῶι κυρίωι, γράφεται ὁ Φράστωρ Στέφανον
τουτονὶ γραφὴν πρὸς τοὺς θεσμοθέτας, Ἀθηναίωι ὄντι ξένης θυγατέρα αὑτῶι
ἐγγυῆσαι ὡς αὑτῶι προσήκουσαν, κατὰ τὸν νόμον τουτονί. καί μοι ἀνάγνωθι
αὐτόν.

ΝΟΜΟΣ

Ἐὰν δέ τις ἐκδῶι ξένην γυναῖκα ἀνδρὶ Ἀθηναίωι ὡς ἑαυτῶι προσήκουσαν, ἄτιμος ἔστω, καὶ ἡ οὐσία αὐτοῦ δημοσία ἔστω, καὶ τοῦ ἑλόντος τὸ τρίτον μέρος. γραφέσθων δὲ πρὸς τοὺς θεσμοθέτας οἷς ἔξεστιν, καθάπερ τῆς ξενίας.

53 Τὸν μὲν τοίνυν νόμον ἀνέγνω ὑμῖν, καθ' ὃν ἐγράφη Στέφανος οὑτοσὶ ὑπὸ

Phrynion's.

49 So then, I have proved in my narrative with the support of witnesses that
she was originally a slave and was sold twice, and that she worked as a
courtesan; that she ran away form Phrynion to Megara, and that she was
required to post bail before the Polemarchos as an alien. But I wish to prove to
you that Stephanos here also has personally testified against her to prove her
50 an alien. Stephanos here gave the daughter of this woman Neaira, whom she
brought to his house as a small child, and who was formerly known as Strybele
but now Phano, in marriage to an Athenian, Phrastor of Aigilia, as though she
were his own daughter, with a dowry of thirty minas. When she went to live
with Phrastor, a working man who had amassed his resources by careful living,
she did not know how to adapt to Phrastor's ways; she hankered after her
mother's habits and the dissolute way of life in her house, since she had, I sup-
51 pose, been brought up among licentiousness of this sort. Phrastor saw that she
was not a decent woman nor willing to obey him, and since also he had
ascertained that she was not Stephanos' daughter but Neaira's, and that he was
tricked to begin with at the betrothal, when he received her in the belief that
she was Stephanos' daughter and not Neaira's, and that she was his daughter
by a citizen wife before he lived in marriage with Neaira; Phrastor was enraged
at all this, and feeling insulted and deceived, he threw the woman out after he
had been living with her for about a year, while she was pregnant, and with-
52 held the dowry. Stephanos brought a suit for maintenance against him at the
Odeion under the law which prescribes that if anyone sends away his wife he
must pay back the dowry, or else pay interest at a rate of nine obols, and that
the guardian may bring a suit for maintenance at the Odeion on behalf of the
woman; so Phrastor brought an indictment against Stephanos before the
Thesmothetai for betrothing to him, an Athenian citizen, the daughter of an
alien as though she were related to him, under the following law. Please read it
out.

LAW

If anyone gives an alien woman in marriage to an Athenian man, representing her as related to him, he is to be disfranchised, his property is to be confiscated, and one third is to go to the successful prosecutor. Those who possess the right may bring an indictment before the Thesmothetai, as for masquerading as a citizen.

53 He has read you the law under which Stephanos here was indicted by Phrastor

τοῦ Φράστορος πρὸς τοὺς θεσμοθέτας. γνοὺς δ' ὅτι κινδυνεύσει ἐξελεγχθεὶς ξένης θυγατέρα ἠγγυηκέναι [καὶ] ταῖς ἐσχάταις ζημίαις περιπεσεῖν, διαλλάττεται πρὸς τὸν Φράστορα καὶ ἀφίσταται τῆς προικός, καὶ τὴν δίκην τοῦ σίτου ἀνείλετο, καὶ ὁ Φράστωρ τὴν γραφὴν παρὰ τῶν θεσμοθετῶν. καὶ ὡς ἀληθῆ λέγω, τούτων ὑμῖν μάρτυρα αὐτὸν τὸν Φράστορα καλῶ, καὶ ἀναγκάσω μαρτ-
54 υρεῖν κατὰ τὸν νόμον. κάλει μοι Φράστορα Αἰγιλιέα.

ΜΑΡΤΥΡΙΑ

Φράστωρ Αἰγιλιεὺς μαρτυρεῖ, ἐπειδὴ ᾔσθετο Νεαίρας θυγατέρα ἐγγυήσαντα αὐτῶι Στέφανον ὡς ἑαυτοῦ οὖσαν θυγατέρα, γράψασθαι αὐτὸν γραφὴν πρὸς τοὺς θεσμοθέτας κατὰ τὸν νόμον, καὶ τὴν ἄνθρωπον ἐκβαλεῖν ἐκ τῆς ἑαυτοῦ οἰκίας καὶ οὐκέτι συνοικεῖν αὐτῆι, καὶ λαχόντος αὐτῶι Στεφάνου εἰς Ὠιδεῖον σίτου διαλύσασθαι πρὸς αὐτὸν [Στέφανον] ὥστε τὴν γραφὴν ἀναιρεθῆναι παρὰ τῶν θεσμοθετῶν καὶ τὴν δίκην τοῦ σίτου ἣν ἔλαχεν ἐμοὶ Στέφανος.

55 Φέρε δὴ ὑμῖν καὶ ἑτέραν μαρτυρίαν παράσχωμαι τοῦ τε Φράστορος καὶ τῶν φρατέρων αὐτοῦ καὶ γεννητῶν, ὡς ἔστι ξένη Νέαιρα αὐτηί. οὐ πολλῶι χρόνωι γὰρ ὕστερον ἢ ἐξέπεμψεν ὁ Φράστωρ τὴν τῆς Νεαίρας θυγατέρα, ἠσθένησε καὶ πάνυ πονήρως διετέθη καὶ εἰς πᾶσαν ἀπορίαν κατέστη. διαφορᾶς δ' οὔσης αὐτῶι παλαιᾶς πρὸς τοὺς οἰκείους τοὺς αὐτοῦ καὶ ὀργῆς καὶ μίσους, πρὸς δὲ καὶ ἄπαις ὤν, ψυχαγωγούμενος ἐν τῆι ἀσθενείαι τῆι θεραπείαι τῆι ὑπό
56 τε τῆς Νεαίρας καὶ τῆς θυγατρὸς αὐτῆς (ἐβάδιζον γὰρ πρὸς αὐτόν, ὡς ἠσθένει καὶ ἔρημος ἦν τοῦ θεραπεύσοντος τὸ νόσημα, τὰ πρόσφορα τῆι νόσωι φέρουσαι καὶ ἐπισκοπούμεναι· ἴστε δήπου καὶ αὐτοὶ ὅσου ἀξία ἐστὶν γυνὴ ἐν ταῖς νόσοις, παροῦσα κάμνοντι ἀνθρώπωι) ἐπείσθη δὴ τὸ παιδίον, ὃ ἔτεκεν ἡ θυγάτηρ ἡ Νεαίρας ταυτησὶ ὅτ' ἐξεπέμφθη ὑπὸ τοῦ Φράστορος κυοῦσα, πυθομένου ὅτι οὐ Στεφάνου εἴη θυγάτηρ ἀλλὰ Νεαίρας, καὶ ὀργισθέντος ἐπὶ τῆι ἀπάτηι, πάλιν
57 λαβεῖν καὶ ποιήσασθαι υἱὸν αὑτοῦ, λογισμὸν ἀνθρώπινον καὶ εἰκότα λογιζ-όμενος, ὅτι πονήρως μὲν ἔχοι καὶ οὐ πολλὴ ἐλπὶς εἴη αὐτὸν περιγενήσεσθαι, τοῦ δὲ μὴ λαβεῖν τοὺς συγγενεῖς τὰ αὑτοῦ μηδ' ἄπαις τετελευτηκέναι ἐποιήσατο τὸν παῖδα καὶ ἀνέλαβεν ὡς αὑτόν· ἐπεὶ ὅτι γε ὑγιαίνων οὐκ ἄν ποτε ἔπραξεν, μεγ-
58 άλωι τεκμηρίωι καὶ περιφανεῖ ἐγὼ ὑμῖν ἐπιδείξω. ὡς γὰρ ἀνέστη τάχιστα ἐξ ἐκείνης τῆς ἀσθενείας ὁ Φράστωρ καὶ ἀνέλαβεν αὑτὸν καὶ ἔσχεν ἐπιεικῶς τὸ σῶμα, λαμβάνει γυναῖκα ἀστὴν κατὰ τοὺς νόμους, Σατύρου μὲν τοῦ Μελιτέως

before the Thesmothetai. Stephanos realized that if it was proved that he had betrothed the daughter of a foreigner he would be subject to the most severe penalties. He reached a settlement with Phrastor, and gave up his claim to the dowry and withdrew the suit for maintenance, and Phrastor withdrew his indictment from the Thesmothetai. To prove the truth of these statements, I shall call Phrastor himself as witness and compel him to give evidence accord-
54 ing to the law. Please call Phrastor of Aigilia.

DEPOSITION

Phrastor of Aigilia deposes that when he realized that Stephanos had betrothed Neaira's daughter to him, representing her as his own daughter, he indicted him before the Thesmothetai according to the law, and ejected the woman from his house and stopped living with her; and when Stephanos brought a suit for maintenance against him at the Odeion he came to terms with him with the result that the indictment was withdrawn from the Thesmothetai and the suit for maintenance which Stephanos brought against me.

55 Now let me produce for you another piece of testimony by Phrastor and the members of his phratry and genos proving that this Neaira is a foreigner. Not long after Phrastor sent away Neaira's daughter, he fell ill; his condition was very serious and he was reduced to complete helplessness. Phrastor had a long-standing quarrel with his relatives, for whom he felt bitter hatred, and he was childless. Beguiled in his illness by the attentions of Neaira and her daugh-
56 ter (they went to call on him, as he was sick and had nobody to treat his illness, bringing all that was needed for his sickness and taking care of him; you know yourselves, I think, how useful a woman is in times of illness as nurse to an invalid), he was persuaded in fact to take back and acknowledge as his son the child which the daughter of this woman Neaira had borne after she was sent away by Phrastor while she was pregnant, because he had discovered that she was not Stephanos' daughter but Neaira's and he was angry at the de-
57 ception. His reasoning was natural and understandable, that his condition was serious and there was not much hope of recovery; and so to prevent his relatives getting his property and himself from dying childless he acknowledged the child as his and received him into his house. That he would never have done this if he had been in health, I shall establish for you with a strong and
58 unambiguous proof. As soon as Phrastor left his bed after that illness and recovered and was reasonably sound in body, he took a wife of citizen birth in accordance with the laws, the legitimate daughter of Satyros of Melite, and

θυγατέρα γνησίαν, Διφίλου δὲ ἀδελφήν. ὥστε ὅτι μὲν οὐχ ἑκὼν ἀνεδέξατο τὸν
παῖδα, ἀλλὰ βιασθεὶς ὑπὸ τῆς νόσου καὶ τῆς ἀπαιδίας καὶ τῆς ὑπ' αὐτῶν
θεραπείας καὶ τῆς ἔχθρας τῆς πρὸς τοὺς οἰκείους, ἵνα μὴ κληρονόμοι γένωνται
τῶν αὐτοῦ, ἄν τι πάθηι, ταῦτ' ἔστω ὑμῖν τεκμήρια· δηλώσει δὲ καὶ τἀκόλουθ'
59 αὐτῶν ἔτι μᾶλλον. ὡς γὰρ εἰσῆγεν ὁ Φράστωρ εἰς τοὺς φράτερας τὸν παῖδα ἐν
τῆι ἀσθενείαι ὧν τὸν ἐκ τῆς θυγατρὸς τῆς Νεαίρας, καὶ εἰς τοὺς Βρυτίδας ὧν
καὶ αὐτός ἐστιν ὁ Φράστωρ γεννήτης, εἰδότες οἶμαι οἱ γεννῆται τὴν γυναῖκα ἥτις
ἦν, ἣν ἔλαβεν ὁ Φράστωρ τὸ πρῶτον, τὴν τῆς Νεαίρας θυγατέρα, καὶ τὴν
ἀπόπεμψιν τῆς ἀνθρώπου, καὶ διὰ τὴν ἀσθένειαν πεπεισμένον αὐτὸν πάλιν
ἀναλαβεῖν τὸν παῖδα, ἀποψηφίζονται τοῦ παιδὸς καὶ οὐκ ἐνεγραφον αὐτὸν εἰς
60 σφᾶς αὐτούς. λαχόντος δὲ τοῦ Φράστορος αὐτοῖς δίκην, ὅτι οὐκ ἐνέγραφον
αὐτοῦ υἱόν, προκαλοῦνται αὐτὸν οἱ γεννῆται πρὸς τῶι διαιτητῆι ὀμόσαι καθ'
ἱερῶν τελείων ἦ μὴν νομίζειν εἶναι αὑτοῦ υἱὸν ἐξ ἀστῆς γυναικὸς καὶ ἐγγυητῆς
κατὰ τὸν νόμον. προκαλουμένων δὲ ταῦτα τῶν γεννητῶν τὸν Φράστορα πρὸς
61 τῶι διαιτητῆι, ἔλιπεν ὁ Φράστωρ τὸν ὅρκον καὶ οὐκ ὤμοσεν. καὶ ὅτι ἀληθῆ
ταῦτα λέγω, τούτων ὑμῖν μάρτυρας τοὺς παρόντας Βρυτιδῶν παρέξομαι.

ΜΑΡΤΥΡΕΣ

Τιμόστρατος Ἑκάληθεν, Ξάνθιππος Ἐροιάδης, Εὐάλκης Φαληρεύς, Ἄνυτος Λακιάδης, Εὐφράνωρ Αἰγιλιεύς, Νίκιππος Κεφαλῆθεν μαρτυροῦσιν εἶναι καὶ αὐτοὺς καὶ Φράστορα τὸν Αἰγιλιέα τῶν γεννητῶν οἳ καλοῦνται Βρυτίδαι, καὶ ἀξιοῦντος Φράστορος εἰσάγειν τὸν υἱὸν τὸν αὑτοῦ εἰς τοὺς γεννήτας, εἰδότες αὐτοὶ ὅτι Φράστορος υἱὸς εἴη ἐκ τῆς θυγατρὸς τῆς Νεαίρας, κωλύειν εἰσάγειν Φράστορα τὸν υἱόν.

62 Οὐκοῦν περιφανῶς ἐπιδεικνύω ὑμῖν καὶ αὐτοὺς τοὺς οἰκειοτάτους Νεαίρας
ταυτησὶ καταμεμαρτυρηκότας ὡς ἔστιν ξένη, Στέφανόν τε τουτονὶ τὸν ἔχοντα
ταύτην νυνὶ καὶ συνοικοῦντ' αὐτῆι καὶ Φράστορα τὸν λαβόντα τὴν θυγατέρα,
Στέφανον μὲν οὐκ ἐθελήσαντα ἀγωνίσασθαι ὑπὲρ τῆς θυγατρὸς τῆς ταύτης,
γραφέντα ὑπὸ Φράστορος πρὸς τοὺς θεσμορέτας ὡς Ἀθηναίωι ὄντι ξένης
θυγατέρα αὐτῶι ἠγγύησεν, ἀλλ' ἀποστάντα τῆς προικὸς καὶ οὐκ ἀπολαβόντα,
63 Φράστορα δ' ἐκβαλόντα τε τὴν θυγατέρα τὴν Νεαίρας ταυτησὶ γήμαντα, ἐπειδὴ
ἐπύθετο οὐ Στεφάνου οὖσαν, καὶ τὴν προῖκα οὐκ ἀποδόντα, ἐπειδή τε ἐπείσθη
ὕστερον διὰ τὴν ἀσθένειαν τὴν αὐτου καὶ τὴν ἀπαιδίαν καὶ τὴν ἔχθραν τὴν πρὸς
τοὺς οἰκείους ποιήσασθαι τὸν υἱόν, καὶ ἐπειδὴ εἰσῆγεν εἰς τοὺς γεννήτας,
ἀποψηφισαμένων τῶν γεννητῶν καὶ διδόντων ὅρκον αὐτῶι οὐκ ἐθελήσαντα
ὀμόσαι, ἀλλὰ μᾶλλον εὐορκεῖν προελόμενον, καὶ ἑτέραν ὕστερον γήμαντα

sister of Diphilos. So this should be proof for you that he did not take back the boy voluntarily but under pressure from his illness, his childlessness, their nursing and his quarrel with his relatives, and his desire to prevent them inheriting his property if anything were to happen to him; what followed will
59 provide still further proof. For when Phrastor tried during his illness to introduce his child by Neaira's daughter into his phratry and into the Brytidai, the genos to which Phrastor belongs, the members of that genos, aware I think of the identity of Phrastor's first wife, Neaira's daughter, and of his ejection of her, and that it was on account of his illness that he was induced to take back
60 the boy, rejected the boy and refused to register him among themselves. When Phrastor brought a suit against them for refusing to register his son, the members of his genos challenged him in the presence of the arbitrator to swear by sacrificial victims that he believed the child to be his son by a woman of citizen birth given in marriage to him in accordance with the law. When the genos members issued this challenge to Phrastor in the presence of the arbitrat-
61 or, Phrastor declined the oath and would not swear. To prove the truth of these statements, I shall provide as witnesses those of the Brytidai who were present.

WITNESSES

Timostratos of Hekale, Xanthippos of Eroiadai, Eualkes of Phaleron, Anytos of Lakiadai, Euphranor of Aigilia and Nikippos of Kephale depose that they and Phrastor belong to the genos called Brytidei, and that when Phrastor claimed the right to introduce his son into the genos, since they knew that it was Phrastor's son by the daughter of Neaira, they prevented him from introducing his son.

62 Thus I offer you clear proof that even the closest relations of this woman Neaira have themselves testified that she is a foreigner, both Stephanos here who now keeps her and is living in marriage with her and Phrastor who married her daughter: Stephanos when he refused to go to trial on behalf of her daughter on being indicted by Phrastor before the Thesmothetai for giving the daughter of a foreign woman in marriage to him, an Athenian citizen, and
63 when he gave up his claim on the dowry rather than recover it; Phrastor when he ejected the daughter of this Neaira after marrying her, upon discovering that she was not Stephanos' daughter, and when he refused to return the dowry; and later, after he was induced to acknowledge his son because of his illness, his childlessness and his quarrel with his relatives, on his attempting to introduce it into his genos, when he refused to swear and preferred to respect the oath after the clan rejected his son and challenged him to swear, and later when he

γυναῖκα ἀστὴν κατὰ τὸν νόμον· αὗται γὰρ αἱ πράξεις περιφανεῖς οὖσαι μεγάλας μαρτυρίας δεδώκασι κατ' αὐτῶν, ὅτι ἔστι ξένη Νέαιρα αὑτηί.

64 Σκέψασθε δὲ καὶ τὴν αἰσχροκερδίαν τὴν Στεφάνου τουτουὶ καὶ τὴν πονηρίαν, ἵνα καὶ ἐκ ταύτης εἰδῆτε ὅτι οὐκ ἔστιν Νέαιρα αὑτηὶ ἀστή. Ἐπαίνετον γὰρ τὸν Ἄνδριον, ἐραστὴν ὄντα Νεαίρας ταυτησὶ παλαιὸν καὶ πολλὰ ἀνηλωκότα εἰς αὐτὴν καὶ καταγόμενον παρὰ τούτοις ὁπότε ἐπιδημήσειεν Ἀθήν-
65 αζε διὰ τὴν φιλίαν τὴν Νεαίρας, ἐπιβουλεύσας Στέφανος οὑτοσί, μεταπεμψάμενος εἰς ἀγρὸν ὡς θύων, λαμβάνει μοιχὸν ἐπὶ τῆι θυγατρὶ τῆι Νεαίρας ταυτησί, καὶ εἰς φόβον καταστήσας πράττεται μνᾶς τριάκοντα, καὶ λαβὼν ἐγγυητὰς τούτων Ἀριστόμαχόν τε τὸν θεσμοθετήσαντα καὶ Ναυσίφιλον τὸν Ναυσινίκου τοῦ ἄρξαντος υἱόν, ἀφίησιν ὡς ἀποδώσοντα αὑτῶι τὸ ἀργύριον.
66 ἐξελθὼν δὲ ὁ Ἐπαίνετος καὶ αὐτὸς αὑτοῦ κύριος γενόμενος γράφεται πρὸς τοὺς θεσμοθέτας γραφὴν Στέφανον τουτονί, ἀδίκως εἰρχθῆναι ὑπ' αὐτοῦ, κατὰ τὸν νόμον ὃς κελεύει, ἐάν τις ἀδίκως εἵρξηι ὡς μοιχόν, γράψασθαι πρὸς τοὺς θεσμοθέτας ἀδίκως εἰρχθῆναι, καὶ ἐὰν μὲν ἕληι τὸν εἵρξαντα καὶ δόξηι ἀδίκως ἐπιβεβουλεῦσθαι, ἀθῶιον εἶναι αὐτὸν καὶ τοὺς ἐγγυητὰς ἀπηλλάχθαι τῆς ἐγγύης· ἐὰν δὲ δόξηι μοιχὸς εἶναι, παραδοῦναι αὐτὸν κελεύει τοὺς ἐγγυητὰς τῶι ἑλόντι, ἐπὶ δὲ τοῦ δικαστηρίου ἄνευ ἐγχειριδίου χρῆσθαι ὅ τι ἂν βουληθῆι, ὡς μοιχῶι
67 ὄντι. κατὰ δὴ τοῦτον τὸν νόμον γράφεται αὐτὸν ὁ Ἐπαίνετος, καὶ ὡμολόγει μὲν χρῆσθαι τῆι ἀνθρώπωι, οὐ μέντοι μοιχός γε εἶναι· οὔτε γὰρ Στεφάνου θυγατέρα αὐτὴν εἶναι ἀλλὰ Νεαίρας, τήν τε μητέρα αὐτῆς συνειδέναι πλησιάζουσαν αὑτῶι, ἀνηλωκέναι τε πολλὰ εἰς αὐτάς, τρέφειν τε ὁπότε ἐπιδημήσειεν τὴν οἰκίαν ὅλην· τόν τε νόμον ἐπὶ τούτοις παρεχόμενος, ὃς οὐκ ἐᾶι ἐπὶ ταύτηισι μοιχὸν λαβεῖν ὁπόσαι ἂν ἐπ' ἐργαστηρίου καθῶνται ἢ πωλῶνται ἀποπεφασμένως, ἐργαστήριον φάσκων καὶ τοῦτο εἶναι, τὴν Στεφάνου οἰκίαν,
68 καὶ τὴν ἐργασίαν ταύτην εἶναι, καὶ ἀπὸ τούτων αὐτοὺς εὐπορεῖν μάλιστα. τούτους δὲ τοὺς λόγους λέγοντος τοῦ Ἐπαινέτου καὶ τὴν γραφὴν γεγραμμένου, γνοὺς Στέφανος οὑτοσὶ ὅτι ἐξελεγχθήσεται πορνοβοσκῶν καὶ συκοφαντῶν, δίαιταν ἐπιτρέπει πρὸς τὸν Ἐπαίνετον αὐτοῖς τοῖς ἐγγυηταῖς, ὥστε τῆς μὲν ἐγγύ-
69 ης αὐτοὺς ἀφεῖσθαι, τὴν δὲ γραφὴν ἀνελέσθαι τὸν Ἐπαίνετον. πεισθέντος δὲ τοῦ Ἐπαινέτου ἐπὶ τούτοις καὶ ἀνελομένου τὴν γραφὴν ἣν ἐδίωκε Στέφανον, γενομένης συνόδου αὐτοῖς καὶ καθεζομένων διαιτητῶν τῶν ἐγγυητῶν, δίκαιον

married another woman of Athenian birth in accordance with the law. For
these actions, which are perfectly clear, have provided convincing testimony
against them, proving that Neaira here is a foreigner.

64 Now observe the greed and unscrupulousness of this man Stephanos, and
you will realize from this too that this woman Neaira is a foreigner. Stephanos
here laid a plot against Epainetos of Andros, a long-standing lover of Neaira's
who had spent a great deal on her, and who used to stay with them whenever
65 he was in Athens because of his affection for Neaira. Stephanos here devised a
plot against him; he invited him to the country on the pretext of making
sacrifice, then caught him in adultery with the daughter of Neaira here; and by
intimidation extorted a ransom of thirty minas. He accepted as sureties for this
sum Aristomachos who had served as Thesmothetes and Nausiphilos the son of
Nausinikos who had been Archon and released Epainetos on an understanding
66 that he would pay the money. Once Epainetos got clear and was his own
master he brought an indictment against this man Stephanos before the
Thesmothetai for false imprisonment under the law which prescribes that if
anyone falsely imprisons another as an adulterer the victim may indict him
before the Thesmothetai for false imprisonment, and that if he secures the
conviction of the man who imprisoned him and it is decided that he has been
the victim of a dishonest plot, he is liable to no penalty and his sureties are quit
of their bail; however, if it is decided that he is an adulterer, the law prescribes
that his sureties are to deliver him to his captor, who may treat him as he
chooses in the court, short of using a knife, on the grounds that he is an adult-
67 erer. It was under this law that Epainetos indicted him. He admitted that he
had had the use of the woman, but denied being an adulterer; he said that she
was not Stephanos' daughter but Neaira's, and that her mother knew that she
was having relations with him, that he had spent a great deal of money on
them, and that whenever he was in town he used to meet the expenses of the
whole household; in addition he cited the law which forbids seizing a man as
an adulterer with any women who sit in a brothel or parade publicly, and he
said that this was what Stephanos' house was, a brothel, that this was their
68 trade, and they made their money chiefly by this means. Because of this line of
argument and the indictment which Epainetos had brought, Stephanos, realizing
that he would be exposed as a brothelkeeper and a blackmailer, submitted his
dispute with Epainetos to the arbitration of the very men who had acted as
surety, on the terms that they were to be quit of their surety, while Epainetos
69 was to withdraw his indictment. Epainetos accepted these terms and withdrew
the indictment on which he was prosecuting Stephanos; there was a meeting at
which men who had stood surety sat as arbitrators. Stephanos had nothing to

μὲν οὐδὲν εἶχε λέγειν Στέφανος, εἰς ἔκδοσιν δ' ἠξίου τὸν Ἐπαίνετον τῆι τῆς
Νεαίρας θυγατρὶ συμβαλέσθαι, λέγων τὴν ἀπορίαν τὴν αὑτοῦ καὶ τὴν ἀτυχίαν
τὴν πρότερον γενομένην τῆι ἀνθρώπωι πρὸς τὸν Φράστορα, καὶ ὅτι ἀπολωλεκὼς
70 εἴη τὴν προῖκα, καὶ οὐκ ἂν δύναιτο πάλιν αὐτὴν ἐκδοῦναι· 'σύ δὲ καὶ κέχρησαι'
ἔφη 'τῆι ἀνθρώπωι, καὶ δίκαιος εἶ ἀγαθόν τι ποιῆσαι αὐτήν', καὶ ἄλλους
ἐπαγωγοὺς λόγους, οὓς ἂν τις δεόμενος ἐκ πονηρῶν πραγμάτων εἴποι ἄν.
ἀκούσαντες δ' ἀμφοτέρων αὐτῶν οἱ διαιτηταὶ διαλλάττουσιν αὐτούς, καὶ
πείθουσι τὸν Ἐπαίνετον χιλίας δραχμὰς εἰσενεγκεῖν εἰς τὴν ἔκδοσιν τῆι θυγατρὶ
τῆι Νεαίρας. καὶ ὅτι πάντα ταῦτα ἀληθῆ λέγω, τούτων ὑμῖν μάρτυρας αὐτοὺς
τοὺς ἐγγυητὰς καὶ διαιτητὰς γενομένους καλῶ.

ΜΑΡΤΥΡΕΣ

71 Ναυσίφιλος Κεφαλῆθεν, Ἀριστόμαχος Κεφαλῆθεν μαρτυροῦσιν ἐγγυηταὶ γενέσθαι Ἐπαινέτου τοῦ Ἀνδρίου, ὅτ' ἔφη Στέφανος μοιχὸν εἰληφέναι Ἐπαίνετον· καὶ ἐπειδὴ ἐξῆλθεν Ἐπαίνετος παρὰ Στεφάνου καὶ κύριος ἐγένετο αὑτοῦ, γράψασθαι γραφὴν Στέφανον πρὸς τοὺς θεσμοθέτας, ὅτι αὐτὸν ἀδίκως εἷρξεν· καὶ αὐτοὶ διαλλακταὶ γενόμενοι διαλλάξαι Ἐπαίνετον καὶ Στέφανον· τὰς δὲ διαλλαγὰς εἶναι ἃς παρέχεται Ἀπολλόδωρος.

ΔΙΑΛΛΑΓΑΙ

Ἐπὶ τοῖσδε διήλλαξαν Στέφανον καὶ Ἐπαίνετον οἱ διαλλακταί, τῶν μὲν γεγενημένων περὶ τὸν εἱργμὸν μηδεμίαν μνείαν ἔχειν, Ἐπαίνετον δὲ δοῦναι χιλίας δραχμὰς Φανοῖ εἰς ἔκδοσιν, ἐπειδὴ κέχρηται αὐτῆι πολλάκις· Στέφανον δὲ παρέχειν Φανὼ Ἐπαινέτωι, ὁπόταν ἐπιδημῆι καὶ βούληται συνεῖναι αὐτῆι.

72 Τὴν τοίνυν περιφανῶς ἐγνωσμένην ξένην εἶναι καὶ ἐφ' ἧι μοιχὸν οὗτος ἐτόλμησε λαβεῖν, εἰς τοσοῦτον ὕβρεως καὶ ἀναιδείας ἦλθεν Στέφανος οὑτοσὶ καὶ Νέαιρα αὑτηί, ὥστε ἐτόλμησαν μὴ ἀγαπᾶν εἰ ἔφασκον αὐτὴν ἀστὴν εἶναι, ἀλλὰ κατιδόντες Θεογένην Κοιρωνίδην λαχόντα βασιλέα, ἄνθρωπον εὐγενῆ μέν, πένητα δὲ καὶ ἄπειρον πραγμάτων, συμπαραγενόμενος αὐτῶι δοκιμαζομένωι καὶ συνευπορήσας ἀναλωμάτων, ὅτε εἰσήιει εἰς τὴν ἀρχήν, Στέφανος οὑτοσί, καὶ ὑπελθὼν καὶ τὴν ἀρχὴν παρ' αὐτοῦ πριάμενος, πάρεδρος γενόμενος, δίδωσι τὴν ἄνθρωπον ταύτην γυναῖκα, τὴν τῆς Νεαίρας θυγατέρα, καὶ ἐγγυᾶι Στέφανος οὑτοσὶ ὡς αὑτοῦ θυγατέρα οὖσαν· οὕτω πολὺ τῶν νόμων καὶ ὑμῶν κατεφρόνη-

say by way of justification, but urged Epainetos to contribute to the marriage of Neaira's daughter; he mentioned his poverty and the girl's earlier misfortune with Phrastor, and the fact that he had lost her dowry and would not be able to
70 marry her off again. 'You have besides had the use of the girl', he said, 'and it is only right that you should do her a good turn', and other coaxing arguments which a man begging in difficult circumstances might use. The arbitrators after listening to both sides arranged a settlement between them; they persuaded Epainetos to contribute a thousand drachmas to the marriage of Neaira's daughter. To prove all I am saying is true, I shall call as witnesses the very men who acted as sureties and arbitrators.

WITNESSES

71 *Nausiphilos of Kephale and Aristomachos of Kephale depose that they acted as sureties for Epainetos of Andros, when Stephanos claimed to have taken Epainetos in adultery; that when Epainetos left Stephanos' house and was his own master he indicted Stephanos before the Thesmothetai for falsely imprisoning him; that they served as conciliators and brought about a settlement between Epainetos and Stephanos; and that the terms of settlement are those produced by Apollodoros.*

SETTLEMENT

These are the terms on which the conciliators arranged a settlement between Stephanos and Epainetos: that they should bear no grudge for the events surrounding the imprisonment, that Epainetos is to give one thousand drachmas for Phano's marriage, since he has had the use of her many times; Stephanos is to offer Phano to Epainetos whenever he is in town and wants to consort with her.

72 Now although this woman was unambiguously judged to be an alien, and although he had had the audacity to take a man in adultery with her, such was the insolence and shamelessness of this Stephanos and this Neaira, that they were not content with claiming she was of citizen birth; observing that Theogenes of the Koironidai, a man of noble birth but poor and inexperienced in public affairs, had been drawn as King-archon, this man Stephanos supported him at his examination and assisted with expenses when he was entering office; he ingratiated himself and bought the post of assessor from him, and gave this woman to him in marriage, Neaira's daughter, betrothing her as though she were his own daughter. Such was his contempt for the laws and

73 σεν. καὶ αὕτη ἡ γυνὴ ὑμῖν ἔθυε τὰ ἄρρητα ἱερὰ ὑπὲρ τῆς πόλεως, καὶ εἶδεν ἃ
οὐ προσῆκεν αὐτὴν ὁρᾶν ξένην οὖσαν, καὶ τοιαύτη οὖσα εἰσῆλθεν οἷ οὐδεὶς
ἄλλος Ἀθηναίων τοσούτων ὄντων εἰσέρχεται ἀλλ' ἢ ἡ τοῦ βασιλέως γυνή,
ἐξώρκωσέν τε τὰς γεραρὰς τὰς ὑπηρετούσας τοῖς ἱεροῖς, ἐξεδόθη δὲ τῶι
Διονύσωι γυνή, ἔπραξε δὲ ὑπὲρ τῆς πόλεως τὰ πάτρια τὰ πρὸς τοὺς θεούς,
πολλὰ καὶ ἅγια καὶ ἀπόρρητα. ἃ δὲ μηδ' ἀκοῦσαι πᾶσιν οἷόν τ' ἐστίν, πῶς
ποιῆσαί γε τῆι ἐπιτυχούσηι εὐσεβῶς ἔχει, ἄλλως τε καὶ τοιαύτηι γυναικὶ καὶ
τοιαῦτα ἔργα διαπεπραγμένηι;
74 Βούλομαι δ' ὑμῖν ἀκριβέστερον περὶ αὐτῶν ἄνωθεν διηγήσασθαι καθ'
ἕκαστον, ἵνα μᾶλλον ἐπιμέλειαν ποιήσησθε τῆς τιμωρίας, καὶ εἰδῆτε ὅτι οὐ μόνον
ὑπὲρ ὑμῶν αὐτῶν καὶ τῶν νόμων τὴν ψῆφον οἴσετε, ἀλλὰ καὶ τῆς πρὸς τοὺς
θεοὺς εὐλαβείας, τιμωρίαν ὑπὲρ τῶν ἠσεβημένων ποιούμενοι καὶ κολάζοντες
τοὺς ἠδικηκότας.

Τὸ γὰρ ἀρχαῖον, ὦ ἄνδρες Ἀθηναῖοι, δυναστεία ἐν τῆι πόλει ἦν καὶ ἡ
βασιλεία τῶν ἀεὶ ὑπερεχόντων διὰ τὸ αὐτόχθονας εἶναι, τὰς δὲ θυσίας ἁπάσας ὁ
βασιλεὺς ἔθυε, καὶ τὰς σεμνοτάτας καὶ ἀρρήτους ἡ γυνὴ αὐτοῦ ἐποίει, εἰκότως,
75 βασίλιννα οὖσα. ἐπειδὴ δὲ Θησεὺς συνώικισεν αὐτοὺς καὶ δημοκρατίαν ἐποίησεν
καὶ ἡ πόλις πολυάνθρωπος ἐγένετο, τὸν μὲν βασιλέα οὐδὲν ἧττον ὁ δῆμος ἡιρεῖτο
ἐκ προκρίτων κατ' ἀνδραγαθίαν χειροτονῶν, τὴν δὲ γυναῖκα αὐτοῦ νόμον
ἔθεντο ἀστὴν εἶναι καὶ μὴ ἐπιμεμειγμένην ἑτέρωι ἀνδρὶ ἀλλὰ παρθένον γαμεῖν,
ἵνα κατὰ τὰ πάτρια θύηται τὰ ἄρρητα ἱερὰ ὑπὲρ τῆς πόλεως, καὶ τὰ νομιζόμενα
76 γίγνηται τοῖς θεοῖς εὐσεβῶς καὶ μηδὲν καταλύηται μηδὲ καινοτομῆται. καὶ
τοῦτον τὸν νόμον γράψαντες ἐν στήληι λιθίνηι ἔστησαν ἐν τῶι ἱερῶι τοῦ
Διονύσου παρὰ τὸν βωμὸν ἐν Λίμναις (καὶ αὕτη ἡ στήλη ἔτι καὶ νῦν ἕστηκεν,
ἀμυδροῖς γράμμασιν Ἀττικοῖς δηλοῦσα τὰ γεγραμμένα), μαρτυρίαν ποιούμενος ὁ
δῆμος ὑπὲρ τῆς αὑτοῦ εὐσεβείας πρὸς τὸν θεὸν καὶ παρακαταθήκην καταλείπων
τοῖς ἐπιγιγνομένοις, ὅτι τήν γε θεῶι γυναῖκα δοθησομένην καὶ ποιήσουσαν τὰ
ἱερὰ τοιαύτην ἀξιοῦμεν εἶναι. καὶ διὰ ταῦτα ἐν τῶι ἀρχαιοτάτωι ἱερῶι τοῦ
Διονύσου καὶ ἁγιωτάτωι ἐν Λίμναις ἔστησαν, ἵνα μὴ πολλοὶ εἰδῶσιν τὰ
γεγραμμένα· ἅπαξ γὰρ τοῦ ἐνιαυτοῦ ἑκάστου ἀνοίγεται, τῆι δωδεκάτηι τοῦ
77 ἀνθεστηριῶνος μηνός. ὑπὲρ τοίνυν ἁγίων καὶ σεμνῶν ἱερῶν, ὧν οἱ πρόγονοι
ὑμῶν οὕτως καλῶς καὶ μεγαλοπρεπῶς ἐπεμελήθησαν, ἄξιον καὶ ὑμᾶς
σπουδάσαι, ὦ ἄνδρες Ἀθηναῖοι, καὶ τοὺς ἀσελγῶς μὲν καταφρονοῦντας τῶν
νόμων τῶν ὑμετέρων, ἀναιδῶς δ' ἠσεβηκότας εἰς τοὺς θεοὺς ἄξιον
τιμωρήσασθαι δυοῖν ἕνεκα, ἵνα οὗτοί τε τῶν ἠδικημένων δίκην δῶσιν, οἵ τ'

73 for you. And this woman made the secret offerings for you as representative of the city, and she saw what as an alien she had no right to see; despite her character she entered where nobody else among the vast Athenian population enters, except the wife of the King-archon, and administered the oath to the Venerable Women who assist in the rites; she was given as bride to Dionysos and she carried out as the city's representative the many ceremonies, holy and secret, which were handed down by our ancestors. How can it accord with piety for just any woman actually to perform rites which it is not permitted for people even to hear of, especially a woman with a character and career such as hers?

74 But I want to go back and tell you about the rites in greater detail, so that you will pay more attention to the punishment, in the knowledge that you will be casting your vote not only in the interest of yourselves and the laws but also of reverence towards the gods, by exacting a penalty for their acts of impiety and punishing the guilty.

In early times, men of Athens, there was a monarchy in the state, a kingship which belonged to those who at my time had most prestige because they were indigenous; the king performed all the sacrifices, and the most solemn and secret sacrifices his wife performed, naturally, since she was queen.
75 After Theseus united the people in one city and created a democracy and the population increased, the people nonetheless continued to choose the King by show of hands from men preselected on grounds of excellence; and they passed a law that his wife should be of citizen birth and he should marry a virgin who had never been with another man, in order that the secret ceremonies should be performed according to ancestral custom, for the city's sake, and the traditional offerings should be made to the gods in accordance with piety without any
76 excision or innovation. They wrote this law on a stone column and set it up in the temple of Dionysos in the Marshes, by the altar (and this column is standing to this day, displaying its inscription in faint Attic characters); thus the people testified to its piety towards the god and left it as a trust to future generations, showing that we expect the woman who is to be given as bride to a god and who is to perform the sacrifices to be like this. This is why they set it up in the most ancient and holy shrine of Dionysos in the Marshes, so that the inscription would not be known to many; for it is opened up once each
77 year, on the twelfth day of the month of Anthesterion. So then these holy and solemn rites, for which your ancestors showed such noble and impressive concern, you too should treat with gravity, men of Athens, and you should punish those who have shown such outrageous contempt for your laws and committed such shameless impiety against the gods, for two reasons: so that

ἄλλοι πρόνοιαν ποιῶνται καὶ φοβῶνται μηδὲν εἰς τοὺς θεοὺς καὶ τὴν πόλιν
ἁμαρτάνειν.

78 Βούλομαι δ' ὑμῖν καὶ τὸν ἱεροκήρυκα καλέσαι, ὃς ὑπηρετεῖ τῆι τοῦ
βασιλέως γυναικί, ὅταν ἐξορκοῖ τὰς γεραρὰς ἐν κανοῖς πρὸς τῶι βωμῶι, πρὶν
ἅπτεσθαι τῶν ἱερῶν, ἵνα καὶ τοῦ ὅρκου καὶ τῶν λεγομένων ἀκούσητε, ὅσα οἷόν
τ' ἐστὶν ἀκούειν, καὶ εἰδῆτε ὡς σεμνὰ καὶ ἅγια καὶ ἀρχαῖα τὰ νόμιμά ἐστιν.

ΟΡΚΟΣ ΓΕΡΑΡΩΝ

Ἁγιστεύω καὶ εἰμὶ καθαρὰ καὶ ἁγνὴ ἀπό τε τῶν ἄλλων τῶν οὐ
καθαρευόντων καὶ ἀπ' ἀνδρὸς συνουσίας, καὶ τὰ θεοίνια καὶ τὰ ἰοβάκχεια
γεραρῶ τῶι Διονύσωι κατὰ τὰ πάτρια καὶ ἐν τοῖς καθήκουσι χρόνοις.

79 Τοῦ μὲν ὅρκου τοίνυν καὶ τῶν νομιζομένων πατρίων, ὅσα οἷόν τ' ἐστὶν
εἰπεῖν, ἀκηκόατε, καὶ ὡς ἣν Στέφανος ἠγγύησεν τῶι Θεογένει γυναῖκα
βασιλεύοντι ὡς αὑτοῦ οὖσαν θυγατέρα, αὕτη ἐποίει τὰ ἱερὰ ταῦτα καὶ ἐξώρκου
τὰς γεραράς, καὶ ὅτι οὐδ' αὐταῖς ταῖς ὁρώσαις τὰ ἱερὰ ταῦτα οἷόν τ' ἐστὶν
λέγειν πρὸς ἄλλον οὐδένα. φέρε δὴ καὶ μαρτυρίαν παράσχωμαι ὑμῖν δι'
ἀπορρήτου μὲν γεγενημένην, ὅμως δὲ αὐτοῖς τοῖς πεπραγμένοις ἐπιδείξω
φανερὰν οὖσαν αὐτὴν καὶ ἀληθῆ.

80 Ὡς γὰρ ἐγένετο τὰ ἱερὰ ταῦτα καὶ ἀνέβησαν εἰς Ἄρειον πάγον οἱ ἐννέα
ἄρχοντες ταῖς καθηκούσαις ἡμέραις, εὐθὺς ἡ βουλὴ ἡ ἐν Ἀρείωι πάγωι, ὥσπερ
καὶ τἄλλα πολλοῦ ἀξία ἐστὶν τῆι πόλει περὶ εὐσέβειαν, ἐζήτει τὴν γυναῖκα
ταύτην τοῦ Θεογένους ἥτις ἦν, καὶ ἐξήλεγχεν, καὶ περὶ τῶν ἱερῶν πρόνοιαν
ἐποιεῖτο, καὶ ἐζημίου τὸν Θεογένην ὅσα κυρία ἐστίν, ἐν ἀπορρήτωι δὲ καὶ διὰ
κοσμιότητος· οὐ γὰρ αὐτοκράτορές εἰσιν, ὡς ἂν βούλωνται, Ἀθηναίων τινὰ
81 κολάσαι. γενομένων δὲ λόγων, καὶ χαλεπῶς φερούσης τῆς ἐν Ἀρείωι πάγωι
βουλῆς καὶ ζημιούσης τὸν Θεογένην ὅτι τοιαύτην ἔλαβεν γυναῖκα καὶ ταύτην
εἴασε ποιῆσαι τὰ ἱερὰ τὰ ἄρρητα ὑπὲρ τῆς πόλεως, ἐδεῖτο ὁ Θεογένης ἱκετεύων
καὶ ἀντιβολῶν, λέγων ὅτι οὐκ ἤιδει Νεαίρας αὐτὴν οὖσαν θυγατέρα, ἀλλ'
ἐξαπατηθείη ὑπὸ Στεφάνου, ὡς αὐτοῦ θυγατέρα οὖσαν αὐτὴν λαμβάνων
γνησίαν κατὰ τὸν νόμον, καὶ διὰ τὴν ἀπειρίαν τῶν πραγμάτων καὶ τὴν ἀκακίαν
τὴν ἑαυτοῦ τοῦτον πάρεδρον ποιήσαιτο, ἵνα διοικήσηι τὴν ἀρχήν, ὡς εὔνουν ὄντ-
82 α, καὶ διὰ τοῦτο κηδεύσειεν αὐτῶι. 'ὅτι δὲ' ἔφη 'οὐ ψεύδομαι, μεγάλωι

these people will pay the penalty for the crimes they have committed and so that others will take care and feel afraid to commit any offence against the gods and the city.

78 I wish also to call before you the Sacred Herald, who assists the King-archon's wife when she puts the oath to the Venerable Women at the baskets near the altar, before they touch the victims, so that you may hear the oath and the words which are spoken, as far as it is allowed to hear them, and know how solemn and holy and ancient the traditional rites are.

OATH OF THE VENERABLE WOMEN

I live a holy life and am pure and clear from all impurity including intercourse with a man, and I shall perform for Dionysos the Feast of the Wine God and the Rites of Bakchos according to ancestral custom and at the appointed times.

79 You have now heard the oath and the customary rites of our ancestors, as far as it is allowed to utter them, and you have heard that the woman whom Stephanos gave as wife to Theogenes when he was serving as King-archon, as though she were his own daughter, carried out these rites and administered the oath to the Venerable Women, and that it is not even permitted for the women who see these rites to divulge them to any other. Let me now offer you a testimony which took place in secret but which I shall prove by the facts themselves to be convincing and true.

80 When these ceremonies had taken place and the nine Archons had gone up to the Areopagos on the appointed days, immediately the Areopagos, which is generally so valuable to the state in matters of piety, enquired about the identity of the wife of Theogenes, and ascertained the truth. It was concerned for the rites, and was inclined to punish Theogenes to the limit of its power, but in secret and with discretion; for they do not have the power to punish an
81 Athenian citizen as they please. A discussion took place, at which the Areopagos expressed its anger and proposed to punish Theogenes for marrying a woman of this sort and for allowing her to perform the secret rites on behalf of the city. Theogenes implored them, begging and pleading, saying that he did not know that she was Neaira's daughter and that he had been tricked by Stephanos and married her according to the law, thinking her Stephanos' legitimate daughter; that it was because of his ignorance of public affairs and innocence that he made this man his assessor, to manage the business of his office, thinking him a friend, and this was why he had become his son-in-law.
82 'I shall prove to you I am not lying,' he said, 'with strong and visible proof.

τεκμηρίωι καὶ περιφανεῖ ἐπιδείξω ὑμῖν· τὴν γὰρ ἄνθρωπον ἀποπέμψω ἐκ τῆς
οἰκίας, ἐπειδὴ οὐκ ἔστιν Στεφάνου θυγάτηρ ἀλλὰ Νεαίρας. κἂν μὲν ταῦτα
ποιήσω, ἤδη πιστοὶ ὑμῖν ἔστωσαν οἱ λόγοι οἱ παρ' ἐμοῦ λεγόμενοι, ὅτι
ἐξηπατήθην· ἐὰν δὲ μὴ ποιήσω, τότ' ἤδη με κολάζετε ὡς πονηρὸν ὄντα καὶ εἰς
83 τοὺς θεοὺς ἠσεβηκότα'. ὑποσχομένου δὲ ταῦτα τοῦ Θεογένους καὶ δεομένου, ἅμα
μὲν καὶ ἐλεήσασα αὐτὸν ἡ ἐν 'Αρείωι πάγωι βουλὴ διὰ τὴν ἀκακίαν τοῦ τρόπου,
ἅμα δὲ καὶ ἐξηπατῆσθαι τῆι ἀληθείαι ἡγουμένη ὑπὸ τοῦ Στεφάνου, ἐπέσχεν. ὡς
δὲ κατέβη ἐξ 'Αρείου πάγου ὁ Θεογένης, εὐθὺς τήν τε ἄνθρωπον τὴν ταυτησὶ
Νεαίρας θυγατέρα ἐκβάλλει ἐκ τῆς οἰκίας, τόν τε Στέφανον τὸν ἐξαπατήσαντα
αὐτὸν τουτονὶ ἀπελαύνει ἀπὸ τοῦ συνεδρίου. καὶ οὕτως ἐπαύσαντο οἱ
'Αρεοπαγῖται κρίνοντες τὸν Θεογένην καὶ ὀργιζόμενοι αὐτῶι, καὶ συγγνώμην
84 εἶχον ἐξαπατηθέντι. καὶ ὅτι ταῦτ' ἀληθῆ λέγω, τούτων ὑμῖν μάρτυρα αὐτὸν τὸν
Θεογένην καλῶ καὶ ἀναγκάσω μαρτυρεῖν. κάλει μοι Θεογένην Ἐρχιέα.

ΜΑΡΤΥΡΙΑ

Θεογένης Ἐρχιεὺς μαρτυρεῖ, ὅτε αὐτὸς ἐβασίλευεν, γῆμαι Φανὼ ὡς Στεφάνου οὖσαν θυγατέρα, ἐπεὶ δὲ ᾔσθετο ἐξηπατημένος, τήν τε ἄνθρωπον ἐκβαλεῖν καὶ οὐκέτι συνοικεῖν αὐτῆι, καὶ Στέφανον ἀπελάσαι ἀπὸ τῆς παρεδρίας καὶ οὐκ ἐᾶν ἔτι παρεδρεύειν αὐτῶι.

85 Λαβὲ δή μοι τὸν νόμον ἐπὶ τούτοις τουτονὶ καὶ ἀνάγνωθι, ἵν' εἰδῆτε ὅτι οὐ
μόνον προσῆκεν αὐτὴν ἀπέχεσθαι τῶν ἱερῶν τούτων τοιαύτην οὖσαν καὶ
τοιαῦτα διαπεπραγμένην, τοῦ ὁρᾶν καὶ θύειν καὶ ποιεῖν τι τῶν νομιζομένων
ὑπὲρ τῆς πόλεως πατρίων, ἀλλὰ καὶ τῶν ἄλλων τῶν 'Αθήνησιν ἁπάντων. ἐφ'
ἧι γὰρ ἂν μοιχὸς ἁλῶι γυναικί, οὐκ ἔξεστιν αὐτῆι ἐλθεῖν εἰς οὐδὲν τῶν ἱερῶν
τῶν δημοτελῶν, εἰς ἃ καὶ τὴν ξένην καὶ τὴν δούλην ἐλθεῖν ἐξουσίαν ἔδοσαν οἱ
86 νόμοι καὶ θεασομένην καὶ ἱκετεύσουσαν εἰσιέναι· ἀλλὰ μόναις ταύταις ἀπ-
αγορεύουσιν οἱ νόμοι ταῖς γυναιξὶ μὴ εἰσιέναι εἰς τὰ ἱερὰ τὰ δημοτελῆ, ἐφ' ἧι ἂν
μοιχὸς ἁλῶι, ἐὰν δ' εἰσίωσι καὶ παρανομῶσι, νηποινεὶ πάσχειν ὑπὸ τοῦ
βουλομένου ὅ τι ἂν πάσχηι, πλὴν θανάτου, καὶ ἔδωκεν ὁ νόμος τὴν τιμωρίαν
ὑπὲρ αὐτῶν τῶι ἐντυχόντι. διὰ τοῦτο δ' ἐποίησεν ὁ νόμος, πλὴν θανάτου, τἄλλα
ὑβρισθεῖσαν αὐτὴν μηδαμοῦ λαβεῖν δίκην, ἵνα μὴ μιάσματα μηδ' ἀσεβήματα
γίγνηται ἐν τοῖς ἱεροῖς, ἱκανὸν φόβον ταῖς γυναιξὶ παρασκευάζων τοῦ
σωφρονεῖν καὶ μηδὲν ἁμαρτάνειν, ἀλλὰ δικαίως οἰκουρεῖν, διδάσκων ὡς, ἄν τι
ἁμάρτηι τοιοῦτον, ἅμα ἔκ τε τῆς οἰκίας τοῦ ἀνδρὸς ἐκβεβλημένη ἔσται καὶ ἐκ
87 τῶν ἱερῶν τῶν τῆς πόλεως. καὶ ὅτι ταῦτα οὕτως ἔχει, τοῦ νόμου αὐτοῦ

For I shall dismiss the woman from my house, since she is not Stephanos' daughter but Neaira's. And if I do this you should trust my statement that I was tricked; if however I fail to do it, then punish me at once as a criminal
83 guilty of impiety against the gods.' When Theogenes made this promise and pleaded with them, the Areopagos held back, both out of pity for him because of his innocent nature and in the belief that he had really been tricked by Stephanos. When Theogenes left the Areopagos, he immediately ejected the person, the daughter of this woman Neaira, from his house and dismissed Stephanos here, the man who tricked him, from the magistrate's board. And so the members of the Areopagos suspended their trial of Theogenes and abandoned their anger against him, and they forgave him since he had been
84 deceived. And to prove I am telling the truth, I shall provide Theogenes himself as witness and I shall force him to give evidences. Call Theogenes of Erchia.

DEPOSITION

Theogenes of Erchia deposes that when he was serving as King-archon he married Phano believing her the daughter of Stephanos, but that when he perceived that he had been deceived he ejected the person and ceased to live with her, and dismissed Stephanos from his assessorship and no longer allowed him to serve as assessor.

85 Take now this law in addition and read it out, so that you may know that not only should she have kept away from these ceremonies, given her character and career, from seeing and sacrificing and carrying out any of the traditional rites of our ancestors on the city's behalf, but from all the other observances in Athens as well. For any woman who is caught with an adulterer is not permitted to enter any of the public temples, to which the laws grant the right to enter as spectator or suppliant even to the foreign woman and the slave.
86 These are the only women the law forbids to enter the public temples, any woman caught with an adulterer; and if they enter illegally, they may be subjected to any mistreatment at all with impunity by anyone who wishes, short of death, and the law has granted the right to punish them to anyone who encounters them. The reason the law prescribed that she might suffer any outrage short of death without any right of redress was to prevent acts of pollution and impiety in the temples; it inspires sufficient fear in women to ensure they will be chaste and avoid wrong but do their duty in the house, and teaches her that if she commits an offence of this sort, she will find herself
87 banished both from her husband's house and from the temples of the city. You

ἀκούσαντες ἀναγνωσθέντος εἴσεσθε. καί μοι λαβέ.

ΝΟΜΟΣ ΜΟΙΧΕΙΑΣ

Ἐπειδὰν δὲ ἕληι τὸν μοιχόν, μὴ ἐξέστω τῶι ἑλόντι συνοικεῖν τῆι γυναικί· ἐὰν δὲ συνοικῆι, ἄτιμος ἔστω. μηδὲ τῆι γυναικὶ ἐξέστω εἰσιέναι εἰς τὰ ἱερὰ τὰ δημοτελῆ, ἐφ' ἧι ἂν μοιχὸς ἁλῶι· ἐὰν δ' εἰσίηι, νηποινεὶ πασχέτω ὅ τι ἂν πάσχηι, πλὴν θανάτου.

88 Βούλομαι τοίνυν ὑμῖν, ὦ ἄνδρες Ἀθηναῖοι, καὶ τοῦ δήμου τοῦ Ἀθηναίων
μαρτυρίαν παρασχέσθαι, ὡς σπουδάζει περὶ τὰ ἱερὰ ταῦτα καὶ ὡς πολλὴν
πρόνοιαν περὶ αὐτῶν πεποίηται. ὁ γὰρ δῆμος ὁ Ἀθηναίων κυριώτατος ὢν τῶν
ἐν τῆι πόλει ἁπάντων, καὶ ἐξὸν αὐτῶι ποιεῖν ὅ τι ἂν βούληται, οὕτω καλὸν καὶ
σεμνὸν ἡγήσατ' εἶναι δῶρον τὸ Ἀθηναῖον γενέσθαι, ὥστε νόμους ἔθετο αὑτῶι
καθ' οὓς ποιεῖσθαι δεῖ, ἐάν τινα βούλωνται, πολίτην, οἳ νῦν προπεπηλακισμένοι
89 εἰσὶν ὑπὸ Στεφάνου τουτουὶ καὶ τῶν οὕτω γεγαμηκότων. ... ὅμως δ' ἀκούοντες
αὐτῶν βελτίους ἔσεσθε, καὶ τὰ κάλλιστα καὶ τὰ σεμνότατα δῶρα τοῖς
εὐεργετοῦσι τὴν πόλιν διδόμενα γνώσεσθε ὡς λελυμασμένοι εἰσίν. πρῶτον μὲν
γὰρ νόμος ἐστὶ τῶι δήμωι κείμενος μὴ ἐξεῖναι ποιήσασθαι Ἀθηναῖον, ὃν ἂν μὴ
δι' ἀνδραγαθίαν εἰς τὸν δῆμον τὸν Ἀθηναίων ἄξιον ἦι γενέσθαι πολίτην. ἔπειτ'
ἐπειδὰν πεισθῆι ὁ δῆμος καὶ δῶι τὴν δωρεάν, οὐκ ἐᾶι κυρίαν γενέσθαι τὴν
ποίησιν, ἐὰν μὴ τῆι ψήφωι εἰς τὴν ἐπιοῦσαν ἐκκλησίαν ὑπερεξακισχίλιοι Ἀθηναί-
90 ων ψηφίσωνται κρύβδην ψηφιζόμενοι. τοὺς δὲ πρυτάνεις κελεύει τιθέναι τοὺς
καδίσκους ὁ νόμος καὶ τὴν ψῆφον διδόναι προσιόντι τῶι δήμωι πρὶν τοὺς ξένους
εἰσιέναι καὶ τὰ γέρρα ἀναιρεῖν, ἵνα κύριος ὢν αὐτὸς αὑτοῦ ἕκαστος σκοπῆται
πρὸς αὑτὸν ὅντινα μέλλει πολίτην ποιήσεσθαι, εἰ ἄξιός ἐστι τῆς δωρεᾶς ὁ
μέλλων λήψεσθαι. ἔπειτα μετὰ ταῦτα παρανόμων γραφὴν ἐποίησε κατ' αὐτοῦ
τῶι βουλομένωι Ἀθηναίων, καὶ ἔστιν εἰσελθόντα εἰς τὸ δικαστήριον ἐξελέγξαι
91 ὡς οὐκ ἄξιός ἐστι τῆς δωρεᾶς, ἀλλὰ παρὰ τοὺς νόμους Ἀθηναῖος γέγονεν. καὶ
ἤδη τισὶ τοῦ δήμου δόντος τὴν δωρεάν, λόγωι ἐξαπατηθέντος ὑπὸ τῶν
αἰτούντων, παρανόμων γραφῆς γενομένης καὶ εἰσελθούσης εἰς τὸ δικαστήριον,
ἐξελεγχθῆναι συνέβη τὸν εἰληφότα τὴν δωρεὰν μὴ ἄξιον εἶναι αὐτῆς, καὶ
ἀφείλετο τὸ δικαστήριον. καὶ τοὺς μὲν πολλοὺς καὶ παλαιοὺς ἔργον
διηγήσασθαι· ἃ δὲ πάντες μνημονεύετε, Πειθόλαν τε τὸν Θετταλὸν καὶ
Ἀπολλωνίδην τὸν Ὀλύνθιον πολίτας ὑπὸ τοῦ δήμου γενομένους ἀφείλετο τὸ
92 δικαστήριον· ταῦτα γὰρ οὐ πάλαι ἐστὶ γεγενημένα ὥστε ἀγνοεῖν ὑμᾶς. οὕτως

will appreciate the truth of this from hearing the law read out. Please take it.

LAW ON ADULTERY

And when he has caught the adulterer, the person who has so caught him may not live in marriage with his wife; if he continues to live with her, he is to be disfranchised. And the woman who is caught with an adulterer may not enter any of the public temples; if she does so enter she is to suffer any mistreatment with impunity, short of death.

88 I now wish, men of Athens, to provide testimony from the Athenian people, to show the gravity with which it treats these rites and how much care it has devoted to them. For the Athenian people, though possessing absolute authority over everything in the city and able to do whatever it wishes, believed that the grant of Athenian citizenship was such a noble and solemn gift that it imposed laws on itself defining terms on which it must admit a man as citizen, if they so wish, laws which have now been treated with contempt by this man
89 Stephanos and people who marry as he has. ... Still, you will be the better for hearing them, and you will realize that the most noble and solemn awards which are given to people who benefit the city have been defiled. First of all there is a law binding on the people forbidding it to admit a man as citizen unless on grounds of excellent conduct towards the Athenian people he deserves to be made citizen. Then when the people has been convinced and made the gift, the law does not ratify the grant unless over six thousand Athen-
90 ians vote for it at the following Assembly in secret ballot. The law bids the Presidents to place the voting urns and submit the vote to the people as they come up, before the foreigners enter and they remove the fences, so that each man on his own authority may consider in his own mind whether the individual he is about to admit as citizen deserves the gift he is about to receive. Next, after this the law has allowed for an indictment for illegality to be brought against him by any Athenian who wishes, who can come into court and prove that he does not deserve the award and has been made an Athenian in contra-
91 vention of the laws. And before now it has happened, when the people have made the award, deceived by the arguments of the proposers, that an indictment for illegality has been lodged, the case has come to court, it was proved that the recipient did not deserve it and the court withdrew it. To list the many examples in the distant past would be a long task; but as for events which you all remember, when Peitholas of Thessaly and Apollonides of Olyn-
92 thos were made citizens by the people the court withdrew it; these are not

τοίνυν καλῶς καὶ ἰσχυρῶς τῶν νόμων κειμένων ὑπὲρ τῆς πολιτείας, δι' ὧν δεῖ
'Αθηναῖον γενέσθαι, ἕτερός ἐστιν ἐφ' ἅπασι τούτοις κυριώτατος νόμος κείμενος·
οὕτω πολλὴν ὁ δῆμος πρόνοιαν ἐποιεῖτο ὑπὲρ αὑτοῦ καὶ τῶν θεῶν ὥστε δι'
εὐσεβείας τὰ ἱερὰ θύεσθαι ὑπὲρ τῆς πόλεως. ὅσους γὰρ ἂν ποιήσηται ὁ δῆμος ὁ
'Αθηναίων πολίτας, ὁ νόμος ἀπαγορεύει διαρρήδην μὴ ἐξεῖναι αὐτοῖς τῶν ἐννέα
ἀρχόντων γενέσθαι, μηδὲ ἱερωσύνης μηδεμιᾶς μετασχεῖν· τοῖς δ' ἐκ τούτων
μετέδωκεν ἤδη ὁ δῆμος ἁπάντων, καὶ προσέθηκεν 'ἐὰν ὦσιν ἐκ γυναικὸς ἀστῆς
93 καὶ ἐγγυητῆς κατὰ τὸν νόμον'. καὶ ὅτι ταῦτ' ἀληθῆ λέγω, μεγάλῃ καὶ
περιφανεῖ μαρτυρίαι ἐγὼ ὑμῖν δηλώσω. βούλομαι δ' ὑμῖν τὸν νόμον πόρρωθεν
προδιηγήσασθαι, ὡς ἐτέθη καὶ πρὸς οὓς διωρίσθη, ὡς ἄνδρας ἀγαθοὺς ὄντας καὶ
βεβαίους φίλους περὶ τὸν δῆμον γεγονότας. ἐκ τούτων γὰρ ἁπάντων εἴσεσθε
τήν τε τοῦ δήμου δωρεάν τὴν ἀπόθετον τοῖς εὐεργέταις προπηλακιζομένην, καὶ
ὅσων ὑμᾶς ἀγαθῶν κωλύουσι κυρίους εἶναι Στέφανός τε οὑτοσὶ καὶ οἱ τὸν
αὐτὸν τρόπον τούτωι γεγαμηκότες καὶ παιδοποιούμενοι.
94 Πλαταιῆς γάρ, ὦ ἄνδρες 'Αθηναῖοι, μόνοι τῶν Ἑλλήνων ὑμῖν ἐβοήθησαν
Μαραθῶνάδε, ὅτε Δᾶτις ὁ βασιλέως Δαρείου στρατηγὸς ἀναχωρῶν ἐξ Ἐρετρίας
Εὔβοιαν ὑφ' ἑαυτῶι ποιησάμενος, ἀπέβη εἰς τὴν χώραν πολλῆι δυνάμει καὶ
ἐπόρθει. καὶ ἔτι καὶ νῆν τῆς ἀνδραγαθίας αὐτῶν ὑπομνήματα ἡ ἐν τῆι ποικίληι
στοᾶι γραφὴ δεδήλωκεν· ὡς ἕκαστος γὰρ τάχους εἶχεν, εὐθὺς προσβοηθῶν γέ-
95 γραπται, οἱ τὰς κυνᾶς τὰς Βοιωτίας ἔχοντες. πάλιν δὲ Ξέρξου ἰόντος ἐπὶ τὴν
Ἑλλάδα, Θηβαίων μηδισάντων, οὐκ ἐτόλμησαν ἀποστῆναι τῆς ὑμετέρας φιλίας,
ἀλλὰ μόνοι τῶν ἄλλων Βοιωτῶν οἱ μὲν ἡμίσεις αὐτῶν μετὰ Λακεδαιμονίων καὶ
Λεωνίδου ἐν Θερμοπύλαις παραταξάμενοι τῶι βαρβάρωι ἐπιόντι συναπώλοντο,
οἱ δὲ λοιποὶ ἐμβάντες εἰς τὰς ὑμετέρας τριήρεις, ἐπειδὴ αὐτοῖς οἰκεῖα σκάφη οὐχ
96 ὑπῆρχεν, συνεναυμάχουν ὑμῖν ἐπί τε 'Αρτεμισίωι καὶ ἐν Σαλαμῖνι. καὶ τὴν
τελευταίαν μάχην Πλαταιᾶσι Μαρδονίωι τῶι βασιλέως στρατηγῶι μεθ' ὑμῶν
καὶ τῶν συνελευθερούντων τὴν Ἑλλάδα μαχεσάμενοι, εἰς κοινὸν τὴν ἐλευθερίαν
τοῖς ἄλλοις Ἕλλησι κατέθηκαν. ἐπεὶ δὲ Παυσανίας ὁ Λακεδαιμονίων βασιλεὺς
ὑβρίζειν ἐνεχείρει ὑμᾶς, καὶ οὐκ ἠγάπα ὅτι τῆς ἡγεμονίας μόνοι ἠξιώθησαν
Λακεδαιμόνιοι ὑπὸ τῶν Ἑλλήνων, καὶ ἡ πόλις τῆι μὲν ἀληθείαι ἡγεῖτο τῆς
ἐλευθερίας τοῖς Ἕλλησιν, τῆι δὲ φιλοτιμίαι οὐκ ἠναντιοῦτο τοῖς Λακεδαιμονίοις,
97 ἵνα μὴ φθονηθῶσιν ὑπὸ τῶν συμμάχων – ἐφ' οἷς φυσηθεὶς Παυσανίας ὁ τῶν
Λακεδαιμονίων βασιλεὺς ἐπέγραψεν ἐπὶ τὸν τρίποδα τὸν ἐν Δελφοῖς, ὃν οἱ
Ἕλληνες οἱ συμμαχεσάμενοι τὴν Πλαταιᾶσι μάχην καὶ τὴν ἐν Σαλαμῖνι
ναυμαχίαν ναυμαχήσαντες κοινῆι ποιησάμενοι ἀνέθηκαν ἀριστεῖον τῶι
'Απόλλωνι ἀπὸ τῶν βαρβάρων,

distant events which you might not know. Now though the laws governing
citizenship, with which grants of citizenship must comply, are so fairly and
firmly laid down, there is another most binding law laid down on top of all of
these; such was the concern the people showed for their own sake and that of
the gods to ensure that the sacrifices on behalf of the city should be carried out
in accordance with piety. For the law expressly forbids all whom the Athenian
people admit as citizens from becoming one of the nine Archons or holding any
priesthood; it admits their descendants without demur to all rights, and adds: 'if
93 they are born of a wife of citizen status married according to the law'. And I
shall prove I am telling the truth with a convincing and unambiguous
testimony. I want to go back in time in my account of the law, to tell how it
was passed and for whom its provisions were intended, as men of worth and
firm loyalty to the Athenian people. From all this you will understand that the
gift of the people which is reserved for benefactors is being degraded and how
important are the privileges which Stephanos here and all who marry and have
children the same way he has are taking from your control.

94 The Plataians, men of Athens, were the only Greek people who came to
your aid at Marathon, when Datis the Persian King's general, on leaving Eretria
after he had gained control over Euboia, disembarked in the area with a large
army and began to pillage it. And to this day the picture in the Painted Portico
displays a reminder of their courage; for each man is painted rushing to support
95 as fast as he could, the ones with the Boiotian caps. And again when Xerxes
advanced on Greece, though the Thebans collaborated with the Medes, the
Plataians refused to abandon their friendship with you, but without the aid of
the other Boiotians, half of them faced the advancing barbarian with Leonidas
and the Spartans and were killed with them, while the rest embarked on your
triremes, since they had no ships of their own, and fought at sea alongside you
96 at Artemision and Salamis. They joined with you and your fellow liberators of
Greece in the final battle at Plataia against Mardonios the King's general and
made common gift of liberty to the rest of Greece. And when the Spartan king
Pausanias tried to insult you and was not satisfied that the Spartans were
honoured with the sole command by the Greeks, and that our city though in
reality leader in winning liberty for Greece did not compete with Sparta for the
97 honour in order to avoid the jealousy of the allies; - the Spartan king,
Pausanias, puffed up with these honours inscribed on the tripod at Delphoi,
which the Greeks who had joined in the battle at Plataia and the sea battle at
Salamis had made jointly and set up in honour of Apollo as a memorial of the
victory over the barbarians:

Ἑλλήνων ἀρχηγός, ἐπεὶ στρατὸν ὤλεσε Μήδων,
Παυσανίας Φοίβωι μνῆμ' ἀνέθηκε τόδε,

ὡς αὐτοῦ τοῦ ἔργου ὄντος καὶ τοῦ ἀναθήματος, ἀλλ' οὐ κοινοῦ τῶν συμμάχων·
98 ὀργισθέντων δὲ τῶν Ἑλλήνων, οἱ Πλαταιεῖς λαγχάνουσι δίκην τοῖς
Λακεδαιμονίοις εἰς τοὺς Ἀμφικτύονας χιλίων ταλάντων ὑπὲρ τῶν συμμάχων,
καὶ ἠνάγκασαν αὐτοὺς ἐκκολάψαντας τὰ ἐλεγεῖα ἐπιγράψαι τὰς πόλεις τὰς
κοινωνούσας τοῦ ἔργου. δι' ὅπερ αὐτοῖς οὐχ ἥκιστα παρηκολούθει ἡ ἔχθρα ἡ
παρὰ Λακεδαιμονίων καὶ ἐκ τοῦ γένους τοῦ βασιλείου. καὶ ἐν μὲν τῶι παρόντι
οὐκ εἶχον αὐτοῖς ὅ τι χρήσωνται οἱ Λακεδαιμόνιοι, ὕστερον δὲ ὡς πεντήκοντα
ἔτεσιν Ἀρχίδαμος ὁ Ζευξιδάμου Λακεδαιμονίων βασιλεὺς εἰρήνης οὔσης ἐνεχείρ-
99 ησεν αὐτῶν καταλαβεῖν τὴν πόλιν. ἔπραξε δὲ ταῦτ' ἐκ Θηβῶν δι' Εὐρυμάχου
τοῦ Λεοντιάδου βοιωταρχοῦντος, ἀνοιξάντων τὰς πύλας τῆς νυκτὸς Ναυκλείδου
καὶ ἄλλων τινῶν μετ' αὐτοῦ, πεισθέντων χρήμασιν. αἰσθόμενοι δ' οἱ Πλαταιεῖς
ἔνδον ὄντας τοὺς Θηβαίους τῆς νυκτὸς καὶ ἐξαπίνης αὐτῶν τὴν πόλιν ἐν εἰρήνηι
κατειλημμένην, προσεβοήθουν καὶ αὐτοὶ καὶ συνετάττοντο. καὶ ἐπειδὴ ἡμέρα
ἐγένετο καὶ εἶδον οὐ πολλοὺς ὄντας τοὺς Θηβαίους, ἀλλὰ τοὺς πρώτους αὐτῶν
εἰσεληλυθότας (ὕδωρ γὰρ γενόμενον τῆς νυκτὸς πολὺ ἐκώλυσεν αὐτοὺς πάντας
εἰσελθεῖν· ὁ γὰρ Ἀσωπὸς ποταμὸς μέγας ἐρρύη καὶ διαβῆναι οὐ ῥάιδιον ἦν,
100 ἄλλως τε καὶ νυκτός), ὡς οὖν εἶδον οἱ Πλαταιεῖς τοὺς Θηβαίους ἐν τῆι πόλει καὶ
ἔγνωσαν ὅτι οὐ πάντες πάρεισιν, ἐπιτίθενται καὶ εἰς μάχην ἐλθόντες κρατοῦσι
καὶ φθάνουσιν ἀπολέσαντες αὐτοὺς πρὶν τοὺς ἄλλους προσβοηθῆσαι, καὶ ὡς
ὑμᾶς πέμπουσιν εὐθὺς ἄγγελον τὴν τε πρᾶξιν φράσοντα καὶ τὴν μάχην
δηλώσοντα ὅτι νικῶσι, καὶ βοηθεῖν ἀξιοῦντες, ἂν οἱ Θηβαῖοι τὴν χώραν αὐτῶν
δηιῶσιν. ἀκούσαντες δὲ οἱ Ἀθηναῖοι τὰ γεγονότα διὰ τάχους ἐβοήθουν εἰς τὰς
Πλαταιάς· καὶ οἱ Θηβαῖοι ὡς ἑώρων τοὺς Ἀθηναίους βεβοηθηκότας τοῖς Πλατ-
101 αιεῦσιν, ἀνεχώρησαν ἐπ' οἴκου. ὡς οὖν ἀπέτυχον οἱ Θηβαῖοι τῆς πείρας καὶ οἱ
Πλαταιεῖς τοὺς ἄνδρας οὓς ἔλαβον αὐτῶν ἐν τῆι μάχηι ζῶντας ἀπέκτειναν,
ὀργισθέντες οἱ Λακεδαιμόνιοι ἀπροφασίστως ἤδη στρατεύουσιν ἐπὶ τὰς
Πλαταιάς, Πελοποννησίοις μὲν ἅπασι πλὴν Ἀργείων τὰ δύο μέρη τῆς στρατιᾶς
ἀπὸ τῶν πόλεων ἑκάστων πέμπειν ἐπιτάξαντες, Βοιωτοῖς δὲ τοῖς ἄλλοις ἅπασι
καὶ Λοκροῖς καὶ Φωκεῦσι καὶ Μαλιεῦσι καὶ Οἰταίοις καὶ Αἰνιᾶσιν πανδημεὶ ἐπ-
102 αγγείλαντες στρατεύειν. καὶ περικαθεζόμενοι αὐτῶν τὸ τεῖχος πολλῆι δυνάμει
ἐπηγγέλλοντο, εἰ βούλοιντο τὴν μὲν πόλιν αὐτοῖς παραδοῦναι, τὴν δὲ χώραν
ἔχειν καὶ καρποῦσθαι τὰ αὑτῶν, ἀφίστασθαι δὲ τῆς Ἀθηναίων συμμαχίας. οὐκ
ἐθελησάντων δὲ τῶν Πλαταιέων, ἀλλ' ἀποκριναμένων ὅτι ἄνευ Ἀθηναίων
οὐδὲν ἂν πράξειαν, ἐπολιόρκουν αὐτοὺς διπλῶι τείχει περιτειχίσαντες δέκα ἔτη,

'The leader of the Greeks, when he destroyed the Mede host,
Pausanias set up this monument to Phoibos.'

as though the achievement and the dedication were his own and not shared by
98 all the allies. The Greeks were enraged; on behalf of the allies the Plataians brought an action for a thousand talents against the Spartans before the Amphiktyons, and compelled them to erase the distich and inscribe the names of the cities which joined in the task. And for this reason not least the hatred of the Spartans and the royal house pursued them. At the time the Spartans would do nothing about them, but about fifty years later the Spartan King Archidamos son of Zeuxidamos attempted to seize their city in time of peace.
99 He did this from Thebes through the agency of Eurymachos the son of Leontiades, who was a Boiotarchos; Nausikleides and some others opened the gates at night for a bribe. The Plataians, discovering that the Thebans were inside at night and that their city had suddenly been seized while at peace, ran to arms too and confronted them. When day broke and they saw that the Thebans were not many in number, and that only the vanguard had entered (for a heavy rainfall in the night had prevented the whole force from entering; the river Asopos was in spate and it was not easy to cross, especially at night) -
100 when the Plataians saw that the Thebans were in the city and realized that the whole force was not present, they attacked, defeated them in battle and succeeded in destroying them before the others could bring further aid. And they sent a messenger to you immediately to tell you of the incident and of their victory in the battle, and to ask for help if the Thebans should pillage their territory. The Athenians on hearing what had happened quickly sent aid to Plataia; and the Thebans, on seeing that the Athenians had reinforced the
101 Plataians, went home. Now when the Thebans failed in their attempt and the Plataians killed those of them whom they had taken alive in battle, the Spartans were angry; without any pretext now they marched against Plataia, having ordered all the Peloponnesians except the Argives to send two thirds of the forces from each city and instructed all the rest of the Boiotians, the Lokrians, Phokians, Malians, Oitaians and Ainianians to take the field in full
102 force. They settled down to besiege their walls with a large force and made overtures asking them if they would agree to hand the city over to them, while keeping their territory and enjoying the use of their own possessions, and abandon their alliance with the Athenians. When the Plataians refused and answered that they would do nothing without the agreement of the Athenians, the enemy built a double wall around them and besieged them for ten years,

103 πολλὰς καὶ παντοδαπὰς πείρας προσάγοντες. ἐπεὶ δ' ἀπειρήκεσαν οἱ Πλαταιεῖς
καὶ ἐνδεεῖς ἦσαν ἁπάντων καὶ ἠποροῦντο τῆς σωτηρίας, διακληρωσάμενοι πρὸς σφᾶς αὐτοὺς οἱ μὲν ὑπομείναντες ἐπολιορκοῦντο, οἱ δὲ τηρήσαντες νύκτα καὶ ὕδωρ καὶ ἄνεμον πολύν, ἐξελθόντες ἐκ τῆς πόλεως καὶ ὑπερβάντες τὸ περιτείχισμα τῶν πολεμίων λαθόντες τὴν στρατιάν, ἀποσφάξαντες τοὺς φύλακας διασῴζονται δεῦρο, δεινῶς διακείμενοι καὶ ἀπροσδοκήτως· οἱ δ' ὑπομείναντές αὐτῶν ἁλούσης τῆς πόλεως κατὰ κράτος ἀπεσφάγησαν πάντες οἱ ἡβῶντες, παῖδες δὲ καὶ γυναῖκες ἐξηνδραποδίσθησαν, ὅσοι μὴ αἰσθόμενοι ἐπιόντ-
104 ας τοὺς Λακεδαιμονίους ὑπεξῆλθον 'Αθήναζε. τοῖς οὖν οὕτω φανερῶς ἐνδεδειγμένοις τὴν εὔνοιαν τῶι δήμωι, καὶ προεμένοις ἅπαντα τὰ αὑτῶν καὶ παῖδας καὶ γυναῖκας, πάλιν σκοπεῖτε πῶς μετέδοτε τῆς πολιτείας. ἐκ γὰρ τῶν ψηφισμάτων τῶν ὑμετέρων καταφανὴς πᾶσιν ἔσται ὁ νόμος, καὶ γνώσεσθ' ὅτι ἀληθῆ λέγω. καί μοι λαβὲ τὸ ψήφισμα τοῦτο καὶ ἀνάγνωθι αὐτοῖς.

ΨΗΦΙΣΜΑ ΠΕΡΙ ΠΛΑΤΑΙΕΩΝ

'Ιπποκράτης εἶπεν, Πλαταιέας εἶναι 'Αθηναίους ἀπὸ τῆσδε τῆς ἡμέρας, ἐπιτίμους καθάπερ οἱ ἄλλοι 'Αθηναῖοι, καὶ μετεῖναι αὐτοῖς ὧνπερ 'Αθηναίοις μέτεστι πάντων, καὶ ἱερῶν καὶ ὁσίων, . . . πλὴν εἴ τις ἱερωσύνη ἢ τελετή ἐστιν ἐκ γένους, μηδὲ τῶν ἐννέα ἀρχόντων, τοῖς δ' ἐκ τούτων. κατανεῖμαι δὲ τοὺς Πλαταιέας εἰς τοὺς δήμους καὶ τὰς φυλάς. ἐπειδὰν δὲ νεμηθῶσι, μὴ ἐξέστω ἔτι 'Αθηναίωι μηδενὶ γίγνεσθαι Πλαταιέων, μὴ εὑρομένωι παρὰ τοῦ δήμου τοῦ 'Αθηναίων.

105 Ὁρᾶτε, ὦ ἄνδρες 'Αθηναῖοι, ὡς καλῶς καὶ δικαίως ἔγραψεν ὁ ῥήτωρ ὑπὲρ
τοῦ δήμου τοῦ 'Αθηναίων, καὶ ἠξίωσε τοὺς Πλαταιέας λαμβάνοντας τὴν δωρεὰν πρῶτον μὲν δοκιμασθῆναι ἐν τῶι δικαστηρίωι κατ' ἄνδρα ἕκαστον, εἰ ἔστιν Πλαταιεὺς καὶ εἰ τῶν φίλων τῶν τῆς πόλεως, ἵνα μὴ ἐπὶ ταύτηι τῆι προφάσει πολλοὶ μεταλάβωσι τῆς πολιτείας· ἔπειτα τοὺς δοκιμασθέντας ἀναγραφῆναι ἐν στήληι λιθίνηι, καὶ στῆσαι ἐν ἀκροπόλει παρὰ τῆι θεῶι, ἵνα σῴζηται ἡ δωρεὰ
106 τοῖς ἐπιγιγνομένοις καὶ ἦι ἐξελέγξαι ὅτου ἂν ἕκαστος ἦι συγγενής. καὶ ὕστερον οὐκ ἐᾶι γίγνεσθαι 'Αθηναῖον ἐξεῖναι, ὃς ἂν μὴ νῦν γένηται καὶ δοκιμασθῆι ἐν τῶι δικαστηρίωι, τοῦ μὴ πολλοὺς φάσκοντας Πλαταιέας εἶναι κατασκευάζειν αὑτοῖς πολιτείαν. ἔπειτα καὶ τὸν νόμον διωρίσατο ἐν τῶι ψηφίσματι πρὸς αὐτοὺς εὐθέως ὑπέρ τε τῆς πόλεως καὶ τῶν θεῶν, [καὶ] μὴ ἐξεῖναι αὐτῶν μηδενὶ

103 making repeated assaults of all sorts. When the Plataians were exhausted and in extreme need and had despaired of being rescued, they drew lots among themselves and one group stayed on to endure the siege while the others, after waiting for a night with much wind and rain, made a sortie from the city, crossed the enemy wall unnoticed by the besieging force, and after massacring the guards reached here safely, against expectation and in a sorry condition. As to those of them who stayed behind, when the city was captured by storm all the grown men were massacred while the women and children were sold into slavery, all of them who had not escaped to Athens when they saw the
104 Spartans approaching. These were men who visibly proved their loyalty to the people and gave up all possessions, children and wives; see now in what way you gave them a share in citizen rights. For your decrees will make the law clear to all, and you will realize that I am speaking the truth. Please take this decree and read it out to them.

DECREE CONCERNING THE PLATAIANS

Hippokrates moved that the Plataians be Athenian citizens from this day forward, with rights as the rest of the Athenians, and that they share in all the privileges which Athenians enjoy, both sacred and profane ... except for any hereditary priesthood or rite, nor the nine Archons, though their descendants may. The Plataians are to be distributed among the demes and tribes. When they have been distributed, it is no longer to be open to any of the Plataians to become an Athenian citizen unless he obtain it as a gift from the Athenian people.

105 You see, men of Athens, how nobly and justly the public speaker drafted the decree on behalf of the Athenian people. And he required that the Plataians receiving the grant should first of all be examined individually in the law court to determine whether each is a Plataian and one of those loyal to our city, to prevent a large number from obtaining citizenship on this pretext; secondly, that the names of those who had been examined should be inscribed on a stone column, which should be placed on the Akropolis by the temple of the goddess, so that the grant might be preserved for their descendants and it
106 might be possible for an individual to prove to which of them he is related. And he does not allow anyone who is not at this point examined in the lawcourt the right to become an Athenian subsequently, to prevent a large number from procuring citizenship for themselves by claiming to be Plataians. Finally he also at once in the decree applying to the Plataians defined the law in defence of the city and the gods, that none of them should have the right to be

τῶν ἐννέα ἀρχόντων λαχεῖν μηδὲ ἱερωσύνης μηδεμιᾶς, τοῖς δ' ἐκ τούτων, ἂν ὦσιν ἐξ ἀστῆς γυναικὸς καὶ ἐγγυητῆς κατὰ τὸν νόμον.

107 Οὔκουν δεινόν; πρὸς μὲν τοὺς ἀστυγείτονας καὶ ὁμολογουμένως ἀρίστους τῶν Ἑλλήνων εἰς τὴν πόλιν γεγενημένους οὕτω καλῶς καὶ ἀκριβῶς διωρίσασθε περὶ ἑκάστου, ἐφ' οἷς δεῖ ἔχειν τὴν δωρεάν, τὴν δὲ περιφανῶς ἐν ἁπάσηι τῆι Ἑλλάδι πεπορνευμένην οὕτως αἰσχρῶς καὶ ὀλιγώρως ἐάσετε ὑβρίζουσαν εἰς τὴν πόλιν καὶ ἀσεβοῦσαν εἰς τοὺς θεοὺς ἀτιμώρητον, ἣν οὔτε οἱ πρόγονοι ἀστὴν κατ-
108 έλιπον οὔθ' ὁ δῆμος πολῖτιν ἐποιήσατο; ποῦ γὰρ αὕτη οὐκ εἴργασται τῶι σώματι, ἢ ποῖ οὐκ ἐλήλυθεν ἐπὶ τῶι καθ' ἡμέραν μισθῶι; οὐκ ἐν Πελοποννήσωι μὲν πάσηι, ἐν Θετταλίαι δὲ καὶ Μαγνησίαι μετὰ Σίμου τοῦ Λαρισαίου καὶ Εὐρυδάμαντος τοῦ Μηδείου, ἐν Χίωι δὲ καὶ ἐν Ἰωνίαι τῆι πλείστηι μετὰ Σωτάδου τοῦ Κρητὸς ἀκολουθοῦσα, μισθωθεῖσα ὑπὸ τῆς Νικαρέτης, ὅτε ἔτι ἐκείνης ἦν; τὴν δὴ ὑφ' ἑτέροις οὖσαν καὶ ἀκολουθοῦσαν τῶι διδόντι τί οἴεσθε ποιεῖν; ἆρ' οὐχ ὑπηρετεῖν τοῖς χρωμένοις εἰς ἁπάσας ἡδονάς; εἶτα τὴν τοιαύτην καὶ περιφανῶς ἐγνωσμένην ὑπὸ πάντων γῆς περίοδον εἰργασμένην ψηφιεῖσθε
109 ἀστὴν εἶναι; καὶ τί καλὸν φήσετε πρὸς τοὺς ἐρωτῶντας διαπεπρᾶχθαι, ἢ ποίαι αἰσχύνηι καὶ ἀσεβείαι οὐκ ἔνοχοι αὐτοὶ εἶναι; πρὶν μὲν γὰρ γραφῆναι ταύτην καὶ εἰς ἀγῶνα καταστῆναι καὶ πυθέσθαι πάντας ἥτις ἦν καὶ οἷα ἠσέβηκεν, τὰ μὲν ἀδικήματα ταύτης ἦν, ἡ δ' ἀμέλεια τῆς πόλεως· καὶ οἱ μὲν οὐκ ἤιδεσαν ὑμῶν, οἱ δὲ πυθόμενοι τῶι μὲν λόγωι ἠγανάκτουν, τῶι δ' ἔργωι οὐκ εἶχον ὅ τι χρήσαιντο αὐτῆι, οὐδενὸς εἰς ἀγῶνα καθιστάντος οὐδὲ διδόντος περὶ αὐτῆς τὴν ψῆφον. ἐπειδὴ δὲ καὶ ἴστε πάντες καὶ ἔχετε ἐφ' ὑμῖν αὐτοῖς καὶ κύριοί ἐστε κολάσαι, ὑμέτερον ἤδη τὸ ἀσέβημα γίγνεται τὸ πρὸς τοὺς θεούς, ἐὰν μὴ ταύτην
110 κολάσητε. τί δὲ καὶ φήσειεν ἂν ὑμῶν ἕκαστος εἰσιὼν πρὸς τὴν ἑαυτοῦ γυναῖκ' ἢ θυγατέρα ἢ μητέρα, ἀποψηφισάμενος ταύτης, ἐπειδὰν ἔρηται ὑμᾶς 'ποῦ ἦτε;' καὶ εἴπητε ὅτι 'ἐδικάζομεν;' 'τῶι;' ἐρήσεται εὐθύς. 'Νεαίραι' δῆλον ὅτι φήσετε (οὐ γάρ;) 'ὅτι ξένη οὖσα ἀστῶι συνοικεῖ παρὰ τὸν νόμον, καὶ ὅτι τὴν θυγατέρα μεμοιχευμένην ἐξέδωκεν Θεογένει τῶι βασιλεύσαντι, καὶ αὕτη ἔθυσε τὰ ἱερὰ τὰ ἄρρητα ὑπὲρ τῆς πόλεως καὶ τῶι Διονύσωι γυνὴ ἐδόθη', καὶ τἆλλα διηγούμενοι τὴν κατηγορίαν αὐτῆς, ὡς καὶ μνημονικῶς καὶ ἐπιμελῶς περὶ ἑκάστου κατηγορ-
111 ήθη. αἱ δὲ ἀκούσασαι ἐρήσονται 'τί οὖν ἐποιήσατε;' ὑμεῖς δὲ φήσετε 'ἀπεψηφίσμεθα'. οὐκοῦν ἤδη αἱ μὲν σωφρονέσταται τῶν γυναικῶν

appointed one of the nine Archons or to any priesthood, though their descendants should, if they are born of a woman of citizen status married according to the law.

107 Is it not grotesque? When, in dealing with men of a neighbouring city
who by common agreement had been the greatest benefactors of our city, you
defined so properly and precisely each of the terms on which they should
receive the grant, will you leave a woman who has blatantly whored throughout
the whole of Greece unpunished for insulting the city so shamefully and
contemptuously and committing sacrilege against the gods, a woman who was
neither bequeathed citizenship by her ancestors nor granted it by the people?
108 For where has she not prostituted herself? Where has she not gone to earn her
daily wage? Has she not been in the whole of the Peloponnese, in Thessaly
and Magnesia with Simos of Larissa and Eurydamas the son of Medeios, in
Chios and in most of Ionia following Sotadas of Crete, hired out by Nikarete
while she still belonged to her? And what do you expect a woman to do when
she is under the control of different men and goes with anyone who pays?
Surely to serve her customers in every type of pleasure? So then, will your
verdict be that a woman of her character who is known for certain by all to
109 have plied her trade over the breadth of the world is a citizen? And what noble
thing will you claim you have achieved when someone asks you; from what
manner of shame and impiety can you claim innocence? For before she was
indicted and brought to trial and everyone learned who she was and what
sacrilege she has committed, the crimes were hers, while the city was guilty
only of neglect. Some of you were unaware, while others had heard and
expressed their anger, but had no practical means of dealing with her, as long
as nobody brought her to trial and provided an opportunity to vote on her. But
now that you all actually know the facts and have her at your mercy and you
have the power to punish her, the impiety against the gods becomes yours
110 now if you fail to punish her. And what could each of you actually say when he
goes home to his own wife or daughter or mother after acquitting this woman,
when she asks you: 'Where were you?' and you say 'we were trying a case.'
'Whom?' she will ask at once. 'Neaira' you will say, of course (what else?)
'because though she is an alien she is living in marriage with a citizen against
the law, and because she gave in marriage to Theogenes who served as
King-archon her daughter who had been caught in adultery, and this woman
carried out the secret sacrifices on behalf of the city and was given as wife to
Dionysos'; and you will narrate the rest of the charge against her, saying how
111 memorably and carefully each detail was presented. And they on hearing this
will ask: 'So what did you do?' and you will say: 'We have acquitted her'. So

ὀργισθήσονται ὑμῖν, διότι ὁμοίως αὐταῖς ταύτην κατηξιοῦτε μετέχειν τῶν τῆς
πόλεως καὶ τῶν ἱερῶν· ὅσαι δ' ἀνόητοι, φανερῶς ἐπιδείκνυτε ποιεῖν ὅ τι ἂν
βούλωνται, ὡς ἄδειαν ὑμῶν καὶ τῶν νόμων δεδωκότων· δόξετε γὰρ ὀλιγώρως
112 καὶ ῥαθύμως φέροντες ὁμογνώμονες καὶ αὐτοὶ εἶναι τοῖς ταύτης τρόποις. ὥστε
πολὺ μᾶλλον ἐλυσιτέλει μὴ γενέσθαι τὸν ἀγῶνα τουτονὶ ἢ γενομένου
ἀποψηφίσασθαι ὑμᾶς. κομιδῆι γὰρ ἤδη [παντελῶς] ἐξουσία ἔσται ταῖς πόρναις
συνοικεῖν οἷς ἂν βούλωνται, καὶ τοὺς παῖδας φάσκειν οὗ ἂν τύχωσιν εἶναι· καὶ
οἱ μὲν νόμοι ἄκυροι ὑμῖν ἔσονται, οἱ δὲ τρόποι τῶν ἑταιρῶν κύριοι ὅ τι ἂν
βούλωνται διαπράττεσθαι. ὥστε καὶ ὑπὲρ τῶν πολιτίδων σκοπεῖτε, τοῦ μὴ ἀν-
113 εκδότους γενέσθαι τὰς τῶν πενήτων θυγατέρας. νῦν μὲν γάρ, κἂν ἀπορηθῆι τις,
ἱκανὴν προῖκ' αὐτῆι ὁ νόμος συμβάλλεται, ἂν καὶ ὁπωστιοῦν μετρίαν ἡ φύσις
ὄψιν ἀποδῶι· προπηλακισθέντος δὲ τοῦ νόμου ὑφ' ὑμῶν ἀποφυγούσης ταύτης,
καὶ ἀκύρου γενομένου, παντελῶς ἤδη ἡ μὲν τῶν πορνῶν ἐργασία ἥξει εἰς τὰς
τῶν πολιτῶν θυγατέρας, δι' ἀπορίαν ὅσαι ἂν μὴ δύνωνται ἐκδοθῆναι, τὸ δὲ τῶν
ἐλευθέρων γυναικῶν ἀξίωμα εἰς τὰς ἑταίρας, ἂν ἄδειαν λάβωσι τοῦ ἐξεῖναι
αὐταῖς παιδοποιεῖσθαι ὡς ἂν βούλωνται καὶ τελετῶν καὶ ἱερῶν καὶ τιμῶν μετέχ-
114 ειν τῶν ἐν τῆι πόλει. ὥστε εἷς ἕκαστος ὑμῶν νομιζέτω, ὁ μὲν ὑπὲρ γυναικός, ὁ δ'
ὑπὲρ θυγατρός, ὁ δ' ὑπὲρ μητρός, ὁ δ' ὑπὲρ τῆς πόλεως καὶ των νόμων καὶ τῶν
ἱερῶν τὴν ψῆφον φέρειν, τοῦ μὴ ἐξ ἴσου φανῆναι ἐκείνας τιμωμένας ταύτηι τῆι
πόρνηι, μηδὲ τὰς μετὰ πολλῆς καὶ καλῆς σωφροσύνης καὶ ἐπιμελείας τραφείσας
ὑπὸ τῶν προσηκόντων καὶ ἐκδοθείσας κατὰ τοὺς νόμους, ταύτας ἐν τῶι ἴσωι
φαίνεσθαι μετεχούσας τῆι μετὰ πολλῶν καὶ ἀσελγῶν τρόπων πολλάκις πολλοῖς
115 ἑκάστης ἡμέρας συγγεγενημένηι, ὡς ἕκαστος ἐβούλετο. ἡγεῖσθε δὲ μήτ' ἐμὲ τὸν
λέγοντα εἶναι Ἀπολλόδωρον μήτε τοὺς ἀπολογησομένους καὶ συνεροῦντας
πολίτας, ἀλλὰ τοὺς νόμους καὶ Νέαιραν ταυτηνὶ περὶ τῶν πεπραγμένων αὐτῆι
πρὸς ἀλλήλους δικάζεσθαι. καὶ ὅταν μὲν ἐπὶ τῆς κατηγορίας γένησθε, τῶν
νόμων αὐτῶν ἀκούετε, δι' ὧν οἰκεῖται ἡ πόλις καὶ καθ' οὓς ὀμωμόκατε δικάσειν,
τί κελεύουσι καὶ τί παραβεβήκασιν· ὅταν δὲ ἐπὶ τῆς ἀπολογίας ἦτε,
μνημονεύοντες τὴν τῶν νόμων κατηγορίαν καὶ τὸν ἔλεγχον τὸν τῶν εἰρημένων,
τήν τε ὄψιν αὐτῆς ἰδόντες, ἐνθυμεῖσθε τοῦτο μόνον, εἰ Νέαιρα οὖσα ταῦτα
διαπέπρακται.

116 Ἄξιον δὲ κἀκεῖνο ἐνθυμηθῆναι, ὦ ἄνδρες Ἀθηναῖοι, ὅτι Ἀρχίαν τὸν
ἱεροφάντην γενόμενον, ἐξελεγχθέντα ἐν τῶι δικαστηρίωι ἀσεβεῖν θύοντα παρὰ
τὰ πάτρια τὰς θυσίας, ἐκολάσατε ὑμεῖς, καὶ ἄλλα τε κατηγορήθη αὐτοῦ καὶ ὅτι
Σινώπηι τῆι ἑταίραι Ἁλώιοις ἐπὶ τῆς ἐσχάρας τῆς ἐν τῆι αὐλῆι Ἐλευσῖνι

then the most decent of the womenfolk will be furious with you, because you thought it right that this woman should have the same share as they in public life and religion; while to all the foolish ones you are giving a clear signal to do whatever they please, since you and the laws have given them complete freedom. For it will seem that you too by treating the matter in a casual and
112 indolent way approve of this woman's way of life. So it would have been far more beneficial if this trial had never taken place than that you should acquit now that it has. For there will then be complete freedom for whores to live in marriage with anyone they please, and to declare anyone at all the father of their children. And your laws will be invalid, while the characters of courtesans will have the power to achieve whatever they wish. So you must also show concern for the women of citizen birth, to prevent the daughters of poor men
113 becoming unmarriageable. For as matters stand, even if a girl is needy, the law contributes an adequate dowry for her, if nature gives her even a remotely moderate appearance. But if the law is brought into contempt by you with this woman's acquittal and becomes invalid, then without a doubt the trade of whores will fall to the daughters of citizens, all those who because of poverty cannot be married, while the status of free women will fall to the courtesans, if they are given the freedom to bear children as they see fit and to share in the
114 civic rituals and ceremonies and rights. So let each one of you believe that he is casting his vote, one in defence of his wife, another his daughter, another his mother, another the city and its laws and religion, so that those women are not seen to be held in equal esteem with this whore, and that women reared by their kinsmen with great and proper decency and care and given in marriage according to the laws are not shown to have equal rights with a woman who has been with many men many times each day, in many lascivious ways, as
115 each man wished. Imagine that the speaker is not I, Apollodoros, nor those citizens who will defend and support her, but that it is the laws and Neaira here who are in dispute with each other over her actions. And when you attend to the prosecution, listen to the laws themselves, by which the city is governed and according to which you have sworn to judge, and ask yourselves what they prescribe and how the defendants have transgressed them; and when you attend to the defence, remember the prosecution made by the laws and the proof offered by their speech, and take a look at her appearance, and consider only this, whether she (Neaira!) has committed these acts.

116 It is worthwhile, men of Athens, to consider this too, that you punished Archias who had served as Hierophant, when it was proved in court that he committed impiety by making sacrifice contrary to ancestral custom. Among the charges against him was that during the Haloa he sacrificed for the

προσαγούσηι ἱερεῖον θύσειεν, οὐ νομίμου ὄντος ἐν ταύτηι τῆι ἡμέραι ἱερεῖα θύειν,
117 οὐδ' ἐκείνου οὔσης τῆς θυσίας ἀλλὰ τῆς ἱερείας. οὔκουν δεινὸν τὸν μὲν καὶ ἐκ
γένους ὄντα τοῦ Εὐμολπιδῶν καὶ προγόνων καλῶν κἀγαθῶν καὶ πολίτην τῆς
πόλεως, ὅτι ἐδόκει τι παραβῆναι τῶν νομίμων, δοῦναι δίκην (καὶ οὔθ' ἡ τῶν
συγγενῶν οὔθ' ἡ τῶν φίλων ἐξαίτησις ὠφέλησεν αὐτόν, οὔθ' αἱ λῃτουργίαι ἃς
ἐλῃτούργησε τῆι πόλει αὐτὸς καὶ οἱ πρόγονοι αὐτοῦ, οὔτε τὸ ἱεροφάντην εἶναι,
ἀλλ' ἐκολάσατε δόξαντα ἀδικεῖν)· Νέαιραν δὲ ταυτηνὶ εἴς τε τὸν αὐτὸν θεὸν
τοῦτον ἠσεβηκυῖαν καὶ τοὺς νόμους, καὶ αὐτὴν καὶ τὴν θυγατέρα αὐτῆς, οὐ
τιμωρήσεσθε;
118 Θαυμάζω δ' ἔγωγε τί ποτε καὶ ἐροῦσι πρὸς ὑμᾶς ἐν τῆι ἀπολογίαι.
πότερον ὡς ἀστή ἐστιν Νέαιρα αὑτηὶ καὶ κατὰ τοὺς νόμους συνοικεῖ αὐτῶι;
ἀλλὰ μεμαρτύρηται ἑταίρα οὖσα καὶ δούλη Νικαρέτης γεγενημένη. ἀλλ' οὐ
γυναῖκα εἶναι αὐτοῦ, ἀλλὰ παλλακὴν ἔχειν ἔνδον; ἀλλ' οἱ παῖδες ταύτης ὄντες
καὶ εἰσηγμένοι εἰς τοὺς φράτερας ὑπὸ Στεφάνου καὶ ἡ θυγάτηρ ἀνδρὶ Ἀθηναίωι
119 ἐκδοθεῖσα περιφανῶς αὐτὴν ἀποφαίνουσι γυναῖκα ἔχοντα. ὡς μὲν τοίνυν οὐκ
ἀληθῆ ἐστιν τὰ κατηγορημένα καὶ μεμαρτυρημένα, οὔτ' αὐτὸν Στέφανον οὔτ'
ἄλλον ὑπὲρ τούτου οἶμαι ἐπιδείξειν, ὡς ἔστιν ἀστὴ Νέαιρα αὑτηί· ἀκούω δὲ
αὐτὸν τοιοῦτόν τι μέλλειν ἀπολογεῖσθαι, ὡς οὐ γυναῖκα ἔχει αὐτὴν ἀλλ'
ἑταίραν, καὶ οἱ παῖδες οὐκ εἰσὶν ταύτης ἀλλ' ἐξ ἑτέρας γυναικὸς αὐτῶι ἀστῆς,
120 ἣν φήσει πρότερον γῆμαι συγγενῆ αὐτοῦ. πρὸς δὴ τὴν ἀναίδειαν αὐτοῦ τοῦ
λόγου καὶ τὴν παρασκευὴν τῆς ἀπολογίας καὶ τῶν μαρτυρεῖν αὐτῶι
παρεσκευασμένων πρόκλησιν αὐτὸν προὐκαλεσάμην ἀκριβῆ καὶ δικαίαν, δι' ἧς
ἐξῆν ὑμῖν πάντα τἀληθῆ εἰδέναι, παραδοῦναι τὰς θεραπαίνας τὰς Νεαίραι τότε
προσκαρτερούσας ὅτ' ἦλθεν ὡς Στέφανον ἐκ Μεγάρων, Θρᾶιτταν καὶ
Κοκκαλίνην, καὶ ἃς ὕστερον παρὰ τούτωι οὖσα ἐκτήσατο, Ξεννίδα καὶ Δροσ-
121 ίδα· αἳ ἴσασιν ἀκριβῶς Πρόξενόν τε τὸν τελευτήσαντα καὶ Ἀρίστωνα τὸν νῦν
ὄντα καὶ Ἀντιδωρίδην τὸν σταδιοδρομοῦντα καὶ Φανὼ τὴν Στρυβήλην
καλουμένην, ἣ Θεογένει τῶι βασιλεύσαντι συνώικησεν, Νεαίρας ὄντας. καὶ ἐὰν
φαίνηται ἐκ τῆς βασάνου γήμας Στέφανος οὑτοσὶ ἀστὴν γυναῖκα καὶ ὄντες
αὐτῶι οἱ παῖδες οὗτοι ἐξ ἑτέρας γυναικὸς ἀστῆς καὶ μὴ Νεαίρας, ἤθελον ἀφίστ-
122 ασθαι τοῦ ἀγῶνος καὶ μὴ εἰσιέναι τὴν γραφὴν ταύτην. τὸ γὰρ συνοικεῖν τοῦτ'
ἔστιν, ὃς ἂν παιδοποιῆται καὶ εἰσάγηι εἴς τε τοὺς φράτερας καὶ δημότας τοὺς
υἱεῖς, καὶ τὰς θυγατέρας ἐκδιδῶι ὡς αὑτοῦ οὔσας τοῖς ἀνδράσιν. τὰς μὲν γὰρ
ἑταίρας ἡδονῆς ἕνεκ' ἔχομεν, τὰς δὲ παλλακὰς τῆς καθ' ἡμέραν θεραπείας τοῦ

courtesan Sinope a victim she brought on the hearth in the courtyard at Eleusis,
though it is not permitted to sacrifice victims on that day, and the sacrifice was
117 not his concern but the priestess's. Is it not monstrous that a man belonging to
the Eumolpidai, born of noble ancestors and a citizen of the state, should be
punished, because it was felt that he had offended against an established
custom (and neither the entreaty of his kin nor that of his friends was of use to
him, nor the many public services which he himself and his ancestors had
performed for the city, nor the fact that he was hierophant, but you punished
him because he was found guilty); – while this woman Neaira, who committed
impiety against the same god and the laws, both herself and her daughter, will
you not punish *her*?
118 For myself, I wonder what on earth they will actually say to you in the
defence. That this Neaira is of citizen birth and that she lives in marriage with
Stephanos according to the laws? But it has been attested that she is a
courtesan and that she was Nikarete's slave. Or that she is not his wife, but he
keeps her in his house as his mistress? But the sons who are hers and who
have been introduced into the phratry by Stephanos and the daughter who was
given in marriage to an Athenian male demonstrate quite clearly that he keeps
119 her as his wife. Now I do not think that either Stephanos himself or anyone
else on his behalf will prove that the allegations and the testimony are untrue,
and that this Neaira is of citizen birth; but I hear that he intends to offer a
defence of this sort, that he keeps her not as his wife but as his mistress, and
that the children are not by her but by another wife of his of citizen birth, a
120 relative of his whom he will say he married previously. In response to the
impudence of his claim and the dishonesty of his defence and of the witnesses
he has suborned I made him a detailed and fair challenge which would have
enabled you to know the whole truth; I challenged him to hand over the
maidservants who remained with Neaira when she came to Stephanos's house
from Megara, Thratta and Kokkaline, and those whom she got later when she
121 was living with him, Xennis and Drosis; they know for certain that Proxenos
who died and Ariston who is still alive and Antidorides the sprinter and Phano
who was called Strybele, who married Theogenes who served as King-archon,
are Neaira's children. And if the examination revealed that Stephanos here
married a woman of citizen birth and that these children are his by another
wife of citizen birth and not Neaira, I was willing to withdraw from the case
122 and to prevent this indictment from coming tocourt. For this is what living in
marriage means: when a man sires children and introduces the sons to phratry
and deme and gives the daughters to their husbands as his own. For we have
courtesans for pleasure, and concubines for the daily service of our bodies, but

σώματος, τὰς δὲ γυναῖκας τοῦ παιδοποιεῖσθαι γνησίως καὶ τῶν ἔνδον φύλακα
πιστὴν ἔχειν. ὥστ' εἰ πρότερον ἔγημεν γυναῖκα ἀστὴν καὶ εἰσὶν οὗτοι οἱ παῖδες
ἐξ ἐκείνης καὶ μὴ Νεαίρας, ἐξῆν αὐτῶι ἐκ τῆς ἀκριβεστάτης μαρτυρίας ἐπιδεῖξαι,
123 παραδόντι τὰς θεραπαίνας ταύτας. ὡς δὲ προὐκαλεσάμην, τούτων ὑμῖν τήν τε
μαρτυρίαν καὶ τὴν πρόκλησιν ἀναγνώσεται. λέγε τὴν μαρτυρίαν, ἔπειτα τὴν
πρόκλησιν.

ΜΑΡΤΥΡΙΑ

Ἱπποκράτης Ἱπποκράτους Προβαλίσιος, Δημοσθένης Δημοσθένους Παιανιεύς, Διοφάνης Διοφάνους Ἀλωπεκῆθεν, Δεινομένης Ἀρχελάου Κυδαθηναιεύς, Δεινίας Φόρμου Κυδαντίδης, Λυσίμαχος Λυσίππου Αἰγιλιεὺς μαρτυροῦσι παρεῖναι ἐν ἀγορᾶι ὅτ' Ἀπολλόδωρος προὐκαλεῖτο Στέφανον, ἀξιῶν παραδοῦναι εἰς βάσανον τὰς θεραπαίνας περὶ ὧν ᾐτιᾶτο Ἀπολλόδωρος Στέφανον περὶ Νεαίρας· Στέφανον δ' οὐκ ἐθελῆσαι παραδοῦναι τὰς θεραπαίνας· τὴν δὲ πρόκλησιν εἶναι ἣν παρέχεται Ἀπολλόδωρος.

124 Λέγε δὴ αὐτὴν τὴν πρόκλησιν, ἣν προὐκαλούμην ἐγὼ Στέφανον τουτονί.

ΠΡΟΚΛΗΣΙΣ.

Τάδε προὐκαλεῖτο Ἀπολλόδωρος Στέφανον περὶ ὧν τὴν γραφὴν γέγραπται Νέαιραν, ξένην οὖσαν ἀστῶι συνοικεῖν, ἕτοιμος ὢν τὰς θεραπαίνας παραλαμβάνειν τὰς Νεαίρας, ἃς ἐκ Μεγάρων ἔχουσα ἦλθεν, Θρᾶιτταν καὶ Κοκκαλίνην, καὶ ἃς ὕστερον παρὰ Στεφάνωι ἐκτήσατο, Ξεννίδα καὶ Δροσίδα, τὰς εἰδυίας ἀκριβῶς περὶ τῶν παίδων τῶν ὄντων Στεφάνωι, ὅτι ἐκ Νεαίρας εἰσίν, Πρόξενός τε ὁ τελευτήσας καὶ Ἀρίστων ὁ νῦν ὢν καὶ Ἀντιδωρίδης ὁ σταδιοδρομῶν καὶ Φανώ, ἐφ' ὧι τε βασανίσαι αὐτάς. καὶ εἰ μὲν ὁμολογοῖεν ἐκ Στεφάνου εἶναι καὶ Νεαίρας τούτους τοὺς παῖδας, πεπρᾶσθαι Νέαιραν κατὰ τοὺς νόμους καὶ τοὺς παῖδας ξένους εἶναι· εἰ δὲ μὴ ὁμολογοῖεν ἐκ ταύτης εἶναι αὐτοὺς ἀλλ' ἐξ ἑτέρας γυναικὸς ἀστῆς, ἀφίστασθαι τοῦ ἀγῶνος ἤθελον τοῦ Νεαίρας, καὶ εἴ τι ἐκ τῶν βασάνων βλαφθείησαν αἱ ἄνθρωποι, ἀποτίνειν ὅ τι βλαβείησαν.

125 Ταῦτα προκαλεσαμένου ἐμοῦ, ὦ ἄνδρες δικασταί, Στέφανον τουτονί, οὐκ ἠθέλησεν δέξασθαι. οὔκουν ἤδη δοκεῖ ὑμῖν δεδικάσθαι ὑπ' αὐτοῦ Στεφάνου τουτουί, ὦ ἄνδρες δικασταί, ὅτι ἔνοχός ἐστι τῆι γραφῆι Νέαιρα ἣν ἐγὼ αὐτὴν ἐγραψάμην, καὶ ὅτι ἐγὼ μὲν ἀληθῆ εἴρηκα πρὸς ὑμᾶς καὶ τὰς μαρτυρίας

wives for the production of legitimate offspring and to have reliable guardian of our household property. So if he had previously married a woman of citizen birth and his children are by her and not by Neaira, it was open to him to prove it by means of the most accurate testimony, by handing over these serv-
123 ant girls. To prove that I issued the challenge, he will read out to you the deposition and the challenge. Read the deposition and then the challenge.

DEPOSITION

Hippokrates son of Hippokrates of Probalinthos, Demosthenes son of Demosthenes of Paiania, Diophanes son of Diophanes of Alopeke, Deinomenes son of Archelaos of Kydathenaion, Deinias the son of Phormos of Kydantidai, and Lysimachos the son of Lysippos of Aigilia depose that they were present in the agora when Apollodoros challenged Stephanos, demanding that he hand over the maidservants for examination in the matter of Apollodoros' charges against Stephanos concerning Neaira; that Stephanos refused to hand over the maidservants; and that the challenge was the one which Apollodoros produces.

124 Read now the actual challenge which I issued to Stephanos here.

CHALLENGE

This challenge was issued by Apollodoros to Stephanos concerning the charge on which he has indicted Neaira, that she is living in marriage with a citizen although she is a foreigner; Apollodoros was ready to take Neaira's maidservants whom she brought with her from Megara, Thratta and Kokkaline, and those whom she acquired later when living with Stephanos, Xennis and Drosis, who possess accurate knowledge about Stephanos' children, that they are by Neaira, Proxenos who is dead and Ariston who is still alive and Antidorides the sprinter, for examination. And if they should admit that these are the children of Stephanos and Neaira, Neaira was to be sold in accordance with the laws and the children were to be aliens; but if they did not admit that these children were by this woman but by another wife of citizen birth, I was ready to withdraw from the case against Neaira, and, if the slaves had suffered any damage from the examination, to pay for any damage suffered.

125 When I issued this challenge, gentlemen of the jury, to Stephanos here, he refused to accept it. Don't you think then that judgement has already been given by this man Stephanos himself that Neaira is guilty of the indictment I brought against her and that I have told the truth to you and the depositions

παρεσχόμην ἀληθεῖς, οὑτοσὶ δ' ὅ τι ἂν λέγηι πάντα ψεύσεται, καὶ ἐξελέγξει αὐτὸς αὐτὸν ὅτι οὐδὲν ὑγιὲς λέγει, οὐκ ἐθελήσας παραδοῦναι εἰς βασάνους τὰς θεραπαίνας ἃς ἐγὼ ἐξήιτουν αὐτόν;

126 Ἐγὼ μὲν οὖν, ὦ ἄνδρες δικασταί, καὶ τοῖς θεοῖς εἰς οὓς οὗτοι ἠσεβήκασιν, καὶ ἐμαυτῶι τιμωρῶν, κατέστησά τε τουτουσὶ εἰς ἀγῶνα καὶ ὑπὸ τὴν ὑμετέραν ψῆφον ἤγαγον. καὶ ὑμᾶς δὲ χρὴ νομίσαντας μὴ λήσειν τοὺς θεούς, εἰς οὓς οὗτοι παρανενομήκασιν, ὅ τι ἂν ἕκαστος ὑμῶν ψηφίσηται, ψηφίσασθαι τὰ δίκαια καὶ τιμωρεῖν μάλιστα μὲν τοῖς θεοῖς, ἔπειτα δὲ καὶ ὑμῖν αὐτοῖς. καὶ ταῦτα ποιήσαντες δόξετε πᾶσι καλῶς καὶ δικαίως δικάσαι ταύτην τὴν γραφήν, ἣν Νέαιραν ἐγὼ ἐγραψάμην, ξένην οὖσαν ἀστῶι συνοικεῖν.

which I provided are true, while everything this man says will be a lie and he will himself prove that he has no sound case to make since he refused to hand over for examination the maidservants I requested.

126 So I, gentlemen of the jury, as avenger both of the gods, against whom these people have committed sacrilege, and of myself have brought them to trial and submitted them to your vote. You too must realize that whatever verdict each of you reaches will not go unnoticed by the gods against whom these people have offended, and vote as justice requires and avenge above all the gods and secondly yourselves. And if you do this you will be thought by all men to have given an honourable and just judgement on this indictment which I have brought against Neaira, that she is living in marriage with a citizen although she is an alien.

COMMENTARY

1-16 *Theomnestos' speech.* This section is both a speech in its own right, containing all the expected elements (introduction §1, narrative §§2-10, argument §§11-13, and epilogue §§14-15) and the introduction to Apollodoros' speech, which has little in the way of formal introduction. Its primary purpose is to remove various sources of jury prejudice against the prosecution and to create prejudice against Stephanos. In this type of case the law allowed for substantial rewards for successful prosecutors (cf. §16); in view of the Athenian hostility against the use of the lawcourts for personal gain it is necessary for Theomnestos to disclaim any desire for profit (cf. esp. 53.1ff.). Secondly, Apollodoros' extensive involvement in litigation may well have made him unpopular with Athenian juries, which disapproved of hasty recourse to the law. Theomnestos redirects this prejudice against Stephanos; he represents Stephanos as the aggressor, and stresses that there was no honourable alternative to litigation. Thirdly, given his youth, the political background and the seriousness of the case, Theomnestos inevitably faces the suspicion that he is merely a tool of Apollodoros; to dispel this suspicion he exaggerates his own role as victim and avenger. This section also establishes to the moral character of prosecution and defence (*ethos*) and contributes to the emotional impact of the speech (*pathos*). The impression is created that Stephanos is persecuting Apollodoros and his relatives, and Theomnestos makes clear that he is not rushing into court in response to a first offence but has been provoked beyond endurance; he thus claims sufficient tolerance to win the respect of the jury without going so far as to make himself seem weak. At the same time, an unfavourable impression of Stephanos is created as ruthless, unscrupulous and venal, and in the process pity for his victims and anger at his offences is stimulated in the jury.

1 **There were many reasons:** only one, the desire for revenge, is dealt with by Theomnestos. To the modern reader revenge is hardly superior to greed as a motive for litigation, but enmity is regularly cited in justification by Greek prosecutors; cf. e.g. 53.1-3, 58.1ff., Lys.14.1, Aischin.1.1. Greek thought saw it as a duty to harm one's enemies (cf. e.g. Solon 13.5, Plat.*Meno* 71e), and there was no objection in principle to the pursuit of personal or political feuds through the courts. However, prosecutors invoking enmity regularly as here stress that they are retaliating, not initiating a quarrel. Moreover, we do not find enmity cited as sole reason for prosecution; the jury are not asked simply to adjudicate a feud. The individual's desire for revenge is a justifiable reason for bringing a public action only where it coincides with the interests of the city and its laws.

though he had never suffered any harm from us: possibly the truth, but certainly

not the whole truth, since it represents the prosecution of Apollodoros as mere malice. As Theomnestos' own account shows, Apollodoros and Stephanos were in opposing political camps.
we were placed in the ... danger of losing both homeland and citizen rights: as explained in §§6-7 and 9. The first person plural effectively presents Theomnestos as Stephanos' victim; but in fact he faced neither exile nor disfranchisement, unlike Apollodoros.

2 Theomnestos begins his narrative by defining his relationship with Apollodoros. This is a necessary prerequisite for his presentation of himself as Stephanos' victim and consequently for his claim to be avenging himself.
Pasion and his descendants: a verbatim quotation of the decree enfranchising Pasion (cf. e.g. *IG* ii[2] 405.8-12). For an attempt to date Pasion's receipt of citizenship see *CQ* 41 (1991) 84-9. For the procedures whereby an alien received Athenian citizenship cf. §§89-90.
because of his benefactions: according to Apollodoros (45.85) these included a gift of one thousand shields to the state and another donation of five triremes.
treated my sister ... well: Apollodoros speaks of his affection for his wife at 50.61; we should bear in mind however that Apollodoros himself wrote these words for Theomnestos.
true relatives share all they have: recasts a Greek proverb *koina ta ton philon*, 'friends share what they have'.
Apollodoros' daughter, my niece: such dynastic exchanges were not uncommon. Marriage between uncle and niece was a frequent occurrence (cf. e.g. Lys.32.4, Isai.10.5 and §22 below), the aim being to keep the property within the immediate family; indeed, when a man died leaving only a daughter the dead man's brother had first claim to her hand (cf. Harrison I 23, 133). Theomnestos was no doubt influenced in part at least by the fact that Apollodoros' daughter will have brought a substantial dowry.

3 **was drawn as member of the Council:** refers to selection by lot. The Council (*Boule*) consisted of five hundred members, fifty from each of the ten tribes; for the selection process see Rhodes *AB* 6-12.
the examination: Greek *dokimasia*. All elected officials had to undergo a scrutiny before assuming office to confirm eligibility and also suitability on grounds of general character; the examination of the Councillors-elect was conducted by the outgoing Council (Arist.*Ath.Pol.*45.3; see Rhodes *AB* 12, 176-8).
the customary oath: for the content of the Councillor's oath see Rhodes *AB* 194ff.
a war crisis: refers to 349-8, the Olythiac crisis and the campaign in Euboia; see

further Introduction 7. Demosthenes was a staunch supporter of the Olynthiac alliance, but unlike Apollodoros he opposed the Euboian expedition (5.5).

to recover once for all your possessions: in particular Amphipolis, taken by Philip in 357. See further Introduction 6.

finally put down Philip: Theomnestos grossly overestimates the rewards for success. Success in the north, and to a lesser extent in Euboia, where Philip's involvement was only indirect (cf. G.L. Cawkwell *CQ* 12 (1962) 129-30), might have slowed the pace of Macedonian expansion, but it is difficult to see how it could have checked Philip permanently. However, in the context of public dissatisfaction with the Peace of Philokrates with Macedon of 346, it is in the interests of the prosecution to represent Stephanos as squandering an opportunity to stop the rise of Macedon.

lack of money: the sudden strain on state finances caused by these two operations was so severe that there was a temporary lack of money to pay the wages of the jurors and the business of the courts was suspended (39.17).

Lemnos, Imbros, Skyros and the Chersonese: stages in Athens' line of communication with the Black Sea, an important source of Athenian grain. Philip had harried Lemnos and Imbros before 351 (4.34) and had threatened the Chersonese in 352 (1.13, 3.4). With Euboia hostile Athens had lost one stepping stone, and with Philip in control of Chalkidike Athens' grain supply could not be safe.

4 **a resolution:** Greek *probouleuma*, a motion from the Council. No matter could be placed before the Assembly except through a *probouleuma* (Arist.*Ath.Pol.*45.4). As Rhodes *AB* 58 (followed by Patteson) notes, formally Apollodoros' motion is an 'open' *probouleuma*, i.e. a motion which simply places an issue before the Assembly without recommending a single course of action.

the laws prescribed: Theomnestos is probably oversimplifying the legal position. See Appendix.

as you all bore witness: Theomnestos means that all attested by their vote that Apollodoros kept his oath by giving the best advice he could. Since the juries sat as representatives of the sovereign people, it is normal for orators addressing a jury to say 'you' when referring to any legislative or executive decision of the Assembly, as here, or to any decision by an Athenian jury.

5 **nobody voted against the use of this money for military purposes:** in the absence of any evidence we cannot assess the truth of this statement.

it is agreed by all: the *locus ab auctoritate* (*Ad Herenn.* 2.30.48). The present example is somewhat similar to the 'everyone knows that ...' topos much used by

Greek orators to embarrass the individual hearer into agreement (Arist. *R.*1408a33-36).

the man who deceived the jurors: it is normal for litigants to ascribe to deception a vote favourable to the opponent (26.20, 37.45, 47.15). This has the dual advantage of maligning the opponent and enabling the speaker to question a decision by a previous jury while avoiding criticism which might alienate the present jury.

indicted the decree as illegal: the *graphe paranomon* could be brought against any motion in the Council or Assembly which was formally or procedurally incorrect or in conflict with an existing law. This action was created at some point in the second half of the fifth century. Its purpose was to prevent hasty legislation. Since like all *graphai* it was open to the volunteer prosecutor, it relied for its effect on, and was much used as a weapon for, political rivalries (according to Aischin.3.194, the politician Aristophon boasted that he had been unsuccessfully indicted on a *graphe paranomon* seventy-five times). If no vote had been taken on the measure under attack, the vote was suspended while the case was heard. If the measure had already been approved, the proposer remained open to prosecution by *graphe paranomon* for a year. Penalty on conviction was a fine (none of the passages advanced by Hansen (cited below) 53 supports his contention that the death penalty was a possibility in such cases); three convictions brought loss of citizen rights. See further H.J. Wolff, *'Normenkontrolle' und Gesetzbegriff in der attischen Demokratie* (Sitzungsberichte der Heidelberger Akademie 1970), M.H. Hansen, *The sovereignty of the people's court in Athens in the fourth century B.C. and the public action against unconstitutional proposals* (Odense 1974), MacDowell *Law* 50-2, Bonner-Smith II 296ff.

that Apollodoros had been a debtor to the Treasury for twenty-five years: this clause in the MSS follows §9 'brought a false charge against him' by a manifest error; the transposition, which was made by Sauppe, is probably correct. Stephanos' allegation may concern an otherwise unknown trierarchy by Apollodoros (Davies *APF* 440), or a fine resulting from litigation. It is not clear whether this was the sole, the main or a subsidiary ground for Stephanos' prosecution. See Appendix.

many accusations irrelevant to the indictment: surviving Greek speeches contain much that we would dismiss as irrelevant; see Carey-Reid 8-12. The importance of moral character in establishing or demolishing credibility, the role of emotion in ancient rhetoric, the system of volunteer prosecutors, which meant that in some cases an habitual malefactor might find himself only rarely in court (cf. 21.2), and the tendency to apportion trials to courts according to the specific offence committed, which meant that a prosecutor pursuing manifold wrongs would have to choose between courts, all favoured the introduction of argument and allegation tangential to the main issue. Only in the case of the Areopagos was there any serious attempt to prevent this. Litigants naturally approach this issue with a kind of 'double think', expecting us to disapprove of the opponent's use of irrelevance while using it themselves.

6 **we have no complaint:** presents the speaker as a tolerant man, responding not to an isolated attack but to systematic persecution. Cf. above §§1-16.
penalty assessment: in those cases for which the law laid down no fixed penalty (such a case was known as an *agon timetos*, 'assessible case'), it was left to the jury to decide between two alternative penalties proposed by prosecution and defence. We have only Theomnestos' unsupported word for the magnitude of the fine proposed by Stephanos; for a comparable case see however 58.1, 30-31.
disfranchising Apollodoros himself and his children: a debtor to the state was subject to *atimia* (loss of citizen rights; cf. on §26) until the debt was paid. If he died with the debt unpaid, the debt and the *atimia* were inherited by his heirs. Apollodoros' sons would therefore be disfranchised only if he died a debtor to the state; but it suits Theomnestos' purpose to aggrandize the potential damage.

7 **three talents:** if so, a fine of fifteen talents would be ruinous. But Davies *APF* 439 calculates that by 350 Apollodoros had received (from his father's estate, from lawsuits concerning his father's bank and from rents) over 43 talents. He had spent heavily on liturgies (cf. Introduction 1 and note on §117) and was allegedly extravagant in his private life (36.8, 45). But it is difficult to believe that he had spent forty talents or more in twenty years; as recently as 352/1 he was in the liturgical class, for which property in excess of three talents was required.
by the ninth prytany: each of the ten tribal contingents of the Council acted as an executive committee for one tenth of the year; they were called *prytaneis* and their term of office *prytaneia*; see Rhodes *AB* 16-23. The ninth prytany was the deadline for many fines and other payments to the state (Arist.*Ath.Pol.*47.3).
inventoried: the procedure referred to here is one of many striking examples of the reliance of the Athenian state on individual initiative. If a man became a state debtor, it was open for any citizen to submit an inventory (*apographe*) of his property with a view to securing payment of the debt to the state. The goods were sold and three quarters of the sum realized went to the denouncer, the remaining quarter to the state. (This in not certain; R. Osborne, cited below, accepts the suggestion of D.M. Lewis, *Ancient society and institutions*, ed. E. Badian (Oxford 1966) 188 with notes 66 and 67, that the reward for the prosecutor in an *apographe* was two-thirds, not three-quarters, of the sum realized; cf. also Millett 265 n.2. The suggestion involves a textual change at [Dem.]53.2). See further

Harrison II 211-17, MacDowell *Law* 166, and R. Osborne, *JHS* 105 (1985) 44ff.

8 his second daughter would be unmarriageable: since marriage was the fulfilment of a woman's main role in life, for a girl to go unmarried was a disaster according to Greek thinking; cf. §112 below. The motif of the unmarriageable daughter is used elsewhere in the orators to excite pity; cf. 40.4, 56, 45.74, Lys.12.21, 13.45 (sister). This emotional vein is mined in a wider context at §112 below, and is allegedly exploited by Stephanos §71.
imposed a fine of one talent: i.e. they accepted Apollodoros' proposal for the scale of the penalty.
pay him back in the same coin: Greek 'to pay him back the same *eranos*'; the *eranos* was a loan (usually interest-free) collected by friends for someone in need. See in general Millett 153-9. The idea of reciprocity was important to the *eranos*; hence the use of the term here of returning a favour (ironic).

9 The second attack involves a false charge of homicide, details of which are unclear. We do not know the precise status of the alleged victim. From i. the probability that the charge is intentional homicide (for the breadth of the Greek definition of intentional homicide see in general W.T. Loomis, *JHS* 92 (1972), 86-95), ii. the involvement of the Palladion, we deduce that the woman was not of citizen status, for while those accused of intentional killing of a citizen were tried by the Areopagos, those accused of killing a slave, resident alien (*metoikos*, 'metic') or foreigner were tried at the Palladion (which also tried cases of uninentional killing of a citizen); see Dem.23.71, Arist.*Ath.Pol.*57.3. The issue is not clarified by the reference to slaves misrepresented as Cyrenaeans, for it is not clear whether these people are meant to be relatives of the dead woman, her owners, or simply witnesses. The description of Stephanos' role suggests that he was the accuser, and therefore that the woman was his slave; the right and the duty to prosecute were confined to the relatives of the victim (see however MacDowell *AHL* 17ff.), though in the case of a slave the owner could prosecute. If this is correct, the 'Cyrenaeans' are presumably witnesses; the trick of disguising slaves as free men may have been intended to prevent their testimony being tested by torture (see on §120 below), and also perhaps to increase the weight of their evidence in the eyes of the jury. Cf. in general Patteson.
Aphidna: in north-east Attica.
publicly summonsed him: the first step in the initiating procedure for homicide cases consisted of a public proclamation in the agora addressed to the accused, ordering him to refrain from social and religious contact with the rest of society (see MacDowell *AHL* 24-6).

the Palladion: probably south-east of the Acropolis (Travlos *PDA* 412ff.).

10 having taken an oath that Apollodoros killed the woman with his own hand: oaths played an important part in homicide trials. Accuser and accused each swore an oath, the former that the accusation was true, the latter that he had not committed homicide. In addition, all homicide witnesses had to swear to the guilt or innocence of the accused. See in general MacDowell *AHL* 90ff.
hired by Kephisophon and Apollophanes: given the date and Apollodoros' political affiliations, the former is probably the Kephisophon mentioned as a supporter of Philokrates at 18.21, 75. This may be Kephisophon son of Kallibios of Paiania (Kirchner *PA* 8417, Davies *APF* 149). This is not certain; since Kephisophon of Paiania may have been prosecuted by Euboulos at some point (19.293), it is odd to find him in Euboulos' camp. However, we are inadequately informed about changes in political affiliation in classical Athens. The alternative is Kephisophon son of Kephalion of Aphidna, who was a significant political figure in the 350s; however, this man appeared as a witness for Apollodoros as recently as 350/9 (45.19). For a good discussion see Trevett *Apollodoros* 148. About Apollophanes nothing is known. Stephanos is consistently presented as a man who abuses the legal system for private gain; cf §§41-3, 64-71.
exile or disfranchisement: the opening of §9 suggests that the penalty faced by Apollodoros in the homicide case was exile. The mention of disfranchisement here (if the text is sound; Gernet, followed by Avezzù wished to excise the words ἢ ἀτιμῶσαι, which would remove the reference to disfranchisement) has been taken to suggest that the penalty for killing a slave was not fixed (cf. MacDowell *AHL* 126-7, Harrison I 170). Lykourg.*Leokr.*65 seems to imply that in the latter part of the fourth century the penalty might be a fine, though he also indicates that at an earlier stage the punishment was more severe. Perhaps Drakon's homicide law allowed only for exile, but subsequent practice mitigated the sentence (cf. Arist.*Ath.Pol.*60 on the laws governing the sacred olives). On this hypothesis, the alternative penalty of *atimia* may be a stage in the process of mitigation which led eventually to the substitution of a monetary penalty. It is however possible that the second penalty mentioned here refers not to the homicide trial but to the case of the *graphe paranomon*, the implication being that Stephanos brought both cases as a hireling and that the homicide case was initiated because of the failure of the preceding attack to ruin Apollodoros. We are given no evidence to prove that Stephanos sold his services.
from five hundred drachmas: so most manuscripts; D has 'from five hundred jurors' (ἐκ πεντακοσίων δικαστῶν), which Q records as a variant. Many editors delete the noun; this gives 'from five hundred' (i.e. votes). The majority MSS reading

is to be preferred. The weight of evidence indicates that the jury at the Palladion (known as the *ephetai*) were fifty-one in number (see MacDowell *AHL* 48-57). We are presumably to imagine the five hundred drachmas as being spent by Stephanos on the suborning of witnesses and perhaps on bribes to individual jurors. Another possibility (suggested to me by Dr. Todd) is that the five hundred drachmas were received by Stephanos as payment for prosecuting Apollodoros (ἐκ = 'as a result of'); this suggestion is appealing, but linguistically more difficult.

12 Since people on all sides urged me: a doubtful claim. Theomnestos would no doubt have been affected by Apollodoros' financial ruin, disfranchisement or exile, since he would have been called upon to give assistance. And according to Greek values it would have been unmanly to leave attacks such as those of Stephanos unavenged (cf. on §1). But Theomnestos was only indirectly affected. He would not have lost his property or citizen rights, nor did he face exile. Apollodoros was the target, and it was for Apollodoros to seek revenge. The effect is to gloss over Theomnestos' role as Apollodoros' instrument. Cf. on §§1-16. The claim that the speaker has received encouragement from a large number of people adds authority to his case; cf. 21.2, 54.1, Lyk.*Leokr*.136. For the confused sentence structure cf. Introduction 19.
so blatantly committing impiety: refers to the incidents narrated in §§72-87.

13 so I too: we might expect Theomnestos to say: 'so I too am trying to deprive Stephanos of his loved ones', but he substitutes a milder statement to avoid creating sympathy for Stephanos or Neaira.
introduced another's children into his phratry and deme: the phratries were subdivisions of the four tribes of archaic Athens; they had lost their political significance as a result of the reforms of Kleisthenes at the end of the sixth century, but they continued to function for religious and social purposes. Membership was hereditary, and was confined to legitimate male issue. Initial enrolment took place in infancy, and there was a second ceremony at puberty, when the boy became a full member of the phratry. Registration in the deme took place at the age of eighteen; this enrolment conferred full political rights. The allegation made here is never substantiated.
gives the daughters of courtesans in marriage as though they were his own: refers to the incidents dealt with in §§49-87.
much expense and trouble: cf. on §2 (Pasion's donations).
if he can get it from Stephanos: this argument is factually weak (Stephanos is allegedly using an illegal marriage to obtain citizen status for Neaira's children; this is clearly not a mechanism he could use to enfranchise large numbers) but

rhetorically effective. It stimulates resentment against Stephanos by presenting the jurors, who represent the demos, as his victims, and at the same time it stresses the enormity of the offence.

14 a young man inexperienced in speaking: the diffidence appeals to the jurors' sense of propriety (for the modesty expected of young men see 54.1, 58.1ff., Lys.16.20); the claim of inexperience in speaking (a commonplace; cf. e.g. 40.4, Ant.5.2-3) likewise lays claim to the goodwill of the jurors.
supporter: Greek *synegoros*. Although a litigant was expected to conduct his own case in court, it was open to him to call upon a supporting speaker; the latter's speech counted against the litigant's time allowance. Theomnestos' request for permission to call a *synegoros* is probably a courtesy only, for such permission is not always sought (cf. 56.50, 58.70). Though technically only the supporting speaker, Apollodoros is the real prosecutor. For other cases in which the *synegoros* conducted the case after a brief introduction from the litigant cf. Lys.32 (where the plaintiff is a very young man) and Dem.36 (where the litigant has imperfect Greek). See further Introduction 4-5 and notes on §§120, 124, 125.

15 the gods, the laws, justice and yourselves: the conclusion of Apollodoros' speech is similar (§126).

16-126 *Apollodoros' speech*. Apollodoros' brief introduction (§§16-17) provides the legal basis for the prosecution.

16 LAW: on the general question of the authenticity of documents in the Demosthenic corpus and in this speech in particular see Introduction 20. We can be reasonably confident that this document is substantially that presented at the trial, for there are three details, the restriction of the right to prosecute to citizens, the reward for the successful prosecutor and the penalty for an Athenian male married to a foreigner, which do not occur in Apollodoros' paraphrase, which would most naturally have formed the basis for any later forgery.
lives in marriage with: the Greek verb used, *synoikein*, means literally 'live with'. But it is regularly used of marriage, and this must be the meaning of the word in the context of the law; see further Introduction 4. The failure to define the offence precisely (as Apollodoros himself seeks to do in §122) is normal for Athenian laws, which were drafted in the language of everyday speech, not in a special legal terminology, and for the use of ordinary citizens rather than professional lawyers. See further on §122.
indict: literally 'bring a *graphe*'. The most important classification of Athenian

lawsuits was the distinction between public and private actions; in private cases the right to prosecute was limited to the victim, while in public cases (of which *graphai* were the most common) anyone could prosecute (see however on §109). In some public cases the right to prosecute was explicitly restricted to citizens as here (cf. 21.47, 24.63, Aischin.1.32). This was not however a general rule (cf. §66 below, 21.175, 24.105; §52 below provides another possible example, though the absence of an explicit restriction there could be due to the cross-reference to the law on *xenia*). See Lipsius 243-4, Harrison I 195 n.1.

who possesses the right: excludes those who were disfranchised totally (such as debtors to the state; for total *atimia* see on §26) or partially (i.e. those who were barred from bringing a particular kind of action; see on §53 and Andok.1.76).

the man ... is to be fined: the discrepancy between the treatment of a male and female of citizen status married to an alien is intelligible in the context of Athenian society. Since the marriage was negotiated between the prospective groom and the bride's father, an Athenian woman who found herself married to an alien could not reasonably be held responsible for any fraud. It is interesting however that the law makes no comparable distinction between the sexes in the case of aliens who were party to such a marriage.

17 or to produce children: i.e. legitimate children. From §§118 and 122 it is clear that it was not illegal for an Athenian to have children by a foreign female; what was illegal was to represent such children as legitimate, for this was to claim citizen status for the alien and so to bestow it on the offspring. See further on §122.

starting at the beginning: signals a detailed narrative; the phrase is a commonplace in the introduction of narrative.

18-84 *Narrative*. Of the narrative section §§18-48 deal with Neaira's career, the rest being devoted primarily to her daughter Phano. For the amount of space given to narrative in this speech see Introduction 12-13.

18 Nikarete: we know nothing of Nikarete beyond what we learn from this speech. Athenaios (XIII.593f) refers to her as 'Nikarete the courtesan' and says that she was mistress of 'Stephanos the orator'. This is clearly a confused recollection of the present speech; likewise his statement that not only Nikarete but all the girls named in chapter 19 were slaves of Kasios (sic) of Elis (in the same passage, Strybele, the given name of Neaira's daughter generally known as Phano, is distorted to Strymbele). It is however likely enough that Nikarete was a prostitute herself before she became a madam, since this was evidently a common progression in the ancient as in the modern world (cf. Hypereides, *Ath.* 3). Her character as it emerges from

Apollodoros' narrative is that of the typical brothelkeeper; cf. on §29 below. We learn from §23 (cf. 26, 28, 29 ff.) that her establishment was in Corinth, a city well known for its prostitutes (Pind.fr.122, Ar. *Wealth* 149, Plat.*Rep.*404d; there was a verb *korinthiazein*, 'to fornicate').

Charisios ... Hippias: otherwise unknown. Probably (Patteson) Hippias like Nikarete was of freedman status.

an expert judge of beauty in small children: like a good judge of wine, Nikarete can predict when purchasing infant slaves which girls will be pretty at puberty. (The words bracketed in the Greek are an explanatory gloss which has found its way into the text; the excision is due to Reiske.)

19 daughters: the fiction that the girls are free enables Nikarete to charge extra for their services, since the status of a prostitute evidently affected the price. In the same way Apollodoros below (§41) represents Neaira as increasing her price while (allegedly) living in marriage with Stephanos. In addition, since Nikarete kept the girls only until they reached womanhood, she could presumably demand higher fees by claiming that the girls were ruining their marriage prospects, especially when dealing with strangers, since she could represent the girls as virgins (customers were prepared to pay extra for the privilege of deflowering a virgin; cf. Epikrates fr.8 *PCG*, Lucian *Dial.mer.*6.1 with H. Herter, *Jahrbuch für Antike und Christentum* 3 (1960) 81 n.192). Youth in prostitutes was anyway highly prized (cf. Ar. fr.148 *PCG* with Herter *loc.cit.*).

have relations with: literally 'draw near to', a regular periphrasis for sexual intercourse. By consistently avoiding detail and using seemly periphrasis Apollodoros is able simultaneously to exploit Neaira's scandalous past and to sustain a moral character which will maintain the hearers' respect for the speaker.

their youth: (Greek *helikia*) probably not youth in the broadest sense (for Neaira was still young and attractive enough to fetch a high price when sold by Nikarete, §29) but the years during and immediately after puberty, say 12-20.

sold them off: literally 'she also sold their bodies' (in contrast to the profit made by hiring them out). The girls will have been sold either to clients who had a passion for a particular girl (for such purchases see on §29) or to a conventional brothel.

together: the narrative in §§29ff. suggests rather that the girls were sold individually as opportunity arose.

Anteia ... Neaira here: most if not all these women had been famous in Athens as courtesans. Anteia was mentioned in Anaxandrides' comedy, *Dotage* (*Gerontomania*, fr. 9, Ath. XIII.570e) in a list of renowned courtesans; the *Anteia*, variously ascribed to Philyllios or Eunikos and according to Athenaios named after a *hetaira*

(XIII.567c), may have been about her. Aristokleia is mentioned in the same context as the famous Lagiska by Athenaios (XIII.592d, citing Lys. *Against Lais*). Metaneira was a favourite of Lysias (§21 below) and also of Isokrates, according to Athenaios (XIII.592b, citing Lysias' *Letters*); Athenaios testifies to her wit (III.107e, XIII. 584f), and Hypereides to her beauty (fr. 13); she is linked by Athenaios (XIII.587d) with the most famous courtesans of the day. Phila was mentioned by Philetairos in his comedy *Huntress* (*Kynagis*, fr.9, Ath. XIII.587e) together with Isthmias, Neaira and the celebrated Lais. Hypereides kept a mistress named Phila at Eleusis (Ath. XIII.590d, citing Hypereides' *Defence of Phryne*). If [Plutarch] is correct in describing Hypereides' mistress as a Theban (*Lives of the Ten Orators* 849d) Apollodoros may have a different woman in mind (Patteson). However, it is to be noted that Apollodoros is our sole authority for the connection between these girls (except for Metaneira and Neaira) and Nikarete. His list may be the result of careful enquiry, but it is also possible (though not provable) that the connection between these girls and Nikarete is an invention intended to give an impression of precision and so lend the narrative an air of authority (compare his treatment of the Spartan forces at Plataia in 429, §101 below). It is on the whole unlikely that members of the jury would have personal knowledge of the background of these foreign courtesans now in their fifties and sixties, if still alive, or of events in Corinth four or five decades before the trial.

20 Which of them each purchaser acquired: if the above identification is correct, Phila was bought then freed by Hypereides. Neaira's purchasers were named in §29 below. On the others we have no information. There is no reason to suppose that Lysias bought Metaneira.
if you wish to hear: the information is not provided. A similar offer of information which is never given is made below, §43. It may be that Apollodoros intended to add something on both subjects but found time lacking; if so, we must suppose that the speech has not been revised before publication, since he has neither added the promised account nor deleted the promise. It is however more likely (given the parallels at Dem. 57.16, 35, 58, 65) that Apollodoros has no intention of providing further information, i.e. that the promise is a rhetorical device designed to create the impression that the speaker has more knowledge than he actually possesses. Such promises could be made with confidence, since although the jury could express its unwillingness to hear in those cases where the speaker does return to the subject (as in Ant. 6.8, 33ff., Dem. 16.3, 6, 50.31, 46) the size of the jury and the nature of the judicial process (continuous speech) made a concerted expression of a desire for further information on a subject already terminated by the speaker unlikely. The formula 'if you wish to hear' adds a gloss of spontaneity to a prefabricated speech.

water to spare: i.e. time to spare, a reference to the use of the water-clock, a simple but effective device which limited the amount of time available for litigants to present their case and ensured that both parties had an equal time-allowance. It consisted of a container of water with a hole in the base. The water was allowed to drain away, and a speaker had to finish once the container was empty. Different amounts of water were allowed for different types of case. In private suits at least the hole was stopped while documents were read out. See further S. Young, *Hesperia* 8 (1939) 174-84, Harrison II 161-2, MacDowell *Law* 249-50, Rhodes on Arist.*Ath.Pol.*67.2, and for 'water' used to mean 'time' cf. e.g. 18.139, 50.2.

21 Lysias the sophist: a rich metic of Syracusan extraction, Lysias lost most of his fortune under the confiscations of the Thirty. After the restoration of the democracy, he worked both as a teacher of rhetoric and as a professional speechwriter. For a brief account of Lysias' life see Carey 1f. The Greek word *sophistes* meant originally someone with knowledge or technical skill. In the late fifth century the word came to be used of the travelling professional teachers of grammar, rhetoric, politics and philosophy who found a congenial place to work and an appreciative clientele in Athens. *Sophistes* can be used pejoratively, but here it is neutral, serving to identify the individual named for the audience; it refers to Lysias' rhetorical activities.

wanted to initiate her: into the Eleusinian Mysteries. These were celebrated during the six days from 15 Boedromion (roughly September). The festival was sacred to Demeter and her daughter Kore (Persephone). Initiation (which was a gradual process culminating in a ceremony on the sixth day in which secret objects were shown to the candidate for initiation) offered the prospect of a better life after death. Further details in Parke 56 ff., Simon 24-35, G. Mylonas, *Eleusis and the Eleusinian Mysteries* (Princeton 1961) 224-85. Initiation was open not merely to non-Athenians but also to slaves of either sex. In the classical period there was a preliminary initiation at the Lesser Mysteries in Anthesterion (roughly February).

asked Nikarete to come to the Mysteries and bring Metaneira: clearly a hard-headed businesswoman like Nikarete would not let a valuable and profitable slave travel unattended. The incident cannot be dated precisely; a date between 390 and 385 seems most likely; see further Introduction 2-3. Clearly Lysias' trade as a speechwriter was lucrative, for although the cost of initiation (15 drachmas) was not enormous, the overall cost, including travel expenses for Metaneira and her party, recompense to Nikarete for inconvenience, (presumably) presents and entertainment, will have involved a large outlay.

promised to initiate her personally: the promise, which is evidently intended to reassure Nikarete that her slave girl is in safe hands, indicates that the role described by the verb 'initiate' (Greek *myein*) involved more than merely paying for the costs of initiation (cf. Andokides 1.132 with MacDowell *Andok.* 156); perhaps the existing initiate accompanied the postulant during the festival and presented him or her at the final ceremony. The initiation itself was carried out by the priests of Eleusis, who belonged to two noble families, the Eumolpidai and the Kerykes.

22 out of respect for his wife: although there was nothing to prevent a man from making use of prostitutes of either sex, it was clearly an affront to his wife to introduce such a woman into her presence. It was claimed that Alkibiades' wife sought to divorce him because he brought prostitutes home ([Andokides] 4.14).
Brachyllos: Lysias had two brothers, Polemarchos and Euthydemos; Brachyllos was evidently the husband of a sister of Lysias, otherwise unknown.
his niece: for such arrangements see on §2 above.
Philostratos of Kolonai: a member of a propertied family (Davies *APF* 552), subsequently active in politics; he prosecuted the general Chabrias for the loss of Oropos to the Thebans in 366/5 (Dem. 21.64).
Neaira here accompanied them: probably Nikarete brought her whole establishment to Athens. The panhellenic appeal of the Eleusinian Mysteries meant that there would be a large influx of visitors to Athens and accordingly a lot of potential custom.
too young: the reference to Neaira's youth is clearly meant to stress her unbridled sexual appetite, so strong that it would not wait for puberty (cf. Lys. 14.25), and so prejudice the jury against her (cf. on §20 above). To the reader, who has leisure to pause, it is clear that if Neaira was already a prostitute as a child this was Nikarete's decision (as her owner), not necessarily Neaira's choice. It is to be noted, however, that (despite Apollodoros' claim in §23) this allegation is not substantiated by the deposition which follows and may therefore be his invention.

23 DEPOSITION: formally this, like all the other depositions inserted in this speech, conforms to the conventions governing depositions in Athenian trials (for which we have reliable evidence at 29.31, 46.5, 54.31), which take the form: 'X/XYZ deposes/depose (μαρτυρεῖ/μαρτυροῦσι)' followed by an attestation in the accusative and infinitive construction (cf. Drerup 309). Although most of the content of the deposition could have been patched together from the surrounding narrative, there is one significant detail which could not. We know the name of Philostratos' father only from an inscription (*IG* ii^2 1622.772-3, with Kirchner, *RhM* 40 (1885) 77f). The presence of this detail probably not available to a later forger suggests that the document is authentic.

24 Simos of Thessaly: known to us only from scattered references; his career can be reconstructed only in broad outline and by conjecture. He was one of the Aleuadai of Larissa (Harpokration), who called on Philip in 352 for assistance against the tyrants of Pherai. Philip subsequently intervened in factional strife among the Aleuadai and eventually expelled them from power (Arist.*Pol.*1306a30, Dem.18.48 with schol.Dem.1.22, 2.14, Polyainos IV.2.11). See N.G.L. Hammond and G.T. Griffith, *A history of Macedonia 550-336* II (Oxford 1979) 256, M. Sordi, *La Lega Tessala fino ad Alessandro Magno* (Rome 1958) 364-8, and especially T.R. Martin, *Sovereignty and coinage in classical Greece* (Princeton 1985) 255-60 for the problems of reconstructing Simos' career.

the Great Panathenaia: the Panathenaia was an annual festival in honour of Athene at the end of Hekatombaion (roughly July). Every fourth year the festival was celebrated with special splendour and included athletic competitions which was inferior in importance only below the big four pan-Hellenic athletic venues (at Olympia, Delphi, the Isthmus and Nemea). It attracted competitors and, as the present passage shows, sightseers from all over Greece. The quadrennial festival was distinguished from the annual by the name Great Panathenaia. For further details see Parke 33ff., Simon 55-72.

Ktesippos the son of Glaukonides: otherwise unknown.

as though she were a courtesan: the ideal for Athenian women was that they should not come into contact with or be exposed to the gaze of males outside the family (see e.g. Eur.*Andr.*876-8, Lyk.*Leokr.*40). The extent to which this ideal reflects the real living conditions of Athenian women has recently been questioned by D. Cohen, 'The social context of adultery at Athens', *Nomos: studies in Athenian law, politics and society*, ed. Cartledge-Millett-Todd (Cambridge 1990) 147ff., and *Law, sexuality and society* (Cambridge 1991) 133ff. Certainly we know from Aristotle that strict seclusion did not extend in practice to the lower levels of Athenian society, where extra working hands were needed (cf. Arist.*Pol.*1300a6). We do not know how far up the social scale this applied. But the persistent treatment of seclusion as the norm in literary sources including the orators suggests that as far as possible Athenians did seek to prevent their wives coming into contact with male outsiders and likewise to avoid coming into contact with decent womenfolk unrelated to them (cf. 47.38, Eur.*I.A.*830 and see further Carey on Lys.3.6). Consequently when a man entertained guests to dinner the only females present would be courtesans or female musicians or dancers (these categories overlapped in practice; cf. Ar. *Wasps* 1345-6 with 1368-9); see esp. Isai.3.14.

25 Euphiletos: a member of a propertied family (Davies *APF* 360), of whom nothing else is known.

Aristomachos: wealthy (he served as trierarch at least once in the 370s) and politically active; in 353/2 he came to Athens as representative of the general Charidemos and the Thracian prince Kersobleptes (23.13f.), and in the late 340s we find him allegedly paying a substantial bribe to secure the passage of a measure concerning Tenedos (58.35). Cf. Davies *APF* 61-2.

WITNESSES: there is nothing in the content of this document to help us determine whether or not it is authentic. There is however one small detail of form which suggests that it is genuine. The phrase 'the defendant in this case' (lit. 'who is now on trial') which occurs here is found again in the depositions at §§28, 32, 34, 40, 47, 48. Whereas witnesses deposed in person during the fifth century, for most of the fourth century depositions presented at the trial were actually drafted by the litigant and not by the witnesses themselves (R.J. Bonner, *Evidence in Athenian courts* (Chicago 1905) 46-7). This recurring detail suggests a single hand, and the combined features of verbal repetitiveness and willingness to restate the obvious suggest the hand of Apollodoros. This conclusion is supported by the fact that the document in §40 is probably to be judged authentic on grounds of content.

26 Xenokleides the poet: a figure known only from this passage and 19.331, where we learn that he was residing in Macedon prior to 343, when he was ejected by Philip. For the significance of this passage for the date of the speech see Introduction 3. It is most suspicious that a man with a grudge against Stephanos should now be claiming to have enjoyed Neaira.

Hipparchos the actor: otherwise unknown. Kirchner *PA* 7599 (cf. Patteson) tentatively identifies him with the Hipparchos who appears in a list of victors in the competition for tragic actors at the Lenaia (*IG* ii^{2} 2325.263).

the laws do not allow him to testify: the penalty on conviction for failure to serve on an expedition for which one was liable (*astrateia*) was loss of citizen rights (*atimia*), that is exclusion from the agora, the public shrines and ceremonies, and debarment from addressing the Council, the Assembly or a lawcourt (Harrison II 171, MacDowell *Law* 73-5; cf. 21.95, Aischin.3.176, Lys.6.24).

27 when you were rescuing the Spartans: when a Theban army invaded the Peloponnese in 369 Sparta requested Athenian aid. Athens sent a force under Iphikrates, but part of the invading force had left Lakonia before he arrived, while the rest were able to slip by the Athenians; all he could do was harry the enemy on their march home (cf. Xen.*Hell*.6.5.49-52). Apollodoros' description is somewhat grandiose; his flattering language is meant to appeal to patriotic pride and so win the goodwill of the jury. It also reflects his hostility to Kallistratos (see next note).

Kallistratos: nephew of the politician Agyrrhios, Kallistratos was prominent in Athenian politics in the 370s and 360s. His first major political act was the prosecution of Andokides and his colleagues for proposing peace with Sparta in 391. He played a major role in organizing the Second Athenian Confederacy in the 370s. At the period in question he was the chief proponent of friendship with Sparta to counter the power of Thebes; he negotiated the peace with Sparta of 371. Kallistratos is reputed to be the orator who inspired Demosthenes to take up politics ([Plut.] *Lives of the Ten Orators* 844b, Souda *s.v. Demosthenes* 454 Adler). He was tried in absence in 361 and executed in the 350s on his return to Athens. See further Kirchner *PA* 8157, R. Sealy, *Historia* 5 (1956) 178ff. Apollodoros' hostility to Kallistratos is made clear already at 50.46ff., almost two decades before the trial of Neaira. Apollodoros later (§43) represents Stephanos as a tool of Kallistratos; the allegation is nowhere proved but on the basis of the present passage it is plausible. The prosecution of Xenokleides is another example of the use of the courts for political purposes, since the aim is clearly to dispose of a political opponent.

he had bought the two-percent tax on grain: all imports and exports were subject to a tax of two percent. This tax was farmed out by the *Poletai* (for whose duties see Arist.*Ath.Pol.*47.2-5) to the highest bidder (individual or group); the successful bidder's profit was the difference between the price paid to the state and the amount actually realized from the tax collection. At the beginning of the fourth century we find Andokides (1.134) buying the whole of the tax. More often it was purchased by a consortium (Andok.1.133) or auctioned by sections, as here with Xenokleides' purchase of the import tax on grain.

each prytany: according to Arist.*Ath.Pol.*47.3 there were different rules governing payment of sums due to the state from those who had leased taxes; some paid in instalments three times per year, others paid each prytany, others a lump sum in the ninth prytany. As one who had to pay each prytany, Xenokleides could not be absent from Athens for a prolonged campaign, and so he enjoyed exemption from service under the law. From 21.166 it seems that tax collection was widely seen as a means of evading service.

he was indicted for failure to serve: for the penalty under the *graphe astrateias* see above on §26. Anyone who stayed behind in Athens when listed for service risked prosecution by an enemy, even if he fell into an exempted category. So Demosthenes was prosecuted for missing the Euboian expedition of 348 because he was serving as choregos (21.103); a chorister at the same festival was likewise prosecuted for failure to serve in Euboia (39.16). The attitude taken by a litigant to such prosecutions varies according to his judgement of the veracity of the reason advanced for failure to serve, and this in turn depends on his rhetorical needs. Here Apollodoros accepts Xenokleides' excuse and disapproves of the prosecution, since it suits his purpose to represent Xenokleides as the victim of Stephanos' vindictiveness.

slandered: we have no evidence other than Apollodoros' narrative that events were exactly as described. Since the jury found for Stephanos, it is possible that Xenokleides' claim to exemption was dubious in some respect, though the conviction may simply reflect the unpopularity of the policy favoured by Xenokleides. The account of Stephanos' conduct agrees with that alleged in his prosecution of Apollodoros (§5); here as elsewhere Apollodoros strengthens his case by astute 'cross-referencing', i.e. by presenting mutually supporting allegations at different points in the speech in order to achieve a persuasive consistency.

28 **oath of disclaimer:** the role of the witness in court during the fourth century was confined to a verbal confirmation of the deposition in his name which had been read out by the clerk of the court. The alternative was to take an oath that he had not been present or knew nothing of the matter (cf. Pol.8.37 with Harrison II 143-4).

subpoena: the Greek verb is *kleteuein*. This process, which was intended to compel a reluctant witness either to depose or to take the oath of disclaimer, involved public proclamation by herald; the person so proclaimed was liable to a fine of one thousand drachmas. See Harrison II 139-41 and most recently S.C. Todd, *Nomos* (cited on §24 above) 24f.; see also Introduction n.38. The threat suggests that Hipparchos is a hostile witness; it is of course possible that this is a rhetorical ploy intended to add weight to the testimony by suggesting that the witness is no friend of the litigant for whom he appears.

29 **Timanoridas ... Eukrates:** otherwise unknown.

Nikarete was extravagant in her demands: pimps and brothelkeepers were stereotypes of unscrupulousness and rapacity in the ancient world; cf. e.g. Arist.*EN1*121b 40-43, Theophrast.*Char*.6.5, Terence *Heaut.Prol*.39. Aischines 1.188 says bluntly to a jury: 'you hate brothelkeepers'.

thirty minas: prices for slaves could vary enormously, according to skill and presumably age and physical condition. In Athens we hear (Dem.27.9) of artisans valued at three, five and six minas; Xen.*Mem*.2.5.2 gives figures of half a mina, two minas and five minas, and even a figure of one talent (sixty minas) for a mine overseer. Neaira's high price presumably reflects her skill in her trade and consequent celebrity (cf. §26), her estimated value to Nikarete (in terms of potential future revenue) and the strength of her admirers' feelings.

in accordance with the law of the city: may reflect some difference between Corinthian and Athenian law (Patteson); the words may be intended to sustain the impression of meticulous research, but equally they may be mere padding (cf. §40).

Such joint purchases for sexual purposes were not unknown in Athens; Lys.4 concerns two men who had acquired a female slave and agreed to share her favours, but who had quarrelled violently out of jealousy.

30 they did not wish to see her working in Corinth: as a perpetual reminder of their wilder days; they were also, as the context shows, motivated by genuine concern for Neaira

a thousand drachmas: a substantial discount, enough to purchase as many as three skilled slaves (preceding note) or (in Athens at least) a small house (§40). But it still left a large amount for Neaira to find. As Patteson notes, what we learn of Nikarete (§21) suggests that Neaira will have been allowed to keep little of her income while under Nikarete's ownership; she may have amassed some possessions by way of gifts from Timanoridas and Eukrates.

Phrynion of Paiania: a member of a wealthy family (Davies *APF* 143-4). Nothing is known of Phrynion beyond what we are told in this speech.

31 in contributions: N.'s solution was to raise an *eranos* (see on §8) from among her former lovers.

pay it for her: Neaira cannot simply pay the money over herself; since a slave lacks legal personality, a third party is required. This is presumably in accordance with Corinthian law, but Athenian law was the same on this point; cf. Ar.*Wasps* 1353 and see M.I. Finley, *Land and credit in ancient Athens*, 500 -200 B.C. (repr. New York 1973) 104-5.

32 on condition that she did not work in Corinth: since we later (§36) find Neaira nervous of violating this condition, it would appear that there was a penalty attached, perhaps (Gernet, Patteson) relapse into slavery. We find conditions (often quite strict) attached to manumission at Delphi, and in Athens too it is likely that conditional manumission was common; see Wyse on Isai.4.9, Harrison I 186.

Philagros of Melite: otherwise known only from two inscriptions of the mid fourth century (IG ii^2 4378, 6874).

DEPOSITION: even in the fourth century many major transactions were carried out without writing (cf. on §54 below); when making an oral agreement or fulfilling an obligation it was necessary to have witnesses to attest that the transaction had actually taken place. Philagros may have acted as Phrynion's witness. For authenticity see on §25.

33 treated her in an outrageous and reckless way: although Neaira is free, Phrynion treats her almost as a possession, allowing her no freedom of movement.

He also (by having intercourse with her in public and by taking her carousing) treats her as a common prostitute rather than a high class courtesan.

his carousals: the Greek uses the verb *komazein*, which like its cognate noun *komos* is used of a variety of occasions, but especially of a noisy progression through the streets by a group of drinkers to visit mistresses or other drinking parties; cf. esp.Ar.*Acharnians* 979ff., *Assemblywomen* 947ff., Plat.*Symp.*212d, Lys.4.7.

Chabrias of Aixone: an Athenian general whose distinguished military career lasted from the 390s until his death in battle at Chios in 357. Nepos *Chabr.*3.2 testifies to his fondness for good living. Dem.19.287 suggests that his private life was scandalous. See in general Kirchner *PA* 15086, Davies *APF* 560-1.

when he won in the Pythian Games ... with the chariot: the Pythian Games, second in prestige only to the Olympics, were held at Delphi every fourth year, in the second year of the Olympiad. Athletic victory was an established way for ambitious politicians to augment their popularity. J.K. Davies, *Wealth and the power of wealth in classical Athens* (New York 1981) 101ff. argues that during the fourth century this form of display declined in political importance.

the archonship of Sokratides: 374/3.

Kolias: the promontary at the south-eastern end of the Bay of Phaleron; site of a temple of Aphrodite. Perhaps this is the location of the 'grand house' of Chabrias (Hypereides fr.137; cf. Davies *APF* 561). It was at victory banquets such as this that the victory odes of Simonides, Pindar and Bakchylides, celebrating athletic successes in the first half of the fifth century, were performed.

There were many there who had intercourse with her: as with much else in the narrative, what is said here is tangential to the indictment; the aim is to arouse jury hostility by representing Neaira as either insatiable (cf. §22) or so jaded and degraded as to be insensitive to abuse and humiliation. It is a fine touch to include the slaves, a calculated appeal to basic prejudice. For all we know it may be true, though even if it were not it would be exceedingly difficult and time-wasting for the defence to disprove.

34 Chionides ... Euthetion: otherwise unknown.

DEPOSITION: for the authenticity of this document cf. on §25.

went to sleep: sloppy drafting; clearly Phrynion is to be understood as sleeping through the proceedings, but we are probably to understand that the other participants remained awake (Drerup 344) or slept only intermittently (Patteson).

35 Thratta and Kokkaline: another example of effective cross-referencing (cf. on §27), here preparing for Apollodoros' account of his challenge demanding the surrender of these slaves for torture (§§120, 124). The first of these names means

'Thracian (woman/girl)'; it was common for slaves to be named from their nationality.

Megara: its proximity to Athens made Megara a natural haven for runaways. Over fifty years before the flight of Neaira we find the Athenians complaining that the Megarians harbour escaped slaves from Attica (Thuc.1.139.2).

Asteios: 373/2.

your second war with Sparta: in 378 after a Spartan force under Sphodrias tried to seize the Peiraeus Athens allied herself with Sparta's enemy Thebes; peace was concluded in 374, but war broke out again almost immediately. Apollodoros refers here to the period of hostilities which began in 374.

36 The lengthy parenthesis and the series of participles (typical of Apollodoros; see Introduction 19) produce a rambling and disorganized sentence.

Alkisthenes: 372/1.

the Megarians are mean and petty: the Athenians generally had a low opinion of their Megarian neighbours; apart from the inevitable hostility to be expected between contiguous states (cf. Thuc.1.139, Dem.13.32, 23.212), we find the comic poets associating Megara with a crude and unimaginative brand of comedy (cf. Ar.*Ach.*738, *Wasps* 57, Ekphantides fr.3*PCG*, Eupolis fr.261 *PCG*). How accurate Apollodoros' claim is we cannot say. Certainly the Megarians were not poor in the fourth century, for Isokrates (8.117) credits them with the largest houses in Greece; but perhaps they preferred to use their money carefully. We have evidence of courtesans in Megara, but if Apollodoros is to be believed they derived much of their livelihood from the foreign merchants who would normally be found in a mercantile centre like Megara (cf. U.E. Paoli, *Uomini e cose del mondo antico* (Florence 1947) 97).

she could not return to Corinth: see on §32. Corinth was an obvious choice, on grounds both of proximity and of ambience (see on §18).

37 Phrasikleides: 371/0, year of the peace of Kallias.

Leuktra: the insistence of Athens and Sparta that Thebes allow the Boiotian cities to sign the peace treaty for themselves led to the exclusion of Thebes, which insisted on retaining control of Boiotia. The Spartan king Kleombrotos, who had occupied Phokis, marched on Thebes. In the battle of Leuktra (in Boiotia) which followed the Spartan army was defeated and Kleombrotos slain. This defeat put paid to Sparta's reputation for invincibility and marked the beginning of the decline of her power.

made Stephanos here her patron: probably (Gernet, Patteson) a reference to the patron (*prostates*) required for anyone registered in Athens as a metic. For a slave manumitted in Athens the patron would usually be the former master. See further on §40.

38 Stephanos spoke encouragement: we are offered no evidence that the conversation recorded here ever took place. Since this is a private conversation between Stephanos and Neaira, the account is probably conjectural. Our attention is diverted from this fact by the vivid and convincing picture of bravadoccio.
introduce the children she had at that time into his phratry: for the phratry see on §13. From §§118-21 and 124 it seems that the male children have received all the privileges due to Stephanos' sons by a citizen wife. The allegation that they are Neaira's children is never substantiated. Apollodoros seeks to convince instead by repetition; cf. §§13, 118ff. and see on §27 for this device. The girl Phano however probably is Neaira's child; cf. on §§50, 61.

This section raises two problems for the reader. The first concerns the ages and origins of these children (cf. Patteson). From the silence in §§30ff. one would suppose that there were no children with Neaira when she moved to Athens. The nature of Phrynion's treatment of her makes it unlikely that her relationship with him lasted long, probably a year (374/3) at most. So we should probably fix on 374 as the earliest date for her move from Corinth to Athens. Yet no more than four years later she has three children. This is physiologically unexceptionable, if we suppose that one was born in Athens (though §35 does not suggest that Neaira had an infant with her when she fled to Megara) or that one was conceived (but not born) in Athens, the others conceived and born in Megara, or again that all three were conceived and born during Neaira's two years in Megara and that two of the children were twins. But all of these conjectures remain implausible in view of two facts: i. Neaira was trying to work as a prostitute during her stay in Megara, a task which semi-permanent pregnancy would render almost impossible; ii. since she needed to maintain an attractive body for her work she had both an incentive and presumably the means to avoid childbirth (which would involve both subsequent stretchmarks and problems with weight and muscle tone). The rapidity with which Apollodoros disposes of this issue here prevents the hearer from registering these chronological problems.

Secondly, the third alleged son of Neaira, Antidorides (§§121, 124), is here ignored. Perhaps Antidorides' age made it implausible to represent him as a small child (the Greek here uses the diminutive *paidion*) in 371/0 (the fact that he was named after Stephanos' father may indicate that he was the oldest of Stephanos' sons), and so Apollodoros saw fit to suppress his name here. Alternatively, Apollodoros may have intended when composing this section of the narrative to represent all but Antidorides as Neaira's children but subsequently changed his mind (for a similar change of mind see on §124). Either way, the interval between §§38 and 121 would prevent a hearer from noting the discrepancy.

39 Whispering Hermes: the location of this statue is unknown. The lexicographers (Suda, Bekker *Anecd.*317.11ff.) state that there were also statues of Aphrodite and Eros with this title, and associate it with the legend of Phaidra's love for Hippolytos.

Dorotheos of Eleusis: a member of a propertied family (Davies *APF* 174); he is known to have served as trierarch in 366/5 and 357 and is mentioned at Isai.3.22.

Kleinomachos: known only from 58.42 as active in Athenian politics.

the house which Spintharos has since bought: the Greek is ambiguous; it is easier syntactically to refer this description to the house of Kleinomachos (as Gernet), but the run of the context favours a reference to the house of Stephanos. The casual mention of Spintharos suggests he is well known, possibly the son of the politician Euboulos, wose father's name was Spintharos.

the sum total of Stephanos' property: the insight into Stephanos' financial circumstances is intended to support the account in §§41-4 of his activities as a pimp, blackmailer and political hireling. If this little house was the sum total of Stephanos' property, we may accept in theory his need to supplement it as described below by Apollodoros, for seven minas was not a particularly high value for a house. However, we are given no evidence that the house was worth no more. Its proximity to properties of wealthy individuals may perhaps suggest that it was more substantial that Apollodoros suggests. Even if it was worth only seven minas, Apollodoros does not prove that this was Stephanos' sole property; Athenians both within and below (see Carey on Lys.1.9) the liturgical class might keep both a residence in Athens and a farm in the country, and §65 may indicate that Stephanos also owned land in the country (Patteson). Some doubt is cast on Apollodoros' claim here by Stephanos' social milieu at the time. Wherever we can identify Stephanos' associates (§§40, 45, 48), with the exception of Theogenes (§72; for Phrastor see on §54), they are found to be men of property; on the assumption (not certain but probable) that Stephanos mixes with people of his own social condition, it is doubtful that he is the pauper depicted by Apollodoros.

sycophant: the verb used here, *sykophantein*, and its cognate noun *sykophantes*, have no precise equivalents in English. The sycophant is basically someone who exploits the law for unfair or illegal gain. The activities covered by the term are very wide, including prosecution for profit in cases where the law allowed rewards to encourage volunteer prosecutors, prosecution for payment from people wishing to embarrass a personal or political enemy or to harass an opponent-at-law, extortion of money by means of the threat of prosecution, and more generally using legal and rhetorical expertise to pursue unjust prosecutions or to escape punishment when prosecuted. In Stephanos we have a prosecutor for hire, as already narrated in §10 and perhaps implied in §27, and a blackmailer, as narrated in §§43, 64ff. The accusation of sycophancy is never satisfactorily proved but gains strength from consistency; for the technique see on §27. For recent discussions of the sycophant see R. Osborne and D. Harvey in *Nomos, essays in Athenian law, politics and society*, ed. Cartledge-Millett-Todd (Cambridge 1990) 83ff., 103ff.

40 bringing some young men with him: it was normal when engaging in activity which might lead to litigation to take friendly witnesses (cf. 57.14, Isai.3.19); the choice of young men suggests further that Phrynion anticipated a fight. The precise legal basis for Phrynion's seizure of Neaira is unclear. A freedman/woman who failed to abide by the conditions of manumission or adopted a new patron in place of his former master was liable to a *dike apostasiou*, and if convicted might be reduced to slavery again (cf. Harpokration *s.v. apostasiou*, Harrison I 185). We do not know: i. whether the right of the former master to act as patron passed to an agent who advanced the sum stipulated for freedom; ii. whether Phrynion had acted as Neaira's patron during her previous stay in Athens; iii. how the legal position was affected by the fact that Neaira's emancipation took place in Corinth. Phrynion's action may be based on the law forbidding a change of patron. If so, the proper course would have been to bring a *dike apostasiou*. Alternatively, he may be claiming that Neaira has not paid her debt to the group who bought her freedom (it is possible that freedom could be revoked in such a case; see W.L. Westermann, *The slave systems of Greek and Roman antiquity* (Philadelphia 1955) 25, Patteson on §§31-2). Again presumably the appropriate course was to bring a *dike apostasiou* (*eranos* members, probably, as Finley (cited on §31) suggests, contributors to a collection for manumission such as that raised by Neaira, appear among the plaintiffs in *dikai apostasiou* in the lists of 'freedmen's bowls' dedicated after acquittal in such actions; acquittal in such cases would most naturally indicate discharge of the debt). However, Phrynion may simply be claiming Neaira untruthfully as a runaway slave, exploiting her weak position, as a woman (who cannot present her case in court) a foreigner (without a wide acquaintance in Athens to support her) and an ex-slave whose manumission took place abroad (and so might be difficult to prove in Athens) and whom Phrynion had publicly treated almost as his slave. On any of these hypotheses Phrynion may not have intended to enslave Neaira but to frighten her into becoming his mistress again. Phrynion's claim appears to have been juristically weak, for it was dismissed by the arbitrators (§46).

asserted her freedom: when a person was seized as a slave by someone claiming

to be the owner, it was open to a third party to oppose the seizure (Greek *aphaireisthai eis eleutherian*, lit. 'take away to freedom'). It was then open to the party claiming ownership to bring an action (*dike aphaireseos*) against the individual who prevented seizure. If the action was successful, the defendant had to pay a fine to the state equal to the value of the slave (58.19, 21; see Lipsius 639ff., Harrison I 178f., II 78, 81). When the summons was issued, the alleged slave's protector was compelled to provide surety to the Polemarchos that the alleged slave would actually appear in court. One of the Polemarchos' duties was the supervision of cases involving metics. This meant that (as here) the charge was originally laid with the Polemarchos, who then passed the case to the relevant court. The involvement of the Polemarchos in cases of dike aphaireseos is due to the fact that the alleged slave is usually claiming metic status (as a freedman/woman).
Aietes of Keiriadai: otherwise unknown.
DEPOSITION: since the individuals named as Stephanos' co-sureties are known only from inscriptions, we can be sure that this deposition is genuine.
Glauketes ... Aristokrates: members of propertied families. Of Glauketes himself we know nothing beyond what we are told here, but a Kleochares son of Glauketes of Kephisia (probably his brother) acted in 341/0 as guarantor of ships for Chalkis and was hieropoios around 330 (Kirchner *PA* 8647, Davies *APF* 89). Aristokrates was victorious choregos for the tragic competition at the Dionysia of 388/7, and held a priesthood at some point early in the fourth century. See Davies *APF* 60.

§§41-44 are a digression devoted to character assassination; the Phrynion affair is resumed in §45.

41 charged larger fees: for the effect of status (here allegedly that of a married citizen female) on prostitutes' rates compare §18. In addition, presumably a married woman could demand higher fees because of the risks she ran in committing adultery (cf. on §§85ff.). We are given no evidence that Stephanos and Neaira were (or claimed to be) married.
in blackmail: the Greek uses the root *sykophant-*; see on §39.
rich and unknown alien: chosen for ability to pay blackmail money and ignorance of Neaira's true status.
he would lock him up indoors and demand a large sum of money: the law gave a man considerable powers against another man caught having illicit sex with a woman under his tutelage and control (see in general Harrison I 32-7, MacDowell *Law* 124-5). The Greek term for the offence is *moicheia* and for the male offender *moichos*. In the case of close female relatives the aggrieved party could legally kill the offender on the spot. He could subject him to degrading treatment. (Popular

punishments according to comic writers included inserting radishes into the adulterer's anus and plucking his pubic hair using hot ash. The reliability of this evidence has been questioned by D. Cohen, *Zeitschrift der Savigny-Stiftung für Rechtsgeschichte, romanistische Abteilung* 102 (1985) 385-7, J. Roy, *LCM* 16 (1991) 73-6, since the orators are silent about such punishments. But given the different conceptions of decorum in the courts and on the comic stage the argument from silence is weak.) As an alternative the aggrieved party could bring a legal action (*graphe moicheias*). Another course open was to hold the offender to ransom. Stephanos and Neaira abused this last power as a source of income from blackmail. If they did in fact regularly practise this trick, then Stephanos has consistently represented Neaira as his wife. But no evidence is offered. The claim is however made more plausible by the inclusion of a similar allegation with reference to Phano (§§64ff.); for the technique see on §27.

42 neither Stephanos nor Neaira had any property: see however on §39.

43 not yet a public speaker: Greek *rhetor*, the term for a regular speaker in the Assembly. Although he received no stipend, the possibilities for financial reward from interested parties open to influential speakers meant that the *rhetor* was in effect a professional politician.
the sort who shout by the speaker's platform: that is, a member of a political claque whose role was to influence opinion in the Assembly. This passage gives a fascinating picture of the activities of the political hanger-on; cf. 13.20, 24.201, 203, Hypereides *Dem.* col.12. Aristophanes vividly describes such minor lights in his description of the successful fifth century politician Kleon at *Wasps* 1033 (=*Peace* 756) as a monster about whose head 'a hundred heads of cursed flatterers licked all around'. No evidence is adduced to support this description of Stephanos, which is one calculated to inspire contempt and hostility.
hire themselves to bring indictments: for Stephanos as hireling prosecutor cf. §10, and for the technique of cross-referencing cf. on §27.
denunciations: Greek *phasis*, a public action available in a variety of cases (Harrison II 218ff.). Since there was a reward (half of the fine estimated by the jury, the other half going to the state) for succesful prosecutors, this was the sort of action to appeal to a sycophant. (Our first encounter with the sycophant as a type, Ar.*Ach.*818ff., associates them with *phasis*.)
put their names to other people's proposals: in order to conceal the real source of a proposal in the Assembly. Apollodoros' own proposal concerning the theoric fund (§4) might well fall into this category.
Kallistratos of Aphidna: cf. on §27.

I shall tell you: the promise is not fulfilled; cf. on §19.

44 claiming to be an Athenian: hints and accusations of foreign extraction were common in Athenian political life, and need not be taken seriously. Apollodoros' real target is clearly visible in §§43-4.

45 and for receiving the property: since only one suit is mentioned here, presumably this was another source of dispute rather than a formal count in Phrynion's suit. It seems clear from §46 that Neaira was in fact still in possession of property belonging to Phrynion.
submit the dispute to their arbitration: there were in Athens two types of arbitration, public and private. All Athenian citizens were liable to to service as public arbitrators on reaching the age of fifty-nine. Most private cases went before a public arbitrator before going to court. In cases not subject to public arbitration, it was open to the parties to appoint mutually acceptable private arbitrators. Although it was possible to appeal to the courts against the judgement of a public arbitrator, the decision of a private arbitrator was binding on both parties, subject to the observation of certain procedures (see Harrison II 65). Here we have private arbitration.
Satyros: otherwise unkown. His brother Lakedaimonios may be the individual named at 57.8.
Saurias: a member of the liturgical class, known to us as the victorious choregos for the tribe Erechtheis in the middle of the century (Davies *APF* 488); cf. on §39.
Diogeiton: treasurer of Athene in 398/7, and also known from a naval list of 377/6 (*IG* ii^2 1388.5, 1392.5-6, 1604.2); cf. Kirchner *PA* 3794.

46 They met in the temple: for the use of temples for this purpose cf. 33.18, 36.15, 40.11. The venue would guarantee solemnity and freedom from interruption, besides of course providing space for the proceedings.
free and her own mistress: evidently any legal claim to ownership by Phrynion was dismissed by the arbitrators. There is still however some ambiguity in Neaira's position, in practice if not in law, since the arbitrators' decision includes the sexual use to be made of her person. The Greek (αὐτὴν αὑτῆς κυρίαν) indicates that Neaira has no male *kyrios* (for this term see on §52) to act for her; cf. Introduction 16.

47 DEPOSITION: for the question of authenticity see on §25.
SETTLEMENT: the full document is not cited, solely the section dealing with Neaira's sex life; it is a further indication of her degraded life that she can be shared

in this way. There is a formal discrepancy between the document here, which would most naturally describe a half-monthly change of hands, and Apollodoros' account in §46, where the language used suggests that Neaira changed hands every second day. The discrepancy could be a sign of forgery, though one would expect a forger to reproduce Apollodoros' words more or less exactly; moreover, common sense suggests that an arrangement along the lines of the text of the agreement (though requiring some adjustment to deal with those months with twenty-nine days) would be the most convenient for all concerned. Probably Apollodoros is being deliberately ambiguous, using language which could fit the arrangement described here but which suggests that Neaira was passed back and forth daily like an object.

48 the people who had supported each party: arbitration was conducted like a court hearing, with the parties producing witnesses and documents as well as narrative and argument.
she dined and drank with them as if she were a courtesan: see on §24. From the past tenses used in this chapter it seems that some other agreement was reached, as allowed in the settlement, unless Phrynion subsequently died; moreover, Apollodoros' prosecution and Stephanos' defence likewise assume that at the date of the present trial Neaira was living only with Stephanos. We are never told how this change came about. Phrynion simply disappears from the story. Indeed, we hear very little of Neaira herself for the rest of the narrative; in §49 the emphasis shifts to her daughter Phano.
Euboulos of Probalinthos: the distinguished politician. His appearance for Apollodoros is surprising, since Stephanos was representing the interests of Euboulos and his group in prosecuting Apollodoros in 348. It is possible that Euboulos has changed sides. See however Introduction 8.
Diopeithes: known elsewhere only as a member of a naval symmory between 356 and 340; see Davies *APF* 160.
Kteson: if Davies' identification is correct (*APF* 338), Kteson was a member of a propertied family. Cf. on §39.
WITNESSES: for the question of authenticity see on §25.

§§49-84 *The career of Phano*. For the rest of the narrative section Apollodoros has little to say of the actions of Neaira. Attention shifts to her daughter Phano. As well as contributing to the factual base for the prosecution, the account is calculated to arouse hostility against Stephanos, who is shown treating the laws, institutions and religion of the city with contempt.

§§49-63 *The Phrastor affair*. For the plausibility of Apollodoros' account see on

§54 and Introduction 11.

49 she was required to post bail before the Polemarchos: as Gernet notes (followed by Patteson), the fact that Neaira had to provide surety before the Polemarchos is not in itself evidence of her status, despite his responsibility for cases involving aliens, since the *dike aphaireseos* inevitably involved the Polemarchos.
Stephanos too has personally testified: that is, by his actions; for the terminology cf. on §62.

50 gave ... in marriage: no date is given, but what we know of ages for marriage suggests that Phano would be at least fourteen (see Lacey 162). If, as Apollodoros claims, Neaira took Phano to Stephanos' household as a small child in 371/0, then this incident (if it took place as narrated; cf. on §54) would be datable to about 360.
formerly known as Strybele but now Phano: since there were no birth registers or certificates in Athens, change of name was a matter of usage rather than legal formality. For the substitution of pet-name for given name cf. Isai.3.30, where we hear of a girl named Kleitarete in infancy but subsequently known as Phile. The name Phano is probably derived from *phainein*, 'show' (it would mean 'splendid one' or 'bright one'). Its connotations of visibility make it an unlikely one for a citizen female (cf. on §24), or indeed a decent woman of metic status; it is however an apt name for a *hetaira*. This supports the claim that Phano is Neaira's daughter; see further on §61.
with a dowry of thirty minas: as Patteson notes, this is a respectable amount for a well-to-do family. According to D. Schaps, *Economic rights of women in ancient Greece* (Edinburgh 1979) 78, available evidence suggests that dowry size ranged from just under 5% to 20% of the paternal estate. This would fix Stephanos' property at 150 minas on a conservative estimate, which would place him just short of the liturgical class. There is some inconsistency between the figure given here for the dowry and the picture of Stephanos' poverty in §§39-43. This is of course a decade after the return from Megara (see above); but in fact Apollodoros still represents Stephanos as poor subsequent to this event (§69).
Phrastor of Aigilia: known only from this speech.
a working man: Greek *ergates*, a term often used of a small-holder who works his own land, which may be what is intended here. It is surprising (and suspicious) to find a man of Stephanos' social milieu marrying a (pretended) daughter to a man who worked with his hands, particularly given the size of the dowry; see on §54.

51 he had ascertained that she was not Stephanos' daughter but Neaira's: we are not told how Phrastor found out Phano's parentage, nor why it took him a year to discover the truth.

while she was pregnant: included to prepare for the further development in §§55ff.

withheld the dowry: the dowry never belonged to the husband, and he had no right to retain it on dissolution of marriage, as the next chapter makes clear.

52 a suit for maintenance: Greek *dike sitou*. It was also possible to sue for the return of the dowry itself. One reason why the *dike sitou* might be preferred (Patteson) is that it might be difficult on occasion to secure repayment of the full amount at once. Success in a *dike sitou* in effect converted the dowry into a loan at a relatively high rate of interest (18%; 12% was the most common rate for non-maritime loans; for evidence and discussion see Millett 104ff.), thus offering some compensation for the withholding of the dowry, and at the same time providing an incentive for the husband to repay the lump sum.

at a rate of nine obols: i.e. nine obols per mina per month (the regular way of calculating interest), equivalent to eighteen per cent per annum.

the guardian: Greek *kyrios*. An Athenian female remained a minor all her life. She was always under the control and protection of a male, her *kyrios*. This was her father until she married, whereupon her husband became her *kyrios*; upon divorce her father, or if he was dead his heir, resumed this role. The *kyrios* acted for the woman in all legal matters; hence here it is the *kyrios* who sues for the dowry.

the Odeion: built by Perikles immediately southeast of the Acropolis and adjacent to the theatre of Dionysos. Its use as a lawcourt is attested already for the fifth century by Ar.*Wasps* 1109.

Phrastor brought an indictment: by bringing a more serious counter-suit Phrastor places his opponent at greater risk (it is a little like raising the stakes in a game of poker); this was an established way of embarrassing or frightening an opponent into dropping proceedings. For instance, Andokides (1.117ff.) claims that he was accused by Kallias on a capital charge while he and Kallias were involved in a legal battle for the hand of an heiress.

LAW: as Harrison I 26f. notes, the formulation of the law is imprecise. 'Anyone' means 'any Athenian'; 'related to him' might have been expressed more lucidly: 'as though she were of citizen birth'. The expression actually used suggests that no familial relationship between a citizen and an alien was formally acknowledged by Athenian law (cf. H.J. Wolff, *Traditio* 2 (1944) 70). For the loose drafting of Athenian laws cf. on §16. In favour of authenticity are two details independent of Apollodoros' paraphrase: the specific reference to loss of citizen rights and confiscation of property as the penalty and the mention of a reward for the prosecutor.

as for masquerading as a citizen: literally 'as for foreignness (*xenia*)', that is the illegal usurpation of citizen rights by an alien (for which see Introduction 3-4).

53 gave up his claim to the dowry: it is this action which Apollodoros regards as proof of Neaira's status; if Phano were Stephanos' daughter by an Athenian wife, he would not so readily give up so large a dowry.
Phrastor withdrew his indictment: to prevent indiscriminate prosecution in public actions there was a rule that a prosecutor who abandoned his action or who failed at the trial to obtain one fifth of the votes cast was liable to a fine of one thousand drachmas. (There is some evidence that he also lost the right to bring the same type of action again; however, the evidence is ambiguous, and MacDowell *Meidias* 328 may be right to accept the statement of Genethlios that partial disfranchisement of this sort was imposed only after a third dereliction; alternatively it may be that partial *atimia* of this sort was an additional penalty explicitly imposed in cases of frivolous prosecution for specific offenses rather than an automatic penalty in all public actions.) In this speech we have two alleged instances (here and §68) in which a *graphe* is withdrawn, with no suggestion of any penalty; see also 20.145. Moreover, it seems unlikely that Phrastor would so readily expose himself to a fine equal to one third of the dowry allegedly retained. In both cases in this speech the verb *anaireisthai* ('take up') is used; this appears to describe a formal termination of the action. Perhaps the law did not punish those who formally terminated a case, only those who failed to appear in court; or perhaps there was a time limit within which a prosecution could legitimately be dropped. G.M. Calhoun, *The Athenian clubs in politics and litigation* (Rome 1946) 59 n.6 suggests that the fine was not automatic but required the intervention of a volunteer prosecutor for its imposition.
compel him to give evidence: see on §28.

54 DEPOSITION: there are two features of this document which might lead one to suspect forgery: i. the deposition begins (as is usual) with the third person but ends with the first person; ii. Phrastor's account, while containing almost all the events found in the narrative, gives a different order (Apollodoros' order is: 1. Stephanos gives Phano in marriage to Phrastor, 2. Phrastor ejects Phano but 3. retains the dowry, 4. Stephanos sues Phrastor, 5. Phrastor indicts Stephanos; Phrastor's deposition omits 3 and gives the other events in the order 1, 2, 5, 4). As to the first problem, there is a similar shift in the challenge quoted in §124, which is probably genuine. We may simply have a case of sloppy drafting. The second problem is more significant. The answer may be (Drerup 347) that Phrastor insisted (as far as the deposition was concerned) on a version which presented him in the best possible light, by omitting the retention of the dowry and representing his *graphe* as intended to punish Stephanos rather than to keep the money. Certainly one would expect a forger to keep much closer to the preceding narrative.

A separate issue concerns the truth of the account verified by Phrastor. Since there was no register of marriages, the only proof that a marriage had ever taken place was the testimony of witnesses. It was normal for the bride's father and the groom to have witnesses present at the betrothal. If Phrastor married Phano, he would inevitably have provided himself with witnesses. In addition, it was common for the groom to hold a marriage feast for his phratry, either as a whole or just his close associates, and the witnesses to this event are elsewhere adduced to prove the existence of a marriage (57.43, Isai.8.18; contrast Isai.3.76). When Phrastor served his summons on Stephanos, he would inevitably under Athenian practice have taken witnesses with him. And of course the magistrates who received the suits of Stephanos and Phrastor would be able to testify to that effect (cf. §40, 58.8-9). Since Stephanos is here accused of an offence punishable by disfranchisement and confiscation of property, it is in Apollodoros' interests to provide witnesses to prove that events were as he describes. Instead we have only Phrastor's testimony that the marriage took place or that there was any legal action between Stephanos and Phrastor. This is highly suspicious. One's suspicions are increased by the striking disparity between the social positions of groom and father-in-law. We are given evidence below (§61) of a connection between Phano and Phrastor. But she may only have been Phrastor's mistress. This would not in itself rule out the possibility of Stephanos settling a sum of money on Phrastor as a quasi-dowry to provide Phano with some security (for such arrangements see Isai.3.39 with Harrison I 14). But where so much is suspect it is difficult to construct a plausible hypothesis.

55 genos: membership of genos, as of phratry, was confined to legitimate male issue. However, the genos was more exclusive than the phratry. Originally these bodies were aristocratic, though by the fourth century membership of a genos presupposed neither social eminence nor great wealth. It appears to have been common for a single genos to form the nucleus of a phratry (A. Andrewes, *JHS* 81 (1961) 1-15), as in the present case (§59).

he fell ill: as Patteson notes, the presentation of Neaira and Phano is calculated to prejudice the jurors against them. They prey on Phrastor's fears and exploit his illness for their own advantage. It should however be noted that the account of their behaviour is not supported by any testimony; cf. on §61.

he was childless: that is, he had no legitimate issue (the alleged marriage with Phano was invalid because of her status). If he left no will his estate would go to his kin (for the order of succession see Harrison I 130ff.). Since he had no legitimate children, he was free to dispose of his property by will; but to let his

oikos die out in this way was scarcely preferable (cf. on §57). The obvious course was to adopt a son or to confer spurious legitimacy on his bastard by the alien Phano. The latter was illegal, but convenient for a sick man.
acknowledge as his son: an Athenian father was not obliged to admit even legitimate children to his family. If he chose to do so, he signified this at the *amphidromia* (literally 'running around'), a ceremony held shortly after birth in which the infant was carried around the family hearth (see Harrison I 70f.). This is probably what Apollodoros has in mind here. The law explicitly excluded bastards from membership of the *oikos* (Harrison I 66).

57 to prevent ... himself from dying childless: the Greeks had a horror of dying childless and so allowing the *oikos* to die out. The reasons were partly economic (a reluctance to allow property to pass outside the family), partly religious and emotional. Inheritance involved not merely succession to the family property but also maintenance of the family cults, prominent among which were the annual offerings to the family dead. The importance of the desire to receive these offerings as a factor in ensuring a succession is attested elsewhere (cf. Isai.2.10, 46, 7.30). The importance of maintaining *oikoi* was recognized by the state; one of the duties of the archon was to take care of *oikoi* which were in danger of extinction (43.75, Isai.7.30).

58 legitimate daughter: since in all probability illegitimacy was not a bar to citizenship and therefore the right to marry a citizen, provided that both parents were Athenian citizens (this issue is controversial; for a recent discussion which argues against the view taken here, with bibliography of the debate, see C. Patterson *Classical Antiquity* 9 (1990) 40-73), this detail is irrelevant from the legal point of view. However, Apollodoros is at pains to heighten the contrast between the alleged marriage with Phano and the subsequent marriage. Since the matter is not directly relevant to the main issue, we should probably draw no conclusion from the absence of evidence for this marriage.
Satyros ... Diphilos: otherwise unknown.

59 introduce his child ... into his phratry and into the Brytidai: the process of acknowledging a child was a gradual one, involving a whole series of acts from infancy to adulthood. After admitting a son to the family, the father next introduced him to his phratry (and where appropriate genos); finally he introduced him to his deme at the age of eighteen. For the process of phratry enrolment see on §13. From the present passage it seems that enrolment in both phratry and genos took place on a single occasion and therefore that the Brytidai formed part of Phrastor's genos (cf. on §55). It is possible that rejection by the genos applied to the phratry also; cf. Andrewes (cited on §55) 6.

refused to register him among themselves: phratry and genos, like deme, had a register of members. A son of Phano and Phrastor could not belong to phratry or genos, since he was neither legitimate nor of citizen status.

60 Phrastor brought a suit: in cases where a youth was rejected by his deme, the law allowed for appeal to the courts. But phratry and genos had no legal significance. Hence all Phrastor could do was bring a private suit. Possibly this was an action for damages (*dike blabes*).

challenged him: formal challenges played an important part in Athenian litigation. They could be issued at any time before the charge was lodged (as a means of avoiding litigation) or (in private cases) once the charge was lodged at any time before arbitration was completed. Challenges took various forms. They could consist of a demand that the opponent fulfil an obligation or accept fulfilment of an obligation, a demand that the opponent submit his slaves for examination or accept the examination of the challenger's slaves (cf. on §§120-4 below), or (as here) that the opponent either swear an oath or accept an oath from the challenger (see in general Harrison II 135-6, 148-9, 150-1, 153). Ostensibly the purpose of the challenge is to avoid litigation or to obtain fresh evidence. In reality challenges are usually issued in the confident expectation that the opponent will decline; since challenges can be introduced as evidence at the trial, the effect is to give the challenger a moral advantage in court.

in the presence of the arbitrator: a public arbitrator (as the absence of any indication of an agreement to arbitration, the mention of a single arbitrator, and the failure to provide any name indicate); cf. on §45.

that he believed the child to be his son by a woman of citizen birth given in marriage to him in accordance with the law: it appears that the father had to swear an oath to this effect when introducing the son to the phratry (57.54, Isai.8.19). Given this fact, and since we find a challenge to swear an oath in the context of a suit concerning disputed parentage or status (39.1, Isai.12.9), Phrastor must have known, as Patteson observes, that he would face such a challenge; so it is difficult to see why, having pressed ahead with his action, he should now hesitate; she suggests that Phrastor may have refused to swear the oath because he was already contemplating the marriage mentioned in §58. Another possible explanation is that the lawsuit is an invention; see on §61.

declined the oath: we are left to understand that the arbitrator found for the genos and that Phrastor did not appeal to a court.

61 WITNESSES: of the witnesses named here, Euphranor is known from an inscription to have served as an arbitrator in the mid-fourth century (*IG* ii[2] 1927.176-7), Nikippos is known to have served as syntrierarch in 322 (Davies *APF* 408, Kirchner *PA* 10833) and to have contributed to a religious dedication in the 320s (*IG* ii[2] 1251). Eualkes has been identified with a Eualkos of Phaleron known from an inscription of 322 (*IG* ii[2] 373.20); this may well be correct, but absence of patronymic makes the identification too uncertain to justify altering the manuscript text. Fortunately, the identification of two figures known only from inscriptions is sufficient to guarantee the authenticity of the document.

If these witnesses are telling the truth, which we have no reason to doubt, there is good evidence for Phrastor's association with Phano, for his unsuccessful attempt to introduce a son believed to be by Phano into his genos, and for a widespread belief that Phano was Neaira's daughter. But the deposition does not substantiate the account of the machinations of Neaira and Phano in §§55ff. or the account of the Phrastor's suit against his genos in §60. Nor does it define the nature of the relationship between Phrastor and Phano; the testimony here is consistent with the supposition that Phano was Phrastor's mistress. We read in Isai.6.21ff. of a man who introduced the son of a prostitute into his phratry as his own (presumably by swearing falsely that this was his son by a wife of citizen status). Such fraud was always possible, and a childless man might well wish to perpetrate it. Be that as it may, Apollodoros still fails to inculpate Stephanos.

62-63 *Résumé of the Phrastor affair.* These chapters display two features common in the speech as a whole. The first is repetitiveness; the summary of §§50-61 is approximately one sixth of the length of the actual narrative. The second is longwindedness in sentence construction.

62 have themselves testified: that is, by their actions. Properly circumstantial evidence of this sort is termed a *tekmerion* ('indication') not *martyria* ('testimony'). The choice of terminology glosses over the paucity of testimony (in the literal sense) for these events. Cf. on §§49, 93, 122, 125.

64-71 *The Epainetos affair.* Here the emphasis falls entirely on the real target, Stephanos. For the plausibility of the account see on §71 and Introduction 11.

64 that this woman Neaira is a foreigner: nothing which is said in this section of the narrative has any bearing on the question of Neaira's status. The role which Stephanos allegedly claims with respect to Phano is however relevant to the question of Neaira's relationship with Stephanos; see Introduction 9-11. And the

account serves to scandalize the jury and arouse hostility against Stephanos.
Epainetos of Andros: known only from this speech.

65 invited him to the country on the pretext of making sacrifice: the location is chosen in order to isolate Epainetos and place him at Stephanos' mercy. Stephanos may have had a country house (Patteson); cf. on §39.
caught him in adultery with the daughter of Neaira: the Greek root *moich-*, which is used here, is broader than the inadequate translation 'adultery' (cf. on §41); hence Stephanos' ability to exercise his rights under *moicheia* law with respect to a (female dishonestly represented as a) daughter; cf. on §41 and see Introduction n.40. The account of Stephanos' alleged trick gains in plausibility from its consistency with the allegation in §41. The same is true of the specific sum of thirty minas, which immediately suggests an attempt to recoup the sum lost to Phrastor (§50); this is made explicit in §69. For the technique see on §27.
extorted a ransom: see on §41.
Aristomachos ... Nausiphilos: otherwise unknown.
Nausinikos: archon in 378/7.

66 he is liable to no penalty and his sureties are quit of their bail: surprisingly there is no suggestion of any penalty for wrongfully imprisoning a man as a *moichos*. Given the fullness of his account of the law and the fact that §68 appears to envisage only exposure as the danger threatening Stephanos, it seems unlikely that Apollodoros has simply omitted this detail. Perhaps the victim would normally seek financial compensation through a private suit or a *graphe hybreos* (for this action see Carey-Reid 75f. with references; for its use in a case of imprisonment cf. Isai.8.41).
treat him as he chooses in the court, short of using a knife: as noted on §41, physical abuse was one of the options open to the aggrieved party who caught a *moichos* in the act. The aggrieved party retains this right in the event of an unsuccessful action for wrongful imprisonment. The option to kill (or even to wound) is no longer open, presumably because the victim waived this right in agreeing to a ransom. The unsuccessful prosecutor is punished for his temerity by the immense publicity now given to his humiliation. Whether the ransom agreed was also to be paid (as one would imagine) is not clear.

67 denied being an adulterer: the defence is based on three arguments. i. Phano was not Stephanos' daughter but Neaira's; so Stephanos was not her *kyrios* (for this term see on §52) and therefore had no right to confine Epainetos. ii. Neaira knew about the affair. Lysias 1.37 indicates that the right to kill was forfeited if the

adulterer was enticed into the house; the present passage suggests further that collusion in the affair removed any right to satisfaction. iii. Phano was a prostitute and as such was explicitly excluded from the categories of women covered by the law on *moicheia*. The *moichos* must actually have threatened the *oikos*, which he can only do if the woman he seduces is chaste (an unmarried girl or decent matron). Unless it is implicit in his first argument, Epainetos apparently did not cite the status of Neaira and Phano as part of his defence; this suggests that non-citizen females were covered by *moicheia* law as well as women of citizen status.
with any women who ... parade publicly: a quotation from the law (cf. Lys.10.19); hence the verb *poleisthai* (translated here 'parade'), which by the classical period at least was confined to poetry, and (according to the text adopted here) the old form of the dative plural feminine ταύτῃσι.
this was what Stephanos' house was, a brothel: this claim has already been made §§39, 41-2; it is never substantiated.

68 a brothelkeeper: for ancient attitudes to this type see on §29.
submitted his dispute ... to the arbitration of the very men who had acted as surety: it is surprising that Stephanos accepted as arbitrators two men close enough to Epainetos to have stood bail for him; contrast §45, where each side has its own representatives on the board of arbitrators. Possibly, as Patteson suggests, Stephanos made this concession in order to induce Epainetos to accept arbitration. However, it does not seem that Stephanos faced any penalty in the trial (see on §66), while in the (perhaps unlikely but not inconceivable) event of failure Epainetos did; so Stephanos was not necessarily at a disadvantage.

69 Epainetos withdrew his indictment: see on §53.
his poverty: see however on §50.
the fact that he had lost her dowry: see on §65. Though there was no legal requirement to give a dowry, it was customary (Harrison I 48f.), and many passages in the orators indicate that the absence of a dowry was a severe disadvantage (cf. §8 above). As Patteson notes, Phano's character as described by Apollodoros would make a dowry vital.

70 you have besides had the use of the girl: the use of direct statement adds vividness and so makes the account more persuasive; cf. §§82, 110.
a thousand drachmas: instead of the thirty minas (three thousand drachmas) demanded by Stephanos. In exchange (§71) Epainetos gets to use Phano whenever he is in Athens. For the arrangement disposing of the favours of a free woman cf. §46.

71 WITNESSES: we have no means of testing the authenticity of this document. However, given its connection with the following settlement document, which is probably genuine (since it includes one detail which could not have been fabricated from Apollodoros' speech, the clause that Epainetos is to have access to Phano when in Athens), we may accept what we have as the document presented at the trial.

It is striking that no evidence from Epainetos is introduced. That Epainetos does not appear in person is not in itself surprising; since he was probably a trader, certainly a foreigner, it might be difficult for him to come to Athens for the trial. But there was a procedure (*ekmartyria*) available to enable testimony to be obtained from people who were sick or abroad; under this procedure the witness deposed to a proxy witness, who then attested in court that the original witness had given the testimony adduced (cf. Harrison II 146-7, MacDowell *Law* 243). Epainetos' testimony could have been obtained in this way during one of his seemingly frequent visits (§§64, 67, 71). It is also noteworthy that no witnesses to the original incident are cited. From Lys.1 it is clear that anyone seeking to trap a *moichos* would arrange for witnesses to the act; even someone abusing the law (as Stephanos allegedly did) would need witnesses to prevent his victim upon release denying that the capture took place. The summons witnesses who accompanied Epainetos when he formally summonsed Stephanos could also have been called, and likewise the magistrate who received Epainetos' *graphe* (cf. §40). Finally, at the arbitration Epainetos presumably introduced witnesses to prove that Phano was Neaira's daughter and that she was a prostitute; these too could have been adduced to confirm the outlines of Apollodoros' account. Since this incident would prove that Stephanos represents Phano as his daughter, it is important for Apollodoros to prove that his account is true. The dearth of witnesses suggests, though it does not prove, that he is inventing.

72-84 *The Theogenes affair.* Though logically placed last according to chronological order, this incident is also well placed for effect as the climax in Stephanos' duplicitous use of Phano, involving not merely breach of marriage law but a sacrilege dangerous to the whole city. For the plausibility of the account see on §87 and Introduction 11.

72 Theogenes of the Koironidai: unknown apart from this speech. The manuscripts give Κοθωκίδην, 'Theogenes of Kothokidai'; but Theogenes' deme is given at §84 as Erchia. The correction accepted in the text introduces a reference to the genos Koironidai, which agrees with the mention of Theogenes' noble birth.

drawn: i.e. selected by lot; for the selection of the archons see Arist.*Ath.Pol.*8.1, 55.1.

King-Archon: Greek *basileus* (lit. 'king'). The duties of the King-Archon (as described by Arist.*Ath.Pol.*57 with 47.4) were primarily religious. He superintended the Eleusinian Mysteries and the Lenaia, arranged all torch-races and administered the majority of ancestral sacrifices. He superintended land belonging to the gods. The cases over which he presided likewise had a religious emphasis, trials for impiety, disputes concerning priesthoods or matters of ritual, homicide cases.

at his examination: for the *dokimasia* see on §3. At their *dokimasia*, which was conducted by the Council, the Archons-elect were asked a series of questions intended to establish birth-qualifications and moral character (see Arist.*Ath.Pol.*55.3.). The candidates introduced witnesses and objections were invited; in the event of an objection, the Council listened to both sides and then voted; any candidate who was rejected could appeal to the courts. The help referred to here could consist of general advice on the *dokimasia* process, including details such as the choice and presentation of witnesses, appearance as witness or (if an objection was lodged) assistance with the presentation of the case.

assisted with expenses: each Archon received a daily maintenance-allowance of four obols (two thirds of a drachma), which may also have had to cover the maintenance of a herald and a flute player (Arist.*Ath.Pol.*62.2 is ambiguous). Even if the allowance was for the Archon alone, it would not meet his personal expenses (which would expand with his new position to include appropriate clothes, furniture and entertainment costs), and so a man of modest means might welcome financial help. The claim that Stephanos provided financial assistance to Theogenes does not square with his alleged poverty.

assessor: the Archon, King-Archon and Polemarchos each had two assistants, *paredroi* (Arist.*Ath.Pol.*56.1), whom they selected themselves. An Archon with no adminisitrative experience could thus (as in the present case) use the selection to obtain the guidance of men with appropriate expertise.

gave this woman to him in marriage: dynastic arrangements of this sort were not uncommon. Since there were important duties prescribed for his wife, one would suppose that only a married man was eligible to serve as King-Archon. Apollodoros presumably intends us to understand therefore either that the marriage took place between ballot and *dokimasia* or that Theogenes had an existing wife whom he divorced after his *dokimasia* in order to marry Phano.

73 the secret offerings: specifically if not exclusively those at the Anthesteria, a festival held on the 11th, 12th and 13th of Anthesterion (roughly February). For details of the festival see Parke 107ff., Simon 92-9. The role of the King-Archon's wife (whose title was *basilinna*, 'queen') was confined to the 'Feast of Pitchers' (*Choes*) on the second day, on which she made secret offerings on behalf of the city; no details of the ritual are known. The climax was a wedding ceremony in which she was given in marriage to Dionysos.

as representative of the city: since by tradition the gods could punish the whole community for the impiety of an individual (cf. Hesiod *Works and Days* 240f. with West's note), the choice of mediators between the city and its gods was very important. As Apollodoros makes explicit elsewhere (§74; cf. 109, 126), the alleged offence threatens the whole city and not merely the guilty parties. The hostility aroused by the breach of the marriage law and abuse of citizen rights is thus accentuated by religious fear.

the Venerable Women: Greek *gerarai*. These priestesses assisted with the secret rites on the second day of the Anthesteria, and participated in other festivals (cf. §78, Bekker, *Anecd.*I,231,2, Hesych. s.v., Pol.8.108, *Et.M.*227,36); according to the lexicographers, there were fourteen, one for each altar in the sanctuary. The oath is quoted at §78.

was given as bride to Dionysos: although the secret offerings were made in the precinct of Dionysos in the Marshes, the marriage took place at a building called the Boukoleion, which was situated near the Prytaneion in the agora (Arist.*Ath.Pol.*3.5).

74-77 *Digression on the history of the role of the Basilinna.* Apollodoros stresses the antiquity and solemnity of the laws and customs flouted by Stephanos, in order to appeal to the strong sense of tradition shared by the Athenians with the Greeks in general. It is not clear whether Apollodoros is drawing on a particular written source or on oral tradition.

74 because they were indigenous: the account is slightly garbled, since it was a source of pride that the entire population of Attica (not only the kings) was native to the territory rather than incomers (Hdt.1.56.2, Thuc.1.2.5). Trevett *CQ* 40 (1990) 418 suggests a borrowing from Thuc.6.2.2.

the king performed all the sacrifices: an inevitable conclusion from the role of the King-Archon in the historical period. For the King-Archon as successor to the kings cf. Arist.*Ath.Pol.*3.

75 united the people in one city: the unification of Attica was ascribed by tradition to Theseus; cf. Thuc.2.15.2, Isok. *Hel.* 35.

created a democracy: anachronistic but not idiosyncratic, for the tradition that Theseus laid the foundations for democracy is found elsewhere (cf. Isok.*Hel.*35-6,

*Panath.*129, [Dem.]60.28, Arist.*Ath.Pol.* cited in Plut.*Thes.*25), and is present already in the fifth century (Eur.*Suppliants* 352-3, 403-8); it may have originated with attempts by the democratic reformers to gain the support of tradition for their constitutional changes.

the people nonetheless continued to choose the King by show of hands from men preselected on grounds of excellence: the point of 'nonetheless' is presumably that despite the (supposed) creation of a democracy the importance of the office of King-Archon was still marked by exclusivity. According to the prevailing traditions, the kingship came to an end either on the death of Kodros or after his son Medon. Either Apollodoros telescopes the period between Theseus and the abolition of the kingship or he believed that Theseus was the last of the kings. Apollodoros may be following a strand of Athenian tradition in presenting the selection of the King-Archon under the post-Thesean constitution as popular election from a preselected list (the evidence is slender and ambiguous; see M.H. Hansen, *CP* 81 (1986) 224f.). However, he may (as suggested by J.C. Trevett, *CQ* 40 (1990) 418) be conflating popular election with selection by lot from a preselected list, which according to Aristotle (*Ath.Pol.*8) was introduced by Solon (this issue is controversial; see most recently M.H. Hansen, *CM* 41 (1990) 55ff.).

his wife should be of citizen birth: before 451/0 the wife of of an Athenian would not necessarily be of Athenian birth; see Introduction 3.

a virgin: this prescription would rule out women who had been widowed or divorced.

76 the temple of Dionysos in the Marshes: location not certain, but possibly in the Ilissos area south of the Acropolis (Travlos *PDA* 184, 332).

faint Attic characters: refers to the local Attic script, which was officially replaced by the Ionic alphabet in 403. Given the other borrowings from Thucydides in this speech (see on §§94-104), the resemblance to Thuc.6.54.6 (who however is referring to a different inscription) probably reflects borrowing by Apollodoros (cf. Trevett (cited on §75) 419). He may mean that the inscription was worn, but (Patteson) since the inscription similarly described by Thucydides is still legible something else may be intended; Meiggs-Lewis 20 suggest the erosion of the paint with which the inscribed letters were picked out.

so that the inscription would not be known to many: probably the reason for placing the inscription in Dionysos' precinct was that it dealt with Dionysiac ritual; it was not until late in the fifth century that Athens acquired anything remotely resembling a central state archive (Thomas 38f.).

it is opened up once each year: as Parke 110 notes, Greek temples were for public worship, not private prayer; hence unlike many Christian churches they were kept locked when not in use.

the twelfth day of Anthesterion: this statement is problematic, since another ceremony (the *Pithoigia*, 'jar-opening') evidently took place at the Limnaion on the eleventh day of Anthesterion, the first day of the festival. Parke 111 resolves the difficulty by suggesting that the part of the *Pithoigia* involving the Limnaion took place on the evening of the first day; he notes that for the Greeks the day began at sunset.

77 so that others will take care: Greek litigants regularly ask the jurors to consider the example their verdict will set; cf. 21.227, Lys.1.47, Lyk.*Leokr.*150.

78 the Sacred Herald: an official of the Eleusinian Mysteries, with which Dionysos was connected; this official was always drawn from the Kerykes ('Heralds') family (cf. on §21). There is no reason to doubt (with Patteson) that this individual was called as witness; it would be very injudicious of Apollodoros to draw attention explicitly to a potential witness without calling him (moreover, one would expect βουλοίμην ἄν/ἐβουλόμην ἄν, 'I could wish/could have wished', not βούλομαι, 'I wish'). See further on §84.

at the baskets near the altar: the baskets will have contained either offerings for Dionysos or (if animal sacrifice is involved) a knife for the slaughter and barley to sprinkle on the victim's head.

the oath and the words which are spoken: since only the oath is actually given, perhaps (Patteson) the other utterances could not be divulged; however, the Greek could mean 'the words which are spoken in the oath'.

OATH: since it contains details which are obviously independent of the narrative, this document is probably genuine. However, we may not have the whole of the oath, but only the clauses (from those which may be divulged) relevant to Apollodoros' aim, which is evidently to stress the purity enjoined by the oath, in contrast to the impurity of the woman who administers it.

including intercourse with a man: sexual abstinence, even for a restricted period, is rarely attested in Greek religion; see R. Parker, *Miasma* (Oxford 1983) 85ff.

Feast of the Wine God: Greek *Theoinia*. According to Harpokration (s.v.) that was a feast of Dionysos celebrated in the demes and involving sacrifice by each genos.

Rites of Bakchos: Greek *Iobakcheia*, a title derived from the ritual cry to the god (*Iô Bakche*). Nothing is known for certain about this festival.

79 a testimony: the terminology is chosen to give weight to what is in fact only unsubstantiated allegation (see on §62); the claim that the following incident took place in secret is meant to explain the lack of hard evidence.

80 had gone up to the Areopagos on the appointed days: at the end of their year of office the archons became members of the Areopagos for life. It is unlikely that Apollodoros refers to this, since from the subsequent dismissal of Stephanos by Theogenes (§83) it seems that the latter's term of office had not yet expired (Rhodes 674f.). Apollodoros seems to envisage a report by the archons during their period of office, perhaps as Patteson suggests at a meeting of the Areopagos to examine the conduct of the Anthesteria. The conduct of the Dionysia and a number of other festivals were examined by the Assembly (21.8,9), but in view of their antiquity the Anthesteria may have been covered by distinct, and older, procedures.
enquired about the identity of the wife of Theogenes: no reason is given for this sudden interest by the Areopagos in the wife of the King-Archon.
they do not have the power to punish an Athenian citizen as they please: the Areopagos had exercised considerable power, including supervision of the magistrates, prior to the democratic reforms of Ephialtes in the fifth century, which had left them with a judicial role in a limited range of offences. Within this range the penalties were severe. But the present case apparently fell outside their judicial competence. It is not clear what penalties they could impose on their own initiative. The Areopagos was not however obliged to impose an inadequate penalty. It could have passed the issue to the assembly or to the courts, using the procedure of *apophasis* (Harrison II 105, MacDowell *Law* 190f.); alternatively one or more members of the Areopagos could have prosecuted Stephanos and Phano before a court.

82 I shall prove to you I am not lying: for the use of direct statement cf. on §70.

83 the magistrate's board: Greek *synedrion*; that is (Gernet) the board made up of the magistrate and his two assessors.

84 I shall force him to give evidence: suggests a reluctant witness. This may be a rhetorical device (cf. on §§28, 53); as an enemy of Stephanos, one would expect Theogenes to welcome an opportunity to harm him, though anyone who had been duped as Theogenes allegedly had might well hesitate between desire for revenge and reluctance to be thought a fool.
DEPOSITION: we have no means of determining the genuineness of this document on internal grounds, but the cumulative evidence of the other documents attached to this speech tells in favour of authenticity. One striking feature of the document is its silence about the examination by the Areopagos. Theogenes admits only to having married Phano in ignorance, divorced her and dismissed Stephanos. The account in

§§80-3 is therefore not supported by Theogenes. In addition Apollodoros could have called upon members of the Areopagos to confirm his account, and Theogenes' other assessor (and possibly Stephanos' replacement, if another appointment was made) could have confirmed the fact and circumstances of Stephanos' dismissal by Theogenes. Apollodoros thus provides no reason to believe his account of the Areopagos incident. But even where it does support Apollodoros, Theogenes' deposition is unsatisfactory. Theogenes testifies that he was married to Phano. This marriage if it took place will have been witnessed (cf. on §54); yet no witness other than Theogenes is adduced. In addition, evidence could have been obtained from others involved in the ceremonies allegedly conducted by Phano. The priestesses could not have testified personally in court; but a woman's guardian (*kyrios*) could testify on her behalf. The Basilinna was presumably seen by many people when she was escorted to the Boukoleion to be married to Dionysos; yet none of these testifies. More significantly, the Basilinna was assisted by the Sacred Herald when she received the oath of the Venerable Women. This official was actually produced in court by Apollodoros (§78) to testify to the content of the oath. Yet apparently he was not asked to confirm that Phano was ever Basilinna.

The reader's dissatisfaction with Apollodoros' account is reinforced by a consideration of the extent of the conspiracy of silence it presupposes. The penalties for impiety were severe. For instance, a woman named Theoris was condemned to death for using magic (Dem.25.79f.); a priestess called Ninos was condemned to death for using magic and for attempting to introduce a new religious cult (Dem.19.281). In Phano's case we have an extreme case of impiety. Phano is disqualified both by birth and by character from being Basilinna. Yet she has been acting as mediator between the Athenian people and its gods. Her crime is much more serious than those of Theoris and Ninos. Yet no action is taken. More significantly, Stephanos could have been prosecuted both for betrothing a foreign female to an Athenian citizen and more importantly for impiety. As Theogenes' assistant Stephanos like other public officials was subject to an examination (*euthyna*) on demitting office (Arist.*Ath.Pol.*56.1). This was an obvious occasion to attack him. As a political figure he had enemies (this we know from the number of public figures appearing against him); yet none of these saw fit to act. Apollodoros disposes of this problem by claiming that the events involving the Areopagos took place in secret. This does not however explain why he himself, despite his knowledge of a well-attested offence for which his enemy could have been severely punished, has used this serious crime solely in his prosecution of Neaira instead of attacking Stephanos directly. Moreover, the secrecy surrounding these events, while it does not surprise the modern reader, accustomed to the use of secrecy as a cloak for abuse and incompetence by governments of every political colour, is itself problematic in the context of a society which lacked the modern concept of government as a narrow, cohesive and continuous administration. This was simply an offence committed by individuals. It is difficult to see why a body traditionally concerned with matters of religion should suppress so heinous a crime, which threatened the relationship between the city and its gods, and thus leave it unpunished. They might well decide to take no action against Theogenes as Stephanos' dupe; but they had no reason to treat Stephanos leniently. And even if the Areopagos as a body declined to take action, it is difficult to see why no individual member took any further action. Any individual could bring an indictment for impiety (*graphe asebeias*) against Stephanos or proceed against him by *eisangelia* (laying information before the assembly, a procedure available for offences against the state, including impiety; this procedure was used after the mutilation of the Herms in 415). The Areopagos consisted of ex-archons, men who would appreciate the seriousness of Stephanos' alleged crimes and were sufficiently well-versed in administration and litigation to conduct a prosecution.

Thus Apollodoros' account is both unconvincing in itself and unsubstantiated by any of the evidence which one might have expected. It is difficult to resist the conclusion that the whole Theogenes affair is an invention. It is however important to bear in mind that these flaws, while obvious in the study, will not necessarily have been evident to the jurors as they listened to the narrative.

85-125 *Proofs*. Of this section only one quarter, §§85-87 (on Phano's capacity to serve as Basilinna) and §§119-125 (refutation of Stephanos' arguments), deals with questions of fact. The rest serves to stimulate hostility towards the accused and to encourage the jurors to deal with her severely. There is a pronounced narrative-descriptive element to the proof section (§§88-93 procedures for the enfranchisement of aliens, §§94-106 the services and reward of the Plataians), with the result that it becomes difficult to divide narrative and proof sections neatly.

85-87 *A fortiori argument against Phano's suitability to be Basilinna*. Apollodoros argues that Phano not only has no right to officiate at state ceremonies, in view of her career she has no right even to enter the temples. The extent of her offence is thereby magnified and the potential for hostility against both her and Stephanos increased.

85 any woman who is caught with an adulterer: a reference to the Epainetos affair. Apollodoros is able both to have his cake and to eat it. Here he accepts that Phano was caught with a *moichos*, while in §67 he uses against Stephanos Epainetos' successful claim that he is not a *moichos* (cf. Patteson). The inconsistency will probably have gone unremarked because of the interval between the two passages and the force of the speaker's indignation. Apollodoros could be confident that the defence could not exploit the inconsistency without appearing to quibble.

86 These are the only women: an exaggeration (as Patteson notes, people accused of murder were also excluded by the public proclamation made by the prosecutor; cf. on §9), but well calculated to stress the severity of the attitude towards unchaste women, as is the emphatic contrast with the rights granted to women of non-citizen and even servile status.
sufficient fear ... to ensure they will be chaste: the deterrent value of the law is a commonplace of Greek thought (Hdt.7.104.4, Aisch.*Eum*.691ff., Lys.14.15, Aischin.3.175). As Patteson notes (citing Dover *GPM* 98ff.), the suggestion that women need such a threat accords with the Greek belief that women were less able to resist desire than men. The punishment for women who committed adultery was less severe than that imposed on male adulterers (for which see on §41 above); this disparity reflected both the limited opportunities for initiative on the part of women and the sexual subservience of women according to Greek belief (see Carey on Lys.1.26). Nonetheless, Apollodoros is correct to emphasize the severity of the treatment of the guilty female. Since religion was the one area of public life in which women played a significant role, and since religious festivals were prominent among the rare occasions on which an Athenian woman of any status would leave the house (even, in the case of festivals confined to women, without male supervision), the punishment described here would be keenly felt (for the extent of female seclusion in classical Athens cf. on §24); so would the shame, both for the woman and her family.
from her husband's house: this statement is clarified by the first clause in the law cited in §87.

87 LAW ON ADULTERY: probably this document is genuine, since while all the other details could have been gleaned from Apollodoros' account of the law, the punishment attached to failure to expel the wife could not. Only the relevant section of the law is quoted. Aischin.1.183 adds that the woman was allowed no personal ornament.
he is to be disfranchised: cf. on §26 for loss of citizen rights (*atimia*).

88-93 *The procedures for enfranchising aliens*. The account is introduced to demonstrate (§88) how seriously the Athenians take their rituals, to the extent of excluding enfranchised aliens from serving as priests (§92). But Apollodoros also seeks to stir resentment against Stephanos by stressing the circumspection with which the Athenian people approaches an act (enfranchisement) which Stephanos allegedly treats in a cavalier fashion. Apollodoros is right to insist on the obstacles to enfranchisement; though bestowed more frequently in the fourth than in the fifth century, it was still a relatively rare honour, and one (as his account shows) obtained with difficulty.

88 testimony from the Athenian people: for the terminology cf. on §62.
imposed laws on itself: that is, the sovereign people saw fit to limit its own powers by law; hence Stephanos, by (allegedly) flouting the laws in elevating Neaira to parity with citizen women and giving citizen status to her children, has set himself above the people; cf. §13.

89 Still, you will be better for hearing them: I follow Herwerden in supposing that something has dropped out before this sentence, for instance: 'These laws are known to you all.' The alternative is to accept Gernet's ὑμεῖς ('you') for MSS. ὅμως ('still'); Gernet is followed by Avezzù. The slightly patronizing tone in this sentence accords with the donnish quality evident in Apollodoros' forays into history; this was a dangerous tone to adopt with an Athenian jury (cf. Aischin.1.141).
excellent conduct: Greek *andragathia*, lit. 'the quality/conduct of a good man'. This reflects the terminology of decrees bestowing citizenship and other honours, which frequently take the form 'because he is/was/showed himself a good man towards the people/city/Athenians' (we also find 'because of his *andragathia*', as *IG* ii^2 25 = Osborne D9.9). The services which might count as *andragathia* towards Athens are discussed by Osborne IV.186ff. For metics this usually involved substantial financial contribution to the state (cf. §13 and see on §2 for Apollodoros' father, Pasion). Osborne IV.143 suggests that the law defining elibigility for enfranchisement was introduced at the same time as and in connection with Perikles' citizenship decree of of 451/0.
over six thousand Athenians vote for it at the following Assembly in secret ballot: both the quorum of six thousand and the secret ballot were normal in laws or decrees directed at an individual (cf. Andok.1.87, Dem.24.59), including ostracism in the fifth century. The second vote of ratification is attested by inscriptions from 369/8 onwards; Osborne IV.161 suggests a date in the 380s for its introduction.

90 the voting urns: as Patteson notes, the procedure appears to have resembled that used in the lawcourts (for which see Arist.*Ath.Pol.*68.1-4); normally voting in the Assembly was by show of hands (M.H. Hansen, *The Athenian Assembly* (Oxford 1987) 41).
as they come up: M.H. Hansen, *GRBS* 26 (1985) 244f. locates this voting in the

area in front of the staircase leading up to the Pnyx from the north.
before the foreigners enter and they remove the fences: the fences in question are wicker barriers (Greek *gerra*) which could control entry to the Pnyx (the hill west of the Acropolis on which the Assembly met). Once all those entitled to attend were seated, spectators were admitted and the barriers removed to clear their view. So Hansen (see preceding note) 247.
indictment for illegality: for the *graphe paranomon* cf. on §5. Although, as Osborne notes (IV.162), the brevity of the interval between initial and ratification vote made a reversal at the latter unlikely, the availability of the *graphe paranomon* allowed for subsequent attack on the proposal. M.H. Hansen (cited on §5) 62-65 notes that over half the cases of *graphe paranomon* known to us concern honorary decrees; he rightly concludes that the purpose of such actions is a political attack on proposer or recipient.
against him: strictly speaking, it was the proposer, not the beneficiary, who was indicted; but since the latter's right to citizenship was on trial Apollodoros' language is natural. It also agrees with his emphasis in this section on the barriers facing a candidate for citizenship.

91 deceived by the arguments of the proposers: like the juries (§5) the Assembly does not make mistakes; it is deceived by unscrupulous speakers.
Peitholas of Thessaly: son of Jason of Pherai in Thessaly, and tyrant of that city with his brother Lykophron. They were allied to the Phokians, whose seizure of Delphi in 356 led to the outbreak of the Sacred War. After the defeat of the Phokian army by Philip of Macedon on the Krokion Plain, the tyrants of Pherai, now isolated in Thessaly, surrendered their city to Philip under truce; they then joined the army of the Phokian Phayllos. That they should be honoured by Athens, another ally of Phokis, is not surprising; why the grant was cancelled is unclear. Aristotle *R.*1410a17 quotes a sentence attacking Peitholas and Lykophron which may have come from the prosecution speech at the trial: 'these men sold you when they were at home, and on coming to you have bought you'. This may be a claim that the passage of the citizenship decree was secured by bribery.
Apollonides of Olynthos: leader of the anti-Macedonian faction in Olynthos in the late 350s (Dem.9.56, 66); he was exiled (probably) in 351 (Hammond and Griffith (cited on §24 above) 303). The reasons for the cancellation of the grant of citizenship are unknown; presumably both enfranchisement and cancellation resulted from the jockeying for power of the rival political groups in Athens, combined with the course of events in the north in 349-8; cf. on §90.

92 one of the nine Archons: this exclusion probably reflects both religious scruple (because of the sacrifices conducted by the Archons) and a desire to preserve the dignity of the archonship, which though of little political importance still enjoyed considerable prestige.

or holding any priesthood: as Gernet notes, in the Plataian decree (§104) this restriction is qualified. He explains the discrepancy by supposing that the law discussed here postdates the Plataian decree. But the unqualified formulation here may be a deliberate oversimplification by Apollodoros to stress the restrictiveness of Athenian practice. Cf. on §93.

if they are born of a wife of citizen status: that is, a man such as Apollodoros, who was born before his father's enfranchisement to a woman of metic status, was excluded; but had Pasion subsequently married a woman of citizen stock, any sons born of this marriage would have been eligible for the archonship or for elective priesthoods.

93 testimony: cf. on §62.

to tell how it was passed: Apollodoros may be correct to date the exclusion provision after the Plataian decree. However, it suits his purpose to present the Plataian decree as the origin of provisions which were subsequently formulated as general law, since the effect is both to increase the authority of the example and to convince the hearer in advance of the relevance of the circumstantial digression which is to follow; the chronological and causal relationship may therefore be his invention.

94-106 *Digression on the Plataians*. This narrative (which takes up one twelfth of the speech) forms the basis of an argument *a fortiori* (§§107-8): if the Athenians imposed restrictions on a people who were consistently loyal to Athens at enormous risk and ultimately at enormous cost to themselves, they cannot show leniency when the laws governing enfranchisement are casually flouted by degraded individuals who have no claim on their gratitude. Though the details are tangential to the main issue, the circumstantial narrative has the effect of substantiating Apollodoros' basic point about the merits of the Plataians; it also (because of the perspective from which the events are presented) engages the emotions of the hearer and so creates a receptive frame of mind for the contrast with Phano and Neaira which follows, though it is possible that the length of the digression undercut this emotional effect for his audience. The narrative is unusual in what remains of Greek oratory in that it derives not from popular tradition but from historiography (cf. Thomas 200-202 with n.19; for the treatment of history in the orators see in general L. Pearson *CP* 36 (1941) 209-29, M. Nouhaud, *L'utilisation de l'histoire par les orateurs attiques* (Paris 1982) *passim*); Apollodoros draws on

Thucydides' account of the career of the Spartan Pausanias in book 1 (§§128-34, specifically 132) and his account of the vicissitudes and ultimate destruction of Plataia in books 2 and 3 (2.1-6, 71-78, 3.20-24, 52-68), even to the extent of echoing Thucydides' phrasing in places, with occasional minor borrowings from elsewhere in Thucydides; these echoes are signalled in the individual notes. His departures from Thucydides are sometimes no more than lapses of memory; more often they are deliberate, and have the effect either of aggrandizing the merits of the Plataians and so reinforcing Apollodoros' argument, or less often of simplifying the narrative to improve its clarity for the purposes of oral presentation. It has been suggested on occasion that where Apollodoros departs from Thucydides he is drawing on an authoritative source (see on §§98, 101); however, since they serve Apollodoros' rhetorical aim these departures are probably his own invention. If he used Herodotos for the Persian Wars his borrowing has been so free as to leave no certain trace.

For all its fullness Apollodoros' narrative is selective. He deals briskly with the Persian Wars, being content to link the Plataians with the most glorious battles in the struggle against the barbarians. For subsequent events, though he follows chronological order, he does not narrate everything; he hurries over some events which his source treats more lavishly and leaps substantial intervals. The result is a narrative which combines rapidity and vividness with strict subservience to the speaker's aim.

94 the only Greeks ... at Marathon: cf. Hdt.6.108. One of the two tumuli near Marathon is probably the burial mound of the Plataians; see R. Barber, *Blue guide to Greece* (repr. London 1990) 237.

Eretria: Athens and Eretria in Euboia were the only cities in mainland Greece to send aid to the Greek cities of the coast and islands of Asia Minor when they revolted from Persia in 499-494. The punitive expedition sent by the Persian king Dareios in 490 sacked Eretria before disembarking at Marathon on the east coast of Attica (cf. Hdt.6.101-2).

the Painted Portico: Greek *stoa poikile*. This building, which was built in the first half of the fifth century, stood on the north side of the agora (R.E. Wycherley, *The stones of Athens* (Princeton 1978) 38), just north of where the Piraeus railway now cuts through the site. Its four wall paintings are described by the traveller Pausanias (1.15). Aischines alludes to the Marathon painting a decade or so later (3.186); it is variously ascribed to Mikon, Panainos and Polygnotos. For a discussion of literary references to this painting and an attempt to reconstruct its overall disposition see E.B. Harrison, *AJA* 76 (1972) 353-78.

95 when Xerxes advanced on Greece: in 480.
without the aid of the other Boiotians: lit. 'alone of the other Boiotians'. The contrast between the Plataians' loyalty to Greece and the Theban collaboration with the Persians comes from the defence speech of the Plataians at the mock trial held by the Spartans after the capture of Plataia in 427, Thuc.3.54.3, 56.4. The phrase 'alone of the Boiotians' is taken from Thuc.3.54.3. This claim is false, for Thespiai and Haliartos also remained loyal to the Greek cause (Hdt.7.132.1, 8.50.2, Paus.9.32.4).
half of them faced the advancing barbarian with Leonidas: in the celebrated stand at Thermopylai. This claim too is false; Herodotos (7.222) says that only Thespian and the Theban contingents were with the Spartan force of Leonidas.
the rest embarked on your triremes ... and fought at sea ... at Artemision and Salamis: Herodotos (8.1.1) says that the Plataians served in Athenian ships at Artemision, and the Plataians in Thucydides (3.54.4) make much of their participation, despite being landlubbers. But the Plataians were not at Salamis (Hdt.8.44.1).

96 at Plataia: where in 479 the Persian land army was defeated.
tried to insult you: as becomes clear below, Apollodoros is treating as an insult to Athens behaviour which insults all the Greeks alike. The aim is to present the Plataians in what follows as benefactors specifically of Athens.
our city ... in reality leader in winning liberty for Greece: cf. Hdt.7.139, Thuc.1.73-4. Sparta as the most powerful state in Greece was leader of the anti-Persian coalition.

97 Pausanias the Spartan king: Pausanias was not in fact king but regent (Hdt.9.10.1, Thuc.1.132.1). The account of his behaviour here, including the epigram, is derived from Thuc.1.132, where it forms part of the tale of his arrogant conduct after the defeat of the Persian invaders.

98 the Plataians brought an action: according to Thucydides, the Spartans themselves were offended by Pausanias' inscription and had it replaced with the names of the cities which had fought against the Persians. Though Apollodoros' account has occasionally found credence (cf. R.J. Bonner and G. Smith, *CP* 38 (1943) 2, H.W. Parke and D.E.W. Wormell, *The Delphic oracle* (Oxford 1956) 182, J.C. Trevett, *CQ* 40 (1990) 409f.), it is quite implausible. In their defence before the Spartans after the capture of the city in 427, the Plataians in Thucydides (3.53-9) represent themselves as consistent friends of Sparta in the period before the Peloponnesian War. Even their enemies the Thebans in their reply (Thuc.3.61-7) can find no enmity between Plataia and Sparta in the past. Even if we suppose that the content of these speeches is largely the creation of Thucydides, it is difficult to believe that he could have ignored such an obvious indication of hostility as the Plataian indictment of Sparta, if it had really occurred. Moreover, the figure of one thousand talents (roughly equal to the annual income of the Athenian empire at its greatest) is preposterously high for the primitive economy of Sparta in the period after the Persian invasions. Almost a century later, after Sparta had acquired an empire, only half that sum was imposed on her as a fine by the Amphictyonic council (Diod.16.29.2). That Sparta should replace the inscription on her own initiative makes perfect sense (*pace* Bonner and Smith), for Pausanias in taking sole credit was slighting Sparta along with the other Greek states; moreover, as Thucydides' narrative makes clear, the Spartans saw Pausanias' act as a sign of dangerous personal ambition. It is possible that Apollodoros derived his account from a pro-Plataian source. But since its aggrandizement of Plataian valour harmonizes so well with his rhetorical aims, it is far more likely that this is his own invention. For the dedication substituted at Delphi see Meiggs-Lewis 57-60.

99 He did this from Thebes: according to Thucydides 2.2.3 the attack on Plataia in 431 was a Theban idea; Plataia had long been an enemy of Thebes, and the Thebans wished to gain control of it before war broke out. Apollodoros reshapes the narrative to fit his version of the Pausanias affair. Cf. Nouhaud (cited above on §§94-106) 263.

Eurymachos ... Naukleides: cf. Thuc.2.2.2-3. Thucydides describes Eurymachos as 'a Theban of great power'. His designation as Boiotarch by Apollodoros may come from an independent source, but equally it may be no more than a false recollection or exaggeration of, or a deduction from, Thucydides' phrase.

for a bribe: according to Thuc.2.2.2, the aim of the Plataian traitors was to destroy the pro-Athenian element and subjugate the city to Thebes in order to secure their own power.

discovering ... had been seized: taken almost verbatim from Thuc.2.3.1. In Thucydides' account, the Plataians initially negotiate with the Thebans; in the process they learn the size of the enemy force and accordingly make a surprise attack in the dark. Apollodoros omits the negotiations; the Plataians range themselves against the enemy force, and on discovering its size at dawn they attack. The change is motivated partly by a desire to avoid imputing any weakness or duplicity to the Plataians, partly perhaps by a desire to make the narrative more readily intelligible by omitting complicating details which while adding nothing of significance for his purpose might confuse the audience.

the vanguard: in Thucydides' account (2.5.1), the Thebans who fail to arrive are a separate body of reinforcements; in Apollodoros there is just one force, of which only the vanguard succeed in entering the city. Again Apollodoros simplifies. The reason for the failure to reinforce is taken almost verbatim from Thuc.2.5.2.

100 they sent a messenger to you: Thucydides 2.6.1-3 speaks of two messengers the first immediately after the Theban seizure of the city, the second after the defeat of the invaders. Apollodoros simplifies, since for his account lucidity is more important than precise historical accuracy.
The Athenians: Apollodoros slips into the historian's manner, using the third person.
on seeing that the Athenians had reinforced the Plataians: according to Thucydides (2.5.5), the Plataians themselves compelled the Theban reinforcements to withdraw by threatening to kill those of the task force who had surrendered to them. The Athenians did not send a force until some time after the Theban withdrawal (2.6.4). Apollodoros gives Athens a more impressive role.

101 killed those of them whom they had taken alive in battle: according to Thucydides (2.6.2), the Athenians on receiving the second message from Plataia (see on §100) sent a messenger advising the Plataians not to kill the prisoners; the Athenian messenger arrived to find that the Plataians had already executed them. Apollodoros by placing the execution after the arrival of Athenian reinforcements involves them in what most Greeks would regard as an immoral act. According to Thucydides (2.5.6-7), the Theban and Plataian accounts of the killing differed. The Thebans claimed that the Plataians promised on oath to free the prisoners unharmed if the Theban reinforcements withdrew, but killed the prisoners even after the Thebans complied. The Plataians denied swearing an oath, and insisted that the promise to release the prisoners was conditional upon successful talks. Even on their own account the Plataians were guilty of a breach of faith, and it is not surprising that Apollodoros omits this detail. It is still surprising that he includes the execution of the prisoners. This may simply be a misjudgement, but (a good hater himself) he may have felt that the Thebans deserved their fate, or that the rhetorical thrust of his narrative made the Plataians' action tolerable or even admirable (as reducing their passivity).

At this point Apollodoros breaks off his account of events of 431. He omits the fact (Thuc.2.6.4) that the Athenians removed the old and infirm, together with the women and children, to Athens, and leaves us with the impression (cf. §103) that virtually the whole population remained in the city. The impression of Plataian loyalty is thereby increased and the extent of their loss exaggerated.
without any pretext now: Apollodoros appears to suggest that the Spartan attack

followed immediately after the Theban failure. In fact he jumps two years, to 429, when instead of invading Attica as in 431 and 430 the Spartan king Archidamos attacked Plataia (Thuc.2.71.1). The misstatement may be due to error, a desire to simplify, or a desire to expand the siege of Plataia to ten years within a period of hostilities which lasted only a decade (see on §102 below). The details of the Peloponnesian forces here are not found in Thucydides' Plataian account. They may come from another source. If so, the source is unreliable. As Trevett, *CQ* 40 (1990) 416 notes, in 427 Sparta founded Herakleia in order to support the Trachinians against the Oitaians (Thuc.3.92.2), and in 419 we find Ainianians and Malians among the forces opposing Herakleia (Thuc.5.51); it is unlikely therefore that these peoples were Spartan allies in the early years of the war. However, it is striking that two phrases in the account are found in close proximity in Thucydides ('all the Peloponnesians except the Argives' Thuc.2.9.2, 'two thirds of the forces from each city' Thuc.2.10.2), while the Boiotians, Lokrians and Phokians appear in the vicinity (Thuc.2.9.2). Since we find Apollodoros elsewhere (see on §§76, 103) lifting phrases from Thucydidean contexts other than those which served as his immediate model for events narrated in this speech, it is likely that Thucydides is the source of these details too. The rest may be deliberate invention by Apollodoros, though equally it could be the result of confusion with another campaign (Haliartos, Xen.*Hell.*3.5.6, suggests itself; cf. Trevett, *CQ* 40 (1990) 416). The intended effect is clearly to exaggerate the forces ranged against Plataia.

102 asking them if they would agree to hand the city over to them: again Apollodoros simplifies. According to Thucydides (2.72.1-2), Archidamos initially demanded that the Plataians either join the Spartan alliance or become neutral. When the Plataians responded that this would expose them to hostility from Athens or attack from Thebes, he offered to take over their city. According to Thucydides (2.72.3), the Spartan suggestion was that the Plataians should hand over both city and land for the duration of the war and receive a rent from the Spartans. Apollodoros' version is probably due to lapse of memory, since his phraseology indicates that Thucydides is his source (with τὴν μὲν πόλιν αὐτοῖς παραδοῦναι here cf. Thuc.2.72.3 πόλιν μὲν καὶ οἰκίας ἡμῖν παράδοτε).

without the agreement of the Athenians: although the wording comes from Thucydides (2.72.2), there it forms part of the Plataian response to the first Spartan overture, as Patteson notes.

a double wall: cf. Thuc.3.21.1.

ten years: since Plataia surrendered in 427 after a two year siege, editors generally accept Palmer's δύο, 'two' in place of δέκα, 'ten', offered by the manuscripts. The manuscript reading is accepted by Trevett *CQ* 40 (1990) 413 n.25. Since it accords with Apollodoros' consistent tendency to overstate the valour and suffering of the Plataians, I accept the manuscript reading. To the modern reader, armed with printed texts and at leisure to pause over details, exaggeration on this scale seems too transparent to be feasible. But it is unlikely that a member of an audience acquainted with history through oral tradition and without the time to reflect would note a misstatement concerning events over eighty years old, particularly in the context of an account whose detail (accurate and invented) gives it a semblance of authority.

repeated assaults of all sorts: in the interests of brevity and relevance Apollodoros here condenses the various attempts by the Peloponnesian forces to take Plataia by storm before they settled down to the siege which are narrated in detail by Thucydides (2.75ff.).

103 When the Plataians ... rescued: Apollodoros leaps to the events of 427. He deals only briefly with the escape, which Thucydides narrates in detail, as tangential to his aim. This clause paraphrases Thuc.3.20.1.

drew lots: according to Thucydides, the original plan was for the whole garrison to escape, but half lost their nerve and stayed behind, though they assisted the escapers by making a diversionary attack on the enemy wall. Apollodoros' account is more creditable to the Plataians, and is probably therefore his own invention. (Gomme *HCT* II 283 finds some inconsistency in Thucydides' narrative between this failure of nerve and the readiness of those who stayed behind to distract the enemy garrison with a diversionary attack; he is therefore inclined to believe Apollodoros. There is no real discrepancy, since i. though the break-out in the event was a remarkable success, it must have seemed in advance a desperate venture (cf. Thuc.3.20.2), unlike a feint on the wall, ii. the break-out required not just courage in battle but nerve in a tense situation.)

after waiting for a night with much wind and rain: taken almost verbatim from Thuc.3.22.1.

captured by storm: in fact (Thuc.3.52.1) the garrison surrendered. Apollodoros substitutes a finale more flattering to the Plataians.

all the grown men ... slavery: according to Thucydides (3.78.3) there were no children present, only a male garrison with one hundred and ten women whose job was to prepare food. Of these, the men were killed, the women enslaved. The punishment narrated by Apollodoros was contemplated (but not executed) by the Athenians after the capitulation of the rebel city of Mitylene in 427 and was actually inflicted on the rebel city of Skione in 421. The former incident is juxtaposed to the capitulation and destruction of Plataia in Thucydides' narrative (3.36.2), while the Plataians appear in the immediate context of the second incident

(5.32.1). This proximity, together with Apollodoros' thoroughgoing use of Thucydides, strongly suggests that he has transposed one of these punishments to the Spartan treatment of Plataia. Given the closer similarity of phrasing (Thucydides has ἀπέκτειναν τοὺς ἡβῶντας, παῖδας δὲ καὶ γυναῖκας ἠνδραπόδισαν, Apollodoros ἀπεσφάγησαν πάντες οἱ ἡβῶντες, παῖδες δὲ καὶ γυναῖκες ἐξηνδραποδίσθησαν), Skione is the likelier model. This may be just a lapse of memory, but since the effect is to exaggerate the suffering of the Plataians it is more likely to be a deliberate change by Apollodoros.

all ... who had not escaped to Athens: see on §101.

104 you gave them a share in citizen rights: Apollodoros evidently believed that the grant of citizenship to the Plataians postdated the destruction of their city; cf. Isok.12.94. He is clearly correct as far as this decree is concerned. The detailed procedures laid down in the decree indicate that it deals with dispossessed Plataians for whom practical arrangements had to be made (cf. *IG* ii² 1.33f.). However, Thucydides twice (3.55.3, 3.63.2) indicates that the Plataians received Athenian citizenship before 427. It is difficult to believe that Thucydides could make such an obvious mistake twice. He had ample opportunity to check his facts, since the capture of Plataia preceded his exile from Athens by three years. Probably we should accept that the Plataians were granted citizenship twice (cf. D.M. MacDowell, *CR* 34 (1985) 319). The first grant (presumably a reward for their intervention at Marathon) was honorary, since Plataia remained a separate state; the second grant took account of the practical problem created by the dispossession of the Plataians and included proposals for integrating them into the Athenian citizen body.

DECREE: the document appears to be genuine, since it contains a number of details absent from the text of the speech (the broad definition of the rights of the Plataians, the clause about hereditary priesthoods (see below), the distribution among the demes, the finality of the gift), while omitting many details from the following account (§§105-6), which one would expect a forger to include. Moreover, Osborne II 13f. points out that the arrangement for distribution into demes and tribes but not phratries agrees with the mass grant of citizenship to the Samians (*IG* ii²1. 33f. = Meiggs-Lewis 94 = Osborne I.D4), and that the opening words of both mass grants are the same. The decree is not quoted in full. Apollodoros has omitted the series of formulae with which Athenian decrees usually commence; in addition, he has chosen to have only the gist of the decree read out by the clerk and to provide much of the detail himself, presumably to enable him to combine fact with comment.

Hippokrates: possibly the Hippokrates who served as strategos in 426/5 (*IG* i²

324.3; cf. Mathieu, *REG* 40 (1927) 74 n.1, Patteson) and again at Delion in Boiotia in 424, where he died (Thuc.4.101.2); see Kirchner *PA* 7640, Davies *APF* 456.
except for any hereditary priesthood or rite: Apollodoros' own statement in §92 suggests a more extensive ban than debarment from hereditary priesthoods, which would anyway by their very nature be closed to the enfranchised alien. Something is missing; possibly the text ran: 'but not the priesthoods [ἀλλὰ μὴ τῶν ἱερωσυνῶν Osborne, following Riehemann], except for any hereditary priesthood or rite ...'. That is, individual Plataians may retain any hereditary priesthoods they already possess, but they may not be chosen to fill any elective priesthood in Athens.
their descendants may: Apollodoros adds a condition that they must be borne of an Athenian woman legally married to the enfranchised alien (§§92, 106). Perhaps this provision has fallen out of the text here; it is however also possible that Apollodoros has himself omitted the clause in transcribing the inscription.

105 public speaker: Greek *rhetor*; see on §43.
be examined individually in the law court: the large number of potential claimants opened the possibility of fraudulent claims, either by non-Plataians or by pro-Theban Plataians (cf. Lys.23).
so that the grant might be preserved for their descendants: that is, the inscription is itself the public document recording the grant; cf. Thomas 73f.

106 one of the nine Archons or to any priesthood: cf. on §92.

107-115 *Arguments against leniency*. These consist of an argument *a fortiori* based on the treatment of the Plataians (107-8), and appeals to religious fear (109), respect and concern for female relatives (110-4), and respect for the laws (115). The powerful emotional appeal of this section does much to offset the weakness of the factual case against Neaira.

107 you defined: for the ascription to the jurors of decisions of the Assembly (here a decree passed by the great-grandparents of Apollodoros' audience) see on §4.
who has blatantly whored throughout the whole of Greece: since Apollodoros moved in §50 from Neaira to her daughter, the hearer might be forgiven for supposing that he is referring here to Phano, whose alleged usurpation of the rights of the Basilinna offers a stark contrast to the limitations imposed by the Athenians even on outstanding benefactors to the city. In fact, as the abuse which follows shows, we are dealing with Neaira. Probably the confusion is intentional. Apollodoros makes no distinction between the alleged crimes of mother and daughter. There is a striking terminological shift at this stage. In his narrative

Apollodoros used the term *hetaira* to describe the status/profession of Neaira. Here and in §§112, 113, 114, as he gives free rein to indignation, he uses the coarser root *porn-*. The suggestion is that Neaira was no more than a common prostitute. In fact, to judge by Apollodoros' account, she was an expensive courtesan, though the distinction will have mattered little to Apollodoros' audience.

sacrilege against the gods: by marrying Phano to Theogenes (§§72ff.). Any responsibility for this alleged crime would strictly devolve on Stephanos under law.

nor granted it by the people: added to emphasize the contrast between Neaira and the Plataians. There is no reason to suppose that a woman could in fact be naturalized in her own right in Athens; indeed it is likely that when an alien male was enfranchised his wife remained an alien (cf. *CQ* 41 (1991) 84-9).

108 the Peloponnese ... Ionia: the list of places where Neaira has prostituted herself is staggering. It is difficult to know how seriously to take it, since we lack information on the mobility of prostitutes. The mention of Nikarete however strongly suggests that the list is Apollodoros' invention. Nikarete was suspicious and possessive. Though she allowed Neaira and Metaneira to travel to Athens (§§22, 24), she insisted on accompanying them. She would presumably have had to accompany Neaira on all these journeys, which besides being unnecessarily arduous (a trip from Corinth to Athens is quite a different matter) would have left little time for business in Corinth. Moreover, Nikarete used only young girls (§§18ff.); it is difficult to see how all this travel could have been accomplished during Nikarete's relatively brief ownership of Neaira. Nor is there anything in Apollodoros' narrative to support the alleged connection with Eurydamas and Sotadas. Apollodoros relies on the wealth of detail to give a ring of authority to his assertions.

Simos of Larisa: cf. on §24.

Eurydamas the son of Medeios: an Aleuad, like Simos, by whom he was killed in a vendetta; see Kallim.fr.588 with Pfeiffer, Ovid *Ibis* 331f. with schol. The manuscripts of Demosthenes give the father's name as Medeios or Meidias; the latter form is found in schol.Hom.*Il*.22.397 (= Kallim.fr.588).

Sotadas of Crete: winner of the Olympic long race in 384; in the next Olympiad he was bribed to accept citizenship of Ephesos, for which he was exiled from Crete (Paus.6.18.6).

to have plied her trade: Hermogenes p.325 Rabe states that the words ἀπὸ τριῶν τρυπημάτων τὴν ἐργασίαν πεποιῆσθαι (literally 'to have made her living from three drill/bore holes'), which are not found in any manuscript of Demosthenes, were 'obelized by some' in the text of this speech on grounds of taste. Blass suggests that the words ἀπὸ τριῶν τρυπημάτων should be inserted here after ὑπὸ πάντων ('known by all to have plied her trade/made her living with/from three holes', a reference to vaginal, oral and anal sex). I doubt that the phrase ever formed part of Apollodoros' speech. From Aischines 1.52 one would suppose that the use of the root *porn-* inthis section is already explicit enough in the context of the lawcourts. It is difficult to believe that Apollodoros would risk offending his audience by using graphic language more at home in comedy (for the register of τρύπημα see J. Henderson, *The maculate muse* (New Haven and London 1975) 142). Moreover, the context is suggestive ('what do you expect a woman to do ...?') rather than graphic. The hearer is invited to conjure up for himself the kind of service Neaira provided for her clients; Apollodoros is thus able to combine titillation with decent imprecision. It would weaken the appeal to imagination for him to define her activities.

109 from what manner of shame and impiety can you claim innocence: that is, failure to punish Neaira for the sacrilege caused by the marriage to Theogenes amounts to condonement. For the specific argument cf. Lyk.*Leokr.*146, and for the attempt to intimidate with reference to divine anger (a powerful appeal to a basic emotion) cf. §126.

others ... had no practical means of dealing with her: since it required considerable confidence in one's forensic knowledge and rhetorical skill to bring someone to trial on a serious charge, particularly in view of the penalties for conspicuous failure, it is not surprising that most public actions of which we know were brought either by the victim (exactly as in private cases) or by a political oppponent (see R. Osborne, *JHS* 105 (1985) 52). Any ordinary Athenian who knew of crimes such as those attributed to Stephanos and Neaira would probably hesitate to take action. There was an additional deterrent in the present case, since any prosecutor would incur the hostility of a seasoned politician and litigant. However, according to Apollodoros the whole of the Areopagos knew of the Theogenes affair; cf. on §84.

110 when he goes home to his own wife or daughter: it is normal for the prosecutor to attempt to make the jurors feel personally threatened by the alleged conduct of the defendant; cf. e.g. 21.220, 23.94, Lys.1.47 and see on §111. For a similar though less graphic appeal to the jurors' feelings for their wives and families cf. Lyk.*Leokr.*141. Closer to the present passage is Aischin.3.245-6, which envisages a dialogue after the trial. But Apollodoros' extended use of direct speech (for which see on §70) makes for a more vivid and effective appeal.

'Where were you?': this exchange gives a very vivid impression of relations between a man and his female relatives. Secluded where financial considerations allowed (see on §24) and excluded from political, judicial and commercial activity, citizen females relied on their husbands for news of the larger world of the polis; cf. Ar.*Lys.*512ff. The readiness of the males to satisfy this curiosity will have varied according to the personalities involved and the warmth of the relationship. The Athenian husband in Aristophanes (as the plot demands) tells his wife to mind her own business, while the present passage suggests that many Athenian men were happy to share their experiences with their womenfolk.

because she gave in marriage: this does not form part of the indictment against Neaira, but if the jury believed the allegation it will have influenced their verdict; cf. on §5.

111 all the foolish ones: the Greeks did not always distinguish strictly between intellectual and moral qualities; 'foolish' here refers to lack of moral restraint. In the same way, the adjective translated here as 'decent', *sophron*, has an intellectual ('prudent', 'reasonable') as well as a moral ('chaste') aspect.

you and the laws have given them complete freedom: it is normal for Greek litigants to treat the trial as a precedent (cf. e.g. 24.243, 54.43, Aischin.1.192). Strictly speaking, if the jury acquits Neaira it will have decided that she is innocent. They are not therefore condoning lawbreaking. But since the litigant always proceeds from the conviction (real or assumed) that his cause is just, a vote for the opponent is by definition a vote for wrongdoing.

112 the daughters of poor men: since they cannot offer a substantial dowry, these females will be unable to compete for husbands in a free market against prostitutes, who can offer the profit from their profession.

113 an adequate dowry: possibly (Patteson) a reference to the law which prescribed that if a girl of thetic class became an *epikleros* (that is, if her father died leaving no male issue; for the *epikleros* see Harrison I 132-8), her nearest male relative must either marry her or provide a dowry of 150, 300 or 500 drachmas according to his status (Dem.43.54). Since however Apollodoros speaks in §§112-3 of poor females in general, and since 'the law' which is in danger of being 'brought into contempt' by Neaira's acquittal is more naturally taken as marriage law, it seems more likely that the reference to a dowry is metaphorical, the 'dowry' being the exclusive right of a female born of citizen parents to marry an Athenian citizen.

the trade of whores will fall to the daughters of citizens: a gross, but effective, exaggeration.

114 one in defence of his wife ... his mother: suggests that the family of each and every juror is threatened; cf. on §110. The contrast which follows between the cloistered life of the average Athenian female and the life of the prostitute Neaira is very effective.

in many lascivious ways, as each man wished: for the appeal to the imagination, combining titillation with the affectation of decent restraint, cf. on §108.

115 it is the laws: Apollodoros' righteous indignation rises to a superb crescendo. At the factual level this passage merely restates the claim that Neaira's acquittal would subvert the laws. However, the personification of the laws (for which cf. 21.188, Lys.1.26, 35, Aischin.3.37 and especially Plat.*Krit.*50a-54e) adds greatly to the force of the argument, offering the jurors a stark choice between the laws and an aging prostitute. The Greeks were proud of their subservience to the laws as distinct from the subjection of the barbarian to the will of an autocrat; cf. Hdt.7.104.4-5, Eur.*Med.*538.

by which you have sworn to judge: at the beginning of the year all jurors swore an oath that they would vote according to the laws and decrees of the Athenian people, or in matters not explicitly covered by law according to their sense of justice; see further Bonner-Smith II 152ff., Harrison II 48. It is common for litigants to remind the jurors of their oath.

take a look at her appearance: K.J. Dover *Lysias and the corpus Lysiacum* (Berkeley and Los Angeles 1968) 34-6 takes this to indicate that Neaira was still an attractive woman. But in that case one would expect a warning to the jury to ignore her appearance. Probably her dress and degree of make-up would clearly mark her out as a courtesan.

whether she (Neaira!) has committed these acts: Apollodoros steers the jury away from the factual issue to Neaira's career.

116-7 *The precedent of Archias.* As in modern trials, it was not unusual for Athenian litigants to cite precedent. However, since no jury was bound by the decisions of another jury, such precedents have only a persuasive value. As with the Plataians, Apollodoros chooses an example where there are mitigating factors (Archias' career, family background and associates, and the fact that his offence was less serious than that attributed to Neaira in the Theogenes affair), in order to use the strictness shown in that case as a yardstick for the treatment to be meted out to Neaira. The case is also selected for its points of contact with the present trial (the identity of the god insulted, the involvement of a courtesan).

116 you punished: for the use of the second person cf. on §4.

Archias: see Kirchner *PA* 2447. As Parke notes (see below), the prosecution of Archias was probably political in origin. In 379/8 he tried to warn the Theban oligarchs (who had the support of a Spartan garrison in Thebes) of a plot by Theban exiles based in Athens to liberate the city (Plut.*Pelop.*10). The attack on

him will have come from pro-Spartan politicians in Athens; cf. on §27.
Hierophant: the chief priest of Demeter at Eleusis, chosen from the family Eumolpidai, who claimed descent from the kings of Eleusis. For his role and prerogatives see Mylonas (cited on §21) 229-30, 237, 247.
Among the charges against him: it is not clear whether the charge cited here was a major element in the prosecution or merely an additional allegation (see on §5), nor therefore whether Archias was formally prosecuted for a religious offence.
Sinope: a well-known *hetaira*, mentioned at 22.56. She was named after the prosperous city on the Black Sea, but according to Athenaios (586a), because she practised her trade when advanced in years, she was nicknamed 'Abydos' after a less salubrious town in the region.
the Haloa: a fertility festival held at Eleusis in Poseideion (roughly December); details in Parke 98ff., Simon 35-7. According to Apollodoros, Archias' offence was twofold: i. since the festival was confined to women, he had no right to participate; ii. animal sacrifice was not allowed (the women's rites at the Haloa involved the produce of the soil, not animal sacrifice).

117 neither the entreaty of his kin nor that of his friends: Athenian courts did not try cases in a vacuum. As well as his own career, a man threw his family and friends into the balance against those of his opponent. It was normal for the relatives and associates of the accused to appear as *synegoroi* (for this term see on §14) and add their pleas for pity to his (cf. e.g. 19.1, 21.208, Lyk.*Leokr*.20).
the many public services: a reference to the *leitourgiai*, costly public services (such as paying the choral costs for tragic, comic or dithyrambic performances), which served as a wealth tax in Athens. It was normal for a litigant to cite his public services in order to stake a claim to the gratitude, and therefore the support, of the jury. The extent to which Athenian society viewed a man in the context of his family (and even his social group - see preceding note), and not merely as an individual, can be seen from the readiness of litigants as here to claim credit for the achievements of ancestors or to draw attention to misdeeds of the opponent's ancestors (as Lys.14.39).
the same god: Dionysos, to whom Phano was allegedly given in marriage, was also connected with the Haloa.

118-125 *Anticipation of Stephanos' defence*. See above on §§85-125.

118 that she is not his wife: §119 indicates that this is the line Stephanos will take.
who are hers and who have been introduced into the phratry by Stephanos: the

second half of this statement is very probably true. §124 indicates that the sons either exercise citizen rights (if old enough for deme membership) or are generally regarded as possessing citizen status. Since illegitimate offspring of two Athenian parents were legally entitled to citizen status (see on §58), it does not follow that these sons enjoyed phratry membership (for the qualifications for phratry membership cf. on §13); however, since Stephanos claims (§119) that the sons are his legitimate issue by a wife of citizen status, he will naturally have introduced them into his phratry. The first half of the statement is never substantiated, at least with reference to the sons. It seems however that Phano was widely held to be Neaira's daughter (cf. on §61). See further on §119.

119 I hear: in those private cases (the majority) which automatically came before a public arbitrator, each litigant would have a reasonably clear idea of the line his opponent proposed to take, since it was a rule that no evidence could be introduced in court which had not been adduced at the arbitration (Arist.*Ath.Pol.*53.2-3). Since this restriction did not apply in other private, or in any public, cases, it was possible to develop a new line of argument supported by evidence at any time up to the trial. This was more problematic for the prosecutor, who spoke first, than for the defendant, who was in a position to make adjustments to take account of unforeseen arguments used by the prosecutor. In such cases a man might approach his opponent's enemies for information and generally listen for rumour (see A.P. Dorjahn *TAPA* 66 (1935) 274-95). For the rest common sense and (where relevant) experience of the lawcourts and knowledge of rhetoric would allow for conjecture about the opponent's arguments. Apollodoros may have obtained information, as his words suggest; but this could be a device to give authority to what is merely educated guesswork.
the children are not by her: Apollodoros suggests that Stephanos' claim embraces all the children. If so, Stephanos is probably telling the truth about the males but not about Phano (see on §§118, 121). However, Apollodoros may be distorting his opponent's argument; Stephanos may claim the males as his legitimate sons, but deny any connection with or responsibility for Phano. The brevity of Apollodoros' treatment of Stephanos' defence suggests that Stephanos has a strong case to make. Certainly he would have abundant testimony if his claim is true. He would be able to adduce witnesses to his marriage (see on §54), to the ceremony after birth in which the father introduced an infant child into his *oikos* (see on §56), to the sons' acceptance by his phratry (see on §59) and (depending on their age) deme. If the mother had died, he could adduce the readiness of her kin to allow the sons to inherit her dowry as evidence of their acceptance of his sons' parentage.

120 I challenged him to hand over the maidservants: for the role of challenges in Athenian litigation see on §60. Here we have the *proklesis eis basanon*, the challenge to the opponent either to submit his slaves for examination or to accept the submission of the challenger's slaves for examination in order to obtain fresh evidence. To be admissible in court, the evidence of slaves had to be extracted under torture. The examination could only take place with the agreement of both parties. In practice (at least as far as extant oratory is concerned) such challenges are always refused either outright or (where there is initial acceptance) after disagreement about terms (see 37.39ff.), and are issued in anticipation of and drafted with a view to refusal by the opponent. Certainly Stephanos had good reason to reject the challenge as formulated by Apollodoros. The latter states (§121) that he was ready to abandon the prosecution if the evidence proved favourable to the defence. But there was another condition (§124), which understandably Apollodoros chooses not to stress, that Neaira would be sold as a slave and the children would lose their citizen status if the evidence favoured the prosecution. The risks to the protagonists were unequal, the dangers for Stephanos from the proposed torture far greater than those from a trial (see on §124), and the outcome of the torture completely unpredictable, dependant as it was on the loyalty and endurance of the slaves, the severity of the torture and the form of the questioning. Apollodoros' account of the issue of the challenge makes his own position, as the originator of the action and not merely *synegoros*, explicit. Since however the jury will have forgotten Theomnestos by this time, it is doubtful that they would notice any inconsistency.
Thratta and Kokkaline: see on §35.
Xennis and Drosis: the latter name is derived from *drosos*, 'dew'. The former means 'foreigner'; the form of the word (the Attic equivalent would be Xenis) suggests that she either originated in or reached Athens by way of an Aeolic-speaking area.

121 Antidorides: since this was the name of Stephanos' father, and since it was a common practice in Athens to name a son after the paternal grandfather, it is likely that this son at least was legitimate. The strong probability that Apollodoros is lying about one son, combined with the complete absence of any hard evidence concerning any of the male offspring, suggests that the other sons too were legitimate.

122 for this is what living in marriage means: although there were no marriage certificates in classical Athens, it was easy in practice to distinguish between marriage proper and cohabitation, since the former was affirmed by a number of acts over a long period. Except in the case of an *epikleros* (see on §113) there was a formal betrothal (*engye*); children of the marriage would be formally admitted to the father's *oikos* shortly after birth (see on §56). The sons would be enrolled in phratry and (where relevant) genos (see on §§13 and 59). Enrolment in the deme too would normally be for a man's legitimate children, though if, as is probable (see on §58), bastards whose parents were both Athenian were entitled to citizen status, this act is ambiguous, since a man might also enrol an illegitimate son by an Athenian mother. The same may be true of the betrothal of a daughter by *engye* to another Athenian citizen. Since a formal betrothal was a prerequisite for marriage (H.J. Wolff, *Traditio* 2 (1944) 46-53, 68), a man who conferred on illegitimate children the marks of legitimacy was simulating, not establishing marriage. However, since the law forbidding marriage between Athenians and foreigners uses the term *synoikein* (see on §16), referring to the relationship between the couple rather than the manner of its inception, and especially since it adds 'by any manner or means', it is likely that any relationship between an Athenian and a foreigner which involved treating the offspring as legitimate would be held by a jury to be in breach of the law.

we have courtesans ... concubines ... wives: Apollodoros is not offering a legal definition of these three categories but explaining his stress on the offspring in his preceding definition. He is using the word *hetaira* here in a restricted sense. There is an overlap in Greek usage between the word *pallake* (here translated 'concubine'), which denotes a female, slave or free, supported by a male in a semi-permanent sexual relationship other than marriage, and the word *hetaira*, which is frequently used with the same value (as §§39, 119 above), as well as denoting a prostitute. Apollodoros here means only the latter. His distinction between pleasure (from the *hetaira*) and servicing of the body (from the *pallake*), both of which refer to sexual gratification, is artificial (cf. J.-P. Vernant, *Myth and society in ancient Greece* (London 1980) 48). His restriction of the role of the wife to child-bearing, to the exclusion of sexual pleasure, while it reflects the legally recognized purpose of marriage (see below), does not correspond with the reality for most Athenian males, for whom the wife was probably the most important source of sexual pleasure; cf. most recently R. Just, *Women in Athenian law and life* (London 1989) 137. An Athenian male owed no duty of fidelity to his wife, as this matter-of-fact statement from a speaker who presents himself as a decent man shows.

for the production of legitimate offspring: this is the principle role of the Athenian wife. It is enshrined in the betrothal formula found in Menander (e.g. *Dyskolos* 842, *Samia* 727): 'I betroth [this woman] to you for the ploughing of legitimate children'.

guardian of our household property: the extent of the wife's role was determined by custom and the individuals concerned, not by law. Supervision of the household stores appears to have been a regular (Ar.*Lys.*494f., *Assemblywomen* 211f., Lys.1.6, Xen.*Oik.*7.36, Theophr.*Char.*18.4) but not inevitable (Ar.*Thesm.*421ff.) function.

the most accurate testimony: the orators are full of confident (and conflicting) assertions of the reliability (cf. Ant.1.18, 6.25, Isai.8.12, Isok.17.54, Dem.30.37, 47.8) or unreliability (Ant.5.32, Lys.5.3ff., Dem.37.41) of the evidence given by slaves under torture. The stance depends on the speaker's immediate rhetorical needs, as can be seen from Lys.7.35, Lyk.*Leokr.*30, Arist.*R.*1376b 31ff. Greek authors usually distinguish between 'testimony' from free individuals (*martyria*, the term used here) and 'torture' (*basanos*), i.e. statements made by slaves under torture. The confusion here may intentional, with the aim of enhancing the importance of the slaves' evidence. Cf. on §62.

123 DEPOSITION: the deposition is likely to be genuine, since it contains names known elsewhere only from inscriptions. From the middle of the fourth century we have inscriptional evidence for a Deinomenes son of Archelaos of Kydathenaion (Kirchner *PA* 3188, Davies *APF* 97). A Diophanes of Alopeke, perhaps a grandson of the man named here, is known from a list of ephebes in an inscription early in the third century (*IG* ii^2 665). The manuscripts give 'Deinias son of Phormides of Kydantidai'; but since a grave inscription (*IG* ii^2 6609) provides us with a Deinias son of Phormos of Kydantidai, I follow Rennie and Kirchner (*PA* 3167) in altering the text here.

The Demosthenes named here is the famous orator. For his association with Apollodoros see Introduction 7.

124 CHALLENGE: the document is likely to be genuine, since it presents plausible details which could not have been derived from the text of the speech (the result in the event of evidence favouring the prosecution, the offer to reimburse Stephanos for any damage sustained by the slaves under torture). Authenticity is also suggested by the formal similarities between this document and a challenge quoted in the text at Aischin.2.126 (G. Thür, *Die Beweisführung vor den Schwurgerichtshöfen Athens* (Vienna 1977) 99ff.). Two features however present difficulties. i. The challenge begins by using the third person of Apollodoros, but switches at the end to the first person. ii. According to the manuscript text, the challenge contradicts Apollodoros' earlier claims (§§13, 38, 50, 51, 52, 67, 81, 82) that these children were Neaira's, not Stephanos', for it maintains that they were Stephanos' children by Neaira. The first point has little weight, since we may simply have slipshod writing of a sort familiar in Apollodoros. The second is the more serious objection. Attempts have been made to change the text at this point to obtain a statement that Stephanos is not the father of the children (see Introduction 21), in order to bring the challenge into line with the rest of the speech. However, as Thalheim, *Hermes* 56 (1921) 433f., observes, §121 agrees with the text of the challenge in representing the children as Stephanos' by Neaira. It is easier therefore to accept the inconsistency offered by the manuscripts, with Thalheim and Patteson (I have however accepted one emendation; see below). As Patteson notes, Apollodoros' case under the law he has invoked would be much stronger if he could prove that the children were both Stephanos' and Neaira's. Ideally, for the relationship to be a marriage, real or feigned, Stephanos should be treating as legitimate his own children by Neaira. Possibly Apollodoros began with the intention of representing these children as Stephanos' offspring by Neaira, but changed his strategy when he realized that their birth could be dated before Stephanos' relationship with Neaira commenced (this is perhaps suggested by §38, where Apollodoros acknowledges that the children named there were born before the relationship began); alternatively, as Patteson suggests, he may simply have wished to cover all possibilities. The interval between the narrative and the presentation of the challenge is probably more than enough to palliate the inconsistency.

The details provided by Apollodoros here, the identity of the slaves to be tortured, the questions to be put or issue to be decided and the consequences for the parties involved were standard components of a formal challenge (Thür (cited above) 107-29). In addition, the identity of the questioner (37.40, Ant.1.10) and the type of torture to be applied (45.61, Ar.*Frogs* 618ff.) might also be included.

on which he has indicted Neaira: this could be an indication that Apollodoros initially brought a *graphe* against Neaira and subsequently withdrew it (for withdrawal of a public action see on §53), after persuading Theomnestos to prosecute in his place. Thür (cited above) 71 n.17 suggests that Apollodoros was forced to step down after Stephanos brought the action for homicide (§10), since the proclamation which began the proceedings would prevent him from appearing in court. However, since we do not know the precise chronological relationship between the homicide case and the current action, this suggestion remains highly conjectural. Moreover, since at §126 Apollodoros represents himself as prosecutor in the present trial, his phraseology here may be no more than a loose expression for his dominant role in the prosecution. Either way, the pretence that he is merely a *synegoros* is abandoned. Cf. on §120.

about Stephanos' children, that they are by Neaira: Baiter's transposition of the names (see Introduction 21; the MSS text would mean 'about Neaira's children, that they are by Stephanos'), though not inescapable, brings the text into line with §121 (cf. also §119); more importantly, it brings the alleged knowledge of the slave girls into line with the question to be put to them later in the challenge, where the disputed issue appears to be maternity, not paternity. Cf. Thür (cited above) 97ff.

Neaira was to be sold in accordance with the laws: that is, testimony unfavourable to Neaira would have exactly the same result for her as conviction in court on the *graphe* (cf. §16).

and the children were to be aliens: if the distinction drawn above between Phano and the male offspring has any validity, it is possible that even if the jurors were to convict on the basis of the account of Phano's career the sons might retain their citizen rights by convincing their deme that both parents were Athenian. The challenge thus offered greater risks than trial by jury. Cf. on §120.

I was ready: for the switch from third to first person cf. §54.

to pay for any damage suffered: the offer adds a veneer of reasonableness to an unacceptable challenge; cf. 37.40, Ar. *Frogs* 618ff., and see on §120.

125 judgement has already been given: the metaphor gives Stephanos' refusal, which amounts to circumstantial evidence (Greek *tekmerion*), the formality of a binding legal judgement. Cf. on §62.

the indictment I brought against her: cf. on §124.

126 *Conclusion* (*epilogos*). Apollodoros closes by stating the grounds for bringing the action, and stressing in particular the religious aspect of the trial. Since the case is not complicated, no elaborate résumé is needed (cf. Arist.*R.*1414b 5-6).

as avenger: the prosecution as a whole ends as it began (ring-composition); cf. §1.

will not go unnoticed by the gods: for the threat cf. §109 above, 19.239, Lys.6.53, Lyk.*Leokr.*146, and for the same motif with a different source of intimidation Lys.12.91. As Patteson notes, the gods involved are firstly Dionysos, who was directly involved in the alleged offence of Phano, and secondly 'the other gods who may be thought to take an interest in the orderly conduct of Athenian citizens according to the laws', including those worshipped by the family and phratry of Stephanos.

secondly yourselves: since the alleged crime devalues both the prestige of citizenship and the power of the demos (cf. §§13 and 93) and threatens the relationship between the city and its gods, the jury are victims of Neaira and Stephanos. It is common for the jurors to be invited to take vengeance upon the defendant rather than act as dispassionate dispensers of justice; cf. e.g. 19.87, 343, 21.142, 24.205, 45.70, 50.64.

this indictment which I have brought against Neaira: cf. on §124. The pedantic precision of this and what follows spoil what might have been a terse and forceful close.

Appendix: Apollodoros and the theoric fund

Theomnestos' brief account of Stephanos' prosecution of Apollodoros by *graphe paranomon* raises two questions. i. What exactly was the legal position concerning the financing of theoric expenditure at the time of the Olynthiac and Euboian campaigns of 349-8? ii. What was the legal basis for Stephanos' prosecution of Apollodoros in 348?

On the first question there is a conflict in the ancient sources. According to Libanios in the hypothesis to Dem.1, at the time of Demosthenes' Olynthiac speeches the arrangements for the funding of the theoric distributions were protected by a law 'threatening death for anyone who formally proposed that this money should be changed to the old status and become military'. There are good parallels for the protection of legislation by penalty clauses.[1] Moreover, Demosthenes' caution as he approaches the subject of the theoric fund in the *First* and *Third Olynthiac* speeches suggests a real anxiety. At 1.19 he says: '"Well, then," someone might say, "do you propose that this money should be put to military use?" No indeed.' At 3.11 he proposes a body of *nomothetai* to examine 'the laws dealing with the theoric monies'. This is a particularly cumbersome procedure to suggest at a time of crisis; but not surprising if there was an obstacle to a direct attack on the theoric laws. At 3.20 he states that until this is done nobody will risk 'destruction', ἀπολέσθαι, by giving good advice (i.e. the diversion of theoric money to the military fund). Demosthenes' anxiety suggests that the obstacle was more than the *graphe paranomon*.

Theomnestos however at 59.4 tells us that 'the laws' order that in time of war the surplus from the administration should go into the military fund. This appears to contradict what we infer from Libanios and Demosthenes about the legal situation. Moreover, when in 348 he tried to divert to military use the money spent on theoric distributions (59.4ff.), Apollodoros was fined, not executed. Thirdly, he was attacked by *graphe paranomon*, not under theoric law.

The contradictions are removed at a single stroke by Hansen.[2] He argues that Demosthenes and Apollodoros are dealing with different issues. Only [Dem.]59 speaks of surplus money (τὰ περιόντα χρήματα τῆς διοικήσεως); all the other sources 'concern the transfer of money from the Theoric Fund to the Stratiotic Fund'. In the 350s, he suggests, Euboulos managed to increase the share of the annual financial distribution which was received by the theoric fund. In the same law the death penalty was prescribed for any attempt to transfer money from the theoric to the military fund, in order to safeguard the new allocation. Demosthenes' aim is to transfer money in this way, but he does not dare to propose the measure bluntly because of the penalty clause. Apollodoros' measure 'deals only with the surplus of the administration and has nothing to do with the law that forbids the use of theoric money for military purposes'. The law prescribed, as Theomnestos says, that this surplus should be used for military purposes in time of war. Apollodoros was afraid that the Boule 'would infringe the law and use the money for theoric distributions. This might have been his motive for suggesting that the decision rest with the Assembly.'

It is however difficult to believe that Apollodoros would expose himself to prosecution as he did if in fact it was the Boule which was about to breach the law. Nor is it easy to see why he should draft his *probouleuma* in the form he did (allowing the Assembly to decide whether the money should be used for theoric or military purposes), if the law prescribed that surplus revenue should go into the military fund, for his proposal was then technically in breach of the very law he was seeking to protect. It would have been safer and simpler to propose that the money should be used for military purposes as the law prescribed. There are however other problems with Hansen's view. The statement that all the other sources deal with the theoric fund allocation, rather than the surplus it received, is erroneous. In fact, the texts are hopelessly imprecise on this subject. Moreover, there is one passage in Demosthenes which suggests that he and Apollodoros are dealing with the same issue. At 3.33 Demosthenes suggests the use of ταῖς περιουσίαις ταῖς οἴκοι ταύταις ('these domestic surpluses') for external affairs. This looks like a reference to what are called τὰ περιόντα χρήματα ('the surplus money') in 59.4. If so, we must accept that there were legal impediments to any attempt to divert the surplus money away from the theoric fund. To this extent Libanios is right.

How then do we explain Theomnestos' statement that the laws prescribed that the surplus should go into the military exchequer? An answer is offered by Harpokration (s.v. *theorika*) and Libanios, who speak of successive uses of the surplus, with the money going originally to the military fund but subsequently to the theoric fund. That is, the law governing the surpluses changed during Euboulos' ascendancy. This is plausible enough in itself.[3] It allows some degree of truth to Theomnestos; this is important, since Theomnestos is addressing a knowledgeable audience whose judgement matters, and whom he cannot therefore afford to alienate with palpable misstatements. He is then simply fudging chronology. However, it is not entirely satisfactory. It makes Apollodoros' measure exceedingly rash. If the legal provision for the administrative surplus was unambiguous, it was very risky to invite the Assembly to set the law aside. Apollodoros' motion makes more sense if we suppose that there was a genuine legal confusion. Theomnestos may be entirely right to state that the laws prescribed that in time of war the surplus should go to the stratiotic fund. He may however be lying by omission.

Possibly the theoric laws prescribed that the surplus should go to the theoric fund without specifying that this was only to be done in time of peace. On the detail of the surplus, they were meant to supplement, not replace, the laws governing the allocation to the military fund. But because this relationship was not made explicit, they were treated in practice as superseding them. If so, the way had been open for someone to attempt to divert the theoric money for years, since Athens had been at war with Philip since the loss of Amphipolis in 357. That no attempt had been made may be due simply to the absence of a crisis which could be presented as an opportunity to put a stop to Macedonian expansion.

This would not of course in itself explain why Apollodoros was not prosecuted under the theoric laws. If the allocation was protected by a penalty clause, why was this not invoked against Apollodoros? One escape route is to follow schol.Dem.1.1, according to which the death sentence was introduced after and because of Apollodoros' attempt to divert the money. However, Cawkwell[4] has given good reasons to doubt the scholiast's authority. Furthermore, it does not really solve the problem. Demosthenes' trepidation in the *First* and *Third Olynthiac* speeches needs to be explained. If there was a penalty clause, it probably predated 349. It is conceivable that the penalty was increased after Apollodoros' motion of 348. But this scholion may rest on an ancient attempt to solve the discrepancy we are now confronting. The answer is probably to be found in the form of Apolodoros' proposal. As Rhodes has pointed out,[5] Apollodoros has attempted to circumvent the legal penalty by bringing an open *probouleuma*. That is, instead of proposing a single course of action he proposed putting alternatives to the Assembly for decision. Demosthenes in the *First Olynthiac* anticipates a question designed to intimidate (1.19): 'Well then ... are you proposing (γράφεις) that this money should be put to military use?' From this Libanios in the hypothesis to Dem.1 concludes that what was proscribed was an attempt to repeal the law. Apollodoros however has not sought to change the law. He has not even formally recommended a single course of action. He has left the decision on the application of the law to the Assembly. Demosthenes in his attack on the theoric laws tried another procedural device, the appointment of a board of *nomothetai* (3.10-11).

If we suppose that Apollodoros evaded the penalty clause by a procedural device, we are free to accept Libanios' statement that the penalty for any meddling with the law was death. This is perfectly compatible with Athenian practice.[6] Libanios is however our only source for this penalty, and it is disquieting that he gives us this information in a context in which he is drawing heavily on Demosthenes. There is therefore no reason to believe that he has any independent authority for the statement. It has been suggested for at least a century that Libanios' statement is a false inference from the reference to destruction in 3.11.

Sandys for instance in his commentary points out that it could as easily refer to *atimia* as death.[7] That Libanios may well be guessing does not necessarily mean that he is wrong. Ultimately, however, the precise penalty is irrelevant. It is enough that there was one, and that it was (or could be, if it was not fixed) severe.

Apollodoros, on the reconstruction I accept, evaded the rigour of the theoric laws by a procedural device. What then was the ground for Stephanos' prosecution? On the basis of Theomnestos' statement, it has been supposed that Apollodoros was tried and convicted on a technicality: as a state debtor he was subject to *atimia* and therefore could not participate in politics.[8] There is reason to doubt Theomnestos, however. Firstly, it is inherently unlikely that Apollodoros was a state debtor. The issue here is not his enormous wealth, which would enable him to pay off even a substantial fine. It is his personality. At the time of the trial Apollodoros had been active in the lawcourts for the best part of two decades. This involved not just his dispute with his stepfather Phormion but also a series of actions relating to his father's bank and, most significant, a number of political trials. It is difficult to believe that all his many enemies failed to unearth a debt which would have removed his legal capacity. Furthermore, when he made his proposal, Apollodoros was a member of the Council. He had passed the *dokimasia* at the commencement of his term of office; there too apparently this disabling debt failed to surface. We must of course remember that innocent men can be wrongly convicted. We must also remember that political trials were at one level popularity polls. Nonetheless one is left with a feeling that this was a charge easily refuted. Secondly, it is far from certain that the Greek actually says that the ground for the *graphe paranomon* was Apollodoros' incapacity. Theomnestos says that false witnesses were adduced ἐπὶ διαβολῆι, 'for the purpose of slander'. The noun *diabole* can certainly be used of a false main charge.[9] It is however also used of attempts to place the opponent in a bad light, that is, of supplementary allegations.[10] This is a role we find played elsewhere in *graphai paranomon* by allegations of indebtedness to the state. Androtion is attacked in Dem.22 for his proposal to crown the Boule on grounds of procedure and substance. But the prosecution adds that he is disfranchised as a state debtor (33-4) and a male prostitute. That we should detect this kind of supplementary *diabole* in the prosecution of Apollodoros is suggested by a further, obvious, fact. It is in Theomnestos' interests to present the prosecution of his kinsman Apollodoros as flimsy, as part of his own *diabole* of the enemy Stephanos. I think it likely therefore that the issue stressed by Theomnestos was merely a legal makeweight, not the main charge.

What then was the main thrust of the case against Apollodoros? I would suggest that it was procedural. In sidestepping the trap set by the theoric laws Apollodoros blundered into another. If as I have conjectured there was a genuine conflict in the laws, Apollodoros was allowing the Assembly to choose between contradictory legal provisions. There were however procedures for dealing with such conflicts. There are many uncertainties concerning the various laws on lawmaking in fourth century Athens.[11] However, the procedures in all cases were designed to prevent hasty revision of the laws. One consistent feature in all attempts to sort out existing legislation and scrutinize new legislation is the empanelling of *nomothetai* ('lawmakers'). Demosthenes in the *Third Olynthiac* proposed such a body of *nomothetai* to sort out the theoric laws. However, according to the reconstruction suggested above, Apollodoros simply proposed that the Assembly should choose by a vote which of the conflicting laws to apply. This was procedurally irregular, and this irregularity was perhaps the main charge in the *graphe paranomon.*

NOTES TO APPENDIX

1 M.H. Hansen, *GRBS* 17 (1976) 237 n.10.

2 Hansen (cited in n.1 above) 244f., followed by Trevett *Apollodoros* 145.

3 Cf. e.g. G.L.Cawkwell, *JHS* 83 (1963) 60f.

4 Cawkwell (cited in n.3 above) 59f.

5 Rhodes *AB* 58.

6 The fifth century decree imposing Athenian coins on the empire includes a clause providing for the death penalty for any attempt to revoke (Meiggs-Lewis 45).

7 J. E. Sandys, *The First Philippic and the Olynthiacs of Demosthenes* (repr. London 1955) 199. We find *atimia* as a penalty in clauses protecting legislation (cf. Meiggs-Lewis 49 and 69).

8 Cf. Patteson on §5, Hansen (cited in n.1 above) 239. Cawkwell (cited in n.3 above) 58f. is more sceptical.

9 Cf. Ant.2A.d.1, 6.7, Lys.19.53.

10 Cf. Dem.37.47, 48.55, Arist.*R.*1354a, 1415a.

11 See in general D.M. MacDowell, *JHS* 95 (1975) 62-74, P.J. Rhodes, *CQ* 35 (1985) 55-60, M.H. Hansen, *GRBS* 26 (1985) 345-71.

INDEX

All references are to page numbers

www.ingramcontent.com/pod-product-compliance
Lightning Source LLC
Chambersburg PA
CBHW071120100726
47908CB00008B/2434

* 9 7 8 0 8 5 6 6 8 5 2 6 2 *